T0369160

Sitting with God

MEDITATING FOR GOD'S DIVINE GUIDANCE

ALLEN C. LILES

WestBow
PRESS
A DIVISION OF THOMAS NELSON

Copyright © 2013 Allen C. Liles.

All rights reserved. No part of this book may be used or reproduced by any means, graphic, electronic, or mechanical, including photocopying, recording, taping or by any information storage retrieval system without the written permission of the publisher except in the case of brief quotations embodied in critical articles and reviews.

WestBow Press books may be ordered through booksellers or by contacting:

WestBow Press
A Division of Thomas Nelson
1663 Liberty Drive
Bloomington, IN 47403
www.westbowpress.com
1-(866) 928-1240

Because of the dynamic nature of the Internet, any web addresses or links contained in this book may have changed since publication and may no longer be valid. The views expressed in this work are solely those of the author and do not necessarily reflect the views of the publisher, and the publisher hereby disclaims any responsibility for them.

Scriptures taken from the Holy Bible, New International Version®, NIV®. Copyright © 1973, 1978, 1984, 2011 by Biblica, Inc.™ Used by permission of Zondervan. All rights reserved worldwide. www.zondervan.com The "NIV" and "New International Version" are trademarks registered in the United States Patent and Trademark Office by Biblica, Inc.™ All rights reserved.

Any people depicted in stock imagery provided by Thinkstock are models, and such images are being used for illustrative purposes only.

Certain stock imagery © Thinkstock.

ISBN: 978-1-4908-0091-2 (sc)
ISBN: 978-1-4908-0093-6 (hc)
ISBN: 978-1-4908-0092-9 (e)

Library of Congress Control Number: 2013912244

Printed in the United States of America.

WestBow Press rev. date: 7/25/2013

For My Dear Wife

INTRODUCTION

The purpose of *Sitting with God* is simple. I want to help demonstrate that a direct human connection with both a transcendent God and the Christ Spirit that I believe dwells within each of us is not only possible but essential to living a happy and fulfilled life. If you are interested in developing such a connection, I hope that my documented experience over a full year will encourage you to explore the possibility.

The key to establishing this sacred connection lies in the practice of meditation. I claim no special relationship with the higher power that I call God. I believe that any committed individual can form a deep and personal bond with God, the Father, and with the Spirit of the Christ that resides at the center of every human being. It only requires a willingness to ask, seek, and knock at the sacred door of meditation and then wait patiently for the response.

A secondary purpose of *Sitting with God* involves the practice of meditation in general. Many doctors, hospitals, and clinics are now recommending meditation as part of restorative and preventive treatment. Research shows that meditation helps lower blood pressure and assists patients with chronic illnesses and depression. The medical benefits of meditation now seem undeniable. Establishing a daily pattern of meditation can pay important health benefits apart from the spiritual aspects.

Although I have been meditating regularly for more than twenty-five years, events of the past year have brought me a renewed commitment to spending time in the silence. My dear wife has been experiencing a serious health challenge, we both have been coping with my retirement as a pulpit minister, and the aging process has continued along for both of us with all its inherent challenges. Family issues have also presented themselves, especially with my two adult children. In addition, world and national events over the past several months have created relevant questions about God's viewpoint regarding these happenings.

This past year presented a unique opportunity to listen for God's wisdom and guidance. I also wanted to transcribe what I was hearing. I have dutifully kept a daily journal since 1985, so writing down Spirit's response seemed natural. However, this particular effort was not a two-way back and forth conversation. I mostly listened. God has so much to tell us, if we only pay attention. In an age of instant information, I believe that sitting with God in quiet meditation provides the defining word regarding the world and our place in it.

The daily meditations presented in this book took place between April 1, 2012, and March 31, 2013. The transcriptions of these meditations cover a spiritual and personal journey of exactly one year. Again, I make no claim to any special insight. Whenever you become ready to activate the relationship with God and your own inner Christ Spirit, I believe Spirit stands ready to respond. Just give your meditation practice time to develop. It requires perseverance, daily commitment, and a nonjudgmental attitude about your progress. Here are three things I discovered as my time in meditation began to flourish: (1) I truly believe God wants this intimate time and deeper relationship with all of us; (2) I am a spiritual as well as a human being, blessed with the gift of perceiving God's wisdom during meditation, and (3) God loves me enough to share time together in the silence. Finally, I found there is nothing to fear from establishing a direct link with Spirit. My life became more peaceful and centered at a time of personal challenge.

I believe God wants an active participation in your spiritual life. If you are reading these words, you are already more aware of your sacred place in the universe. I urge you to gratefully answer God's call in the silent realm of meditation. Pray for the knowledge of God's will for you and the power to carry it out. Pray, listen, and trust that God has a specific divine plan for your life. That plan could be revealed

Allen C. Liles

in the silence. If you are not already practicing meditation, it is never too late to begin. There is no perfect formula or set guideline for your meditations. Do not set a high bar for yourself, create unrealistic expectations, or strive for absolute perfection. Your meditations, like your fingerprints, are unique to you alone. A meditation of sixty seconds, in dedicated contact with God, can be more powerful than an hour of unfocused silence. If your mind wanders, take a time out and read scripture or an uplifting passage in a book. I have found that Sarah Young's *Jesus Calling* (Thomas Nelson), A. J. Russell's *God Calling* (Spire Books), or Joel Goldsmith's *The Art of Meditation* (HarperSanFrancisco) represented excellent companions to my morning meditations. The televised worship services presented by Dr. Charles Stanley of the First Baptist Church each Sunday from Atlanta also were weekly inspirational boosts. Utilize whatever helps your meditation practice: a mantra, an affirmation, a Bible verse, and so on. The main requirement is that you commit to meeting with God on a regular basis. Spirit will gladly take it from there.

You are on a sacred path that leads to the kingdom of heaven. Enjoy the journey. Enjoy your time with *Sitting with God*.

Allen C. Liles
Minneapolis, Minnesota
June 2013

JANUARY

Christ in you, the hope of glory ...

—Colossians 1:27 (NIV)

JANUARY 1

The New Year

Open your arms, mind, and heart to the infinite possibilities of the new year. Let your expectations of My generous blessings flow.

Allow your dreams to come true. Dream only big dreams, but look closely for small signs of progress. Watch for My presence, for even the tiniest glimmer of hope amid the chaos and confusion. I AM always there in the darkest of sad and tragic moments. If you stumble, I will lift you up. When you backslide, I will pull you forward.

Reach out for Me when the depths of life threaten to crush you. Rise again to the glorious heights that I have planned for you. One step at a time, walk steadfastly toward the sun of opportunity and fulfillment. Your path leads to My kingdom, the ultimate destination. I stand ready to welcome you. I open My loving arms to receive you. Then the journey will seem easy in retrospect when you come home to Me, your loving Father. Until that day, bless the earth with your light.

Comfort, encourage, and love others. Bestow My grace on everyone you encounter. You are My precious instrument. I use you to carry hope and compassion to those in need. Do My will. I provide every resource. Trust Me. Banish fear. Bolster your courage. Increase your faith to the maximum. Keep your thoughts on Me, and lean not on your own understanding. Expect a divine year of progress and completion. Believe it. I love you dearly, My precious child.

JANUARY 2

Quiet Surrender

Spiritual growth comes in the silence. In quietness, you discover strength. In surrender to Me, you experience the peace that passes all understanding. Resist the urge to control your spiritual or earthly quest. Sit down. Take a break from the constant striving. Rest in Me, for Me, with Me. Do not struggle for anything. Allow everything to flow toward you. Depend on Me, and you will receive everything. In the stillness, the abundance of heaven descends upon you. Quiet your busy mind.

Make no great plans without Me. Let Me sort out and manage your life. Trust that I place all in divine order. Scrap your need to control outcomes. Watch as your life falls into place under My direction. Surrender to My will. Have faith in My judgment.

My knowledge exceeds yours. Put little or no trust in your human planning. You mean well, but the scope of your understanding remains limited. The ways of the world have the power to thwart and confuse you. I eliminate confusion. I know the correct path. I AM your guide. I also accompany you on the journey. Relax and enjoy the trip, secure in My plan for your life. You travel with My protection and blessing. I prepay your expenses.

Surrendering control guarantees that you experience the adventure of a lifetime. Watch gratefully as I clear the path before you. Indecision and chaos vanish as we walk together.

Release all resistance. Embrace Me. Let go of the reins. Take away the burden of human responsibility for every outcome. Partner with Me. You travel light when we move forward as one. Everything becomes clear and discernible. Indecision, chaos, and confusion vanish. Surrender now to Me. Surrender and find peace.

JANUARY 3

Healthy Living

Respect your body as a temple. It represents My divine gift to you. Please do not abuse this gift.

Whether the world sees you as stunningly beautiful does not matter. You are My perfect child. I created you in My image and likeness. How do you perceive Me? Do you think of Me as a beautiful God or as a God filled with anger and hate, with a countenance to match? However you view Me matches the same reflection that you show the world.

Your body serves as a sacred image of Me. Treat it with great care. Love the form that I provide to you, no matter how the world judges it. Put nothing into your body that brings harm. Poisonous substances abound in a world fixated on short-term pleasure and instant gratification. Let your body remain pure and unadulterated. Preserve the form that I gave you. Feed it properly. Exercise it with consistency. Protect your human temple at all costs.

Do not wear out your body with stress or worry. Your body craves peace and quiet. Stress and chaos upset its natural rhythms. Avoid people who may upset your body's balance.

Your body has feelings and a perfect memory. It seeks to avoid situations that once caused it harm. Honor your body's feelings. Love your form. See it as a glorious expression of Me.

Your body also stands as My sacred temple. Consecrate it. Be satisfied and proud of what I bestowed on you. Treat your body well. Let your body serve as your badge of honor. It shines forth as a singular treasure, the only one of its kind on earth.

Allen C. Liles

JANUARY 4

My Presence

I AM here, My beloved. I AM in you, around you, before you, and behind you. Believe it. Never waver or question.

I AM holding you up when you want to fall down. I absorb the heavy blows of life for you. I give you the strength to continue. I help you recover from the most grievous losses. I restore your spirit when the world crushes it. I provide the divine ideas that bless you and make you wealthy.

I AM the one true source of everything. Turn to Me in times of loneliness. I comfort and reassure you. When the world tempts you, look to Me for guidance. Together, we can walk past any distraction or threat to your spiritual journey.

Trust Me in all things big and small. I AM always here to listen and counsel with you. I AM a committed partner. Hold My hand when you feel down and out. I provide the confidence to press on.

I know you. I love you. I AM certain of your success. I guarantee it. Lock on to Me. Refuse to falter. Cling to Me tightly when strong winds threaten to carry you away. Tether yourself to Me. Together we ride out the storms of life.

JANUARY 5

Endings

Any ending represents a new beginning. Prepare for changes. Follow the path I set out before you. Take one step at a time. Avoid giant leaps or retracing your steps

Take My hand. Move onward and upward to the next rung of the ladder. I do not let you fall or fail. Never look back over your shoulder and obsess about what has gone before. Watch the past recede until it no longer looms large in the rearview mirror of your mind. Bid memories, both good and bad, a fond good-bye. You are rising toward new experiences that promise blessings for you and others.

I AM giving you a new assignment. All the pieces are falling into place. A brand new play has been written by Me, just for you. The stage awaits your entrance as the lead actor. Your initial appearance on stage signals the first act of an important new drama.

I have carefully authored the words for you to say. You wait nervously in the wings now, ready for your big moment. The stage lights dim. The audience sits with great anticipation. You find yourself filled with the confidence of someone who painstakingly learned his or her lines. You faithfully prepared and rehearsed for this moment. You are the true star of this new play entitled *My Life*.

At the end of the evening, a grateful audience rises as one in standing applause. Enjoy this much-deserved ovation for your powerful performance. You deserve it. Reap the lavish praise and appreciation with genuine humility. Know that you allowed Me to use you as My blessed instrument. Enjoy your shining moment.

Allen C. Liles

JANUARY 6

Asking for Help

Ask and you shall receive. Seek and you will find. Knock and the door will be opened unto you.

Whenever you call to Me, I answer. I eagerly await your requests. One of My most important qualities is being available under any circumstance.

Do not wait until things become dire. Talk to Me constantly. Share your innermost thoughts and vulnerabilities. I AM already aware of anything you might bring Me. I want to help. I AM here to comfort and reassure you. Your needs are My concern.

Will I rescue you from negative choices? Yes, sometimes. But often your decisions, even the bad ones, become great learning opportunities for your spiritual growth. I help you understand the lessons involved.

Never hesitate to get down on your knees in times of trouble. This never indicates weakness. It demonstrates spiritual surrender and acknowledgment of your human limitations.

I deem no request as too unimportant. I want to guide you in all of life's crucial decisions and daily challenges. Call My name quickly when life closes in on you. I AM here, ready to share My wisdom, compassion, and comfort. I AM your counselor, your friend, your mentor, and your protector. Ask for My help and you shall receive it.

JANUARY 7

Being Fully Alive

Live purposefully and with intention. Do not drift or let material winds carry you off My path. Walk forward boldly.

I breathed life into you for a reason. I AM fulfilling an extraordinary goal through you. I sent you to comfort and bless others. I made you with the greatest of care. You possess many spiritual gifts encoded into your being. Use them openly and with gusto.

Stay alert for ways to serve Me. Breathe deeply. Fill your physical body with My divine essence. Let the Holy Spirit guide your path in every way.

Keep your eyes always focused, your mind clear, and your thoughts pure. Cast aside any negativity or useless distractions. Make each day count. Do something helpful for yourself or others. Learn a new thing about the world around you.

I created it, this wondrous earth. You can never grasp the entirety of its incomparable beauty. Open yourself to the splendor. Find treasure in a sunrise or sunset. Luxuriate in a gentle rain or soft breeze. Be grateful for a majestic mountain or a placid lake. Look with awe at the ocean's vastness.

And, to think, you are a part of all this grandeur. You have been given a designated place in the midst of incredible beauty. Be grateful.

You are alive at an exciting moment in the history of the world. Marvel at the technological feats that the human brain produces. Vow to make your own spiritual contribution to the world's betterment.

Carefully follow My divine plan for your life. Every individual lives more successfully when he or she aligns with Me. Listen for My daily guidance. Live your life to the maximum. I watch over your daily progress.

Allen C. Liles

JANUARY 8

I AM Here

Never doubt My presence. I AM closer than your hands or feet. I AM here within you. I conceived you, and I AM residing forever at your core. Therefore, you can never separate yourself from Me.

Yes, you may occasionally choose to separate. You forget our oneness. You set out on another path, one that may appear more attractive. You deem people, situations, and distractions more important than our relationship. I understand your humanity and planned for it. You are allowed the gift of free will. I give you the freedom to travel any path of your choice. But though you may temporarily leave Me, I never leave you. I AM a constant and steadfast presence that patiently awaits your eventual return. When you come back to Me, I do not admonish or judge you.

We could never be eternally separated. At the very least, we are finally reunited when you make your earthly transition. Then, as we once again meld into oneness, I gather you into My loving arms. I carry you back home to the heaven from whence you came. I was there for you at the beginning and I AM here for you at the end of days. I always wait patiently for you to acknowledge and bond with Me.

JANUARY 9

Staying Calm

I lead you beside the still waters. Behold their calmness. Yes, much can be happening out of your sight beneath those serene waters. But, on the surface, calm exists.

Roiled waters hide a churning and underlying fear that causes upset. They indicate a confused and chaotic state. Let your mind be peaceful as the stillest waters. Do not stir things up with thoughts that create distraction or turmoil.

Steering your ship of life across a sea of tranquility proves much easier. When the human brain fragments itself with negativity and temptation, your ship begins taking on water. Hold to the correct course. Stay centered. Find the proper balance and sail ahead with confidence and purpose.

Remember, you are the primary source of any unrest. Skewed thinking results in questionable actions and poor outcomes. Keep your focus on Me. I AM the one and only captain of your ship. I set the proper course. I keep you headed in the right direction. I instruct the waters of life to remain still while you glide safely over the whitecaps.

Calm waters lead to ordered thinking. A peaceful mind better navigates the most dangerous part of the ocean. Remain at peace despite any threat or storm. Nothing can harm you. I promise it.

Allen C. Liles

JANUARY 10

What's Next?

Life, as you know it on the physical earthy plane, has one constant theme. It is forever and always changing. No two days unfold exactly alike. One day the sun shines. On another day the clouds roll in. One afternoon may be dry, but the next afternoon could be rainy. The snow falls heavily some days, but the next day after a snowstorm you may shed your coat and walk forth in sweet warmth.

This remains true for everything in your life. You may be wealthy one day and totally broke the next. You could be enjoying a longtime career on Monday and be without gainful employment on Friday. Today may find you giddy with happiness. Just twenty-four hours later, your tears could be overflowing. Do you understand what I AM saying? The world fluctuates. Stability eludes it. Nothing stays the same. Relationships start and end. People, even those closest to you, come and go for various reasons. Even the dearest pets get old and die. Not one thing, including you, ever remains exactly the same. This represents temporal life as you know it.

In heaven, everything stays consistently beautiful. Peace prevails. You revel in each glorious moment. Time has no meaning. You remain forever safe and secure, content and happy. Your soul resides in constant splendor and unimaginable beauty. Your happiness continues throughout eternity. Your soul travels in a stunningly glorious environment. Physical pain has no place in My kingdom. If you experience ill health on earth, in heaven you know only perfect health. I AM only giving you the barest preview of what awaits you. Be comforted. I guarantee that the next place greatly exceeds any of your earthly experiences. Expect only the best.

JANUARY 11

Letting Go of Control

Thinking that you can completely control people, situations, and events demonstrates an unwillingness to accept reality. Trying to control anyone or anything outside yourself leads to a lifetime of frustration. You are simply not meant to control the unfolding of someone else's path. Another's destiny never rests in your hands. Trying to control how things happen and people act causes unnecessary emotional pain. Forcing your will on others sooner or later ends badly. On occasion, certain people may allow you to dominate them for a brief time. Then, when your attention strays elsewhere, they quickly dart away from you.

Save your time and energy. Give up your need to direct outcomes. Allow Me to do My job. I AM fully present at all times with each individual and in every situation. Focus any efforts to control someone on yourself. You are the only person who may pay heed, but sometimes even your own receptivity lags. Remember that you also possess free will. If you want to ignore My advice, you are certainly free to proceed otherwise.

Human nature abhors being controlled. Feel free to suggest or cajole. Those are common characteristics in human relationships. However, expect considerable rejection and blatant inattention to your wisdom. If you persist, today's attempt at control may lead to tomorrow's estrangement or total abandonment. Is that what you really want? Your time proves much better used when you work on changing yourself. Praying for divine order in the lives of others works best. Let go. Let Me be God and watch over everyone. Keep the focus on yourself.

Allen C. Liles

JANUARY 12

Praise Me

Praise Me in the good times. Praise Me even more in times of trouble. When you waver, praise Me. When you revel in material good fortune, do not forget to praise Me. When you enjoy wonderful health, praise Me. When you struggle to take a breath, praise Me. When people seek your presence, praise Me. When the same people ignore or reject you, praise Me. When you feel spiritually grounded, praise Me. When you sense moral bankruptcy threatening you, praise Me. Praise Me in the morning of life, and praise Me as you watch the sun start to set. In the spring, summer, fall, or winter, praise Me.

Never let a day go by without praising Me. Praise Me when happy days flow like wine. Praise Me when the nights become long and bitterness knocks at your door. Praise Me with passion and enthusiasm. Do not withhold praise, even when your energy wanes. Praise Me through the happiest laughter and the saddest tears. Rise above your current circumstances, and send your praise to the heavens. Find a reason to praise Me in the darkness or when the sun dawns for another day. Praise Me for My presence in your life. Praise Me when you think I AM gone forever. Praise Me without worry.

I hear everything. Give praise. I AM glad in it.

JANUARY 13

Humility

Find humility and embrace it. Hold it close. Honor it. Look for and treasure humility in others.

Becoming and remaining truly humble is one of the most important factors in anyone's life. On the flip side, being spiritually arrogant ranks as an especially undesirable trait. Regarding yourself as spiritually better than someone else affirms that the ego remains in charge. Even if your religious title includes minister, pastor, chaplain, choir director, lay leader, Father, or Sister, your human-based credentials do not raise you above others. If anything, your religious affiliation demands a much greater sense of humility.

You should know that only I ordain My disciples. I routinely give credentials to the lowest among you. Sometimes I travel into prisons to bestow My official blessing and spiritual ordination. There are times when I search through the homeless to locate the perfect recipient of My grace. Often, I must bypass the largest and richest cathedrals when looking for someone to do My work. I appreciate and bless the efforts of all clergy. It stands as a thankless occupation in many ways. But when I comb the world for potential advocates, I do not rule out anyone because of poverty or lack of academic credential. I search primarily for those who are teachable, truly humble, and possess loving and caring hearts.

The heart never lies. The mind can become arrogant and boastful, but deep in the heart of every human being rests his or her true self. I treasure the pure in heart. I know whether the heart really loves Me or just uses Me for the ego's selfish purposes.

Humility never means humiliating yourself before Me. True humility appears as quiet strength and powerful meekness. You instantly recognize real humility when you see it.

JANUARY 14

Spiritual Health

Your spiritual health ranks as My paramount concern. Eventually you shed your physical body and leave it behind. Only your soul travels forward to My kingdom. Any physical ills disappear forever when your soul enters heaven. Let Me repeat: no matter how many afflictions or diseases ravage your human body on earth, My kingdom operates pain free. You bring only one thing with you from your worldly experience: the consciousness your soul attained while living its earthly existence.

However high or low your conscious mind evolved during the material life, you carry it forward to eternity. Every soul rises, stays the same, or falls during its allotted time on earth. If you pursued oneness with Me, chances are that your conscious awareness advanced. If, on the other hand, your life focused on ego gratification, human sensations, carnality, and the pursuit of fame, wealth, or celebrity, your soul has probably slipped to a lower rung of consciousness.

Many people do not see either great advancement or precipitous decline during their worldly time spans. I always want you to increase your soul's progress. However, I receive you gladly into My kingdom wherever you stand.

JANUARY 15

Anxiety about the Future

Be anxious about nothing. Stay strong in Me. I guard you. I AM your shield. Do not fear the future. I protect you. Do not quake or tremble. Look only to Me for strength. I carry you over the blazing coals.

If someone or something wants to scare and intimidate you, that can mean only one thing: the person or spirit fears your presence and commitment to Me. Your spiritual progress threatens the forces of evil. Some of your foes may use "fear of the future" as ammunition in their attacks. If you spend precious time fretting about unrealized problems, you become distracted from our primary relationship.

Take solace in My ongoing promise to protect you. Eliminate any doubt regarding My power. It greatly exceeds that of your tormentors. Nestle under the comforting shadow of My wings. Cling ever closer when poisonous barbs fly your way. Be comforted and remain peaceful. The world may clamor at the gates, shouting for your destruction. But the loudness of those menacing cries fades over time. Meanwhile, I stand in front of you to deflect and absorb any blows. I AM your great protector, always more powerful than the most cunning foes. I can withstand any force or any threat. Be at peace.

JANUARY 16

Renewing the Mind

Protect the sanctity of your mind at all costs. Keep it pure and uncluttered as possible. Eliminate and avoid the multiple distractions of the world.

Your beautiful and unique mind represents a great spiritual gift. Never ruin or debase it. Feed your brain daily with only the positive. Filter out filth and negativity. You cannot imagine the awesome power contained in your mind. It can create miracles, construct the most beautiful architecture, and invent technological wonders.

Of course, a downside does exist. Your mind can also plan and carry out murder, direct destructive criminal enterprises, cast stones at the innocent, and inflict unimaginable harm to multitudes.

Free will often causes the human mind to falter and travel down questionable paths. Yet, I shaped your lovely mind so that it exists essentially as a spiritual tool. It usually responds to visions of love and caring. Your mind skews naturally toward the good and positive aspects of life. The world tries to corrupt its natural inclinations with negative images that infect your mind with the ugly and mean aspects of the human condition. A battle for control always rages inside your mind. Opposing forces strive daily for the upper hand. Because the visible world exists ever presently around you, it usually maintains an advantage. You are subject to the sights and sounds of the world's preoccupations.

Fight to keep your mind stayed on Me. Resist the ease of allowing the world to dominate your thoughts. Renew your mind constantly. Keep it filled with conscious thoughts of Me. Choose Me before any crassness that brings you lower. Your mind more easily embraces the possibilities of transformation when filled with thoughts of Me.

JANUARY 17

Patience

Be patient. Calm yourself. All unfolds in My time. Stay firm in your focus. Take all twenty-four hours as they appear every day. Keep alert for My daily guidance.

There is absolutely no need for you to retake control. I set the calendar. I reveal everything in its own time. Humanity wants answers now. It demands to know the outcome ahead of time for any situation or endeavor. Relax. Do today's work, and tomorrow will arrive in perfect order.

Worrying about the future fouls the present. Place your energy squarely on this moment, and go after your immediate tasks with determination. All is well. I take great care in helping you meet My schedule.

"Not too fast, not too slow" is My motto for completing the work spread before you. "Just right" is the way I characterize My divine order. I have constructed your day with ample time for both work and rest. And, yes, I also throw in a little "play" every now and then. I want your life to reflect balance and pace. Patience with the unfolding of your journey plays a key role in successfully fulfilling your spiritual destiny. All is well. Trust Me.

Allen C. Liles

JANUARY 18

Lost in the Wilderness

Life in the visible world can indeed become a complex wilderness. One beautiful day you travel easily on a smooth eight-lane freeway with no traffic in sight. Overnight, you might find yourself lost in a dense jungle with no discernible path. At times, you skip along happily singing a song at the top of your lungs. At other moments, you lie spent, battered, and defeated. Every tissue in the world cannot dry your tears. For years, you successfully pursue a business career or profession. Then the sun rises one day and everything has suddenly disappeared, taking your stature and identity along with it. What do all of these common and natural occurrences say about the material world? *Everything changes.* The earth stays forever in flux. A human being can feel forever lost in a changing and complex world.

How do you make sense of this confounding maze? When you seem lost in any situation, I AM but a quick summons away. Call My name. I come in a hurry, bringing a spiritual compass that leads you back to safety. Disorientation strikes frequently as you traverse the world. So many side roads beckon invitingly. They often appear interesting, attractive, and pleasurable. You know them well by their earthly names: power, wealth, fame, sex, drugs, and various addictions. Most of these unpaved roads lead to the nearest cliff. Everyone gets tempted at some point by the allure of a lovely, new, and promising side path. So many lives wind up at the bottom of a ravine because of poorly marked roads. The moral wilderness exists everywhere. A correct path to safety and freedom begins and ends with Me. I AM the way, the truth, and the life in every situation. No matter how lost or defeated you may feel, I stand ready to lead you home. I always hold the divine plan for your life in My hands. I know your final destination. Whenever you become ready to get back on track, I AM waiting with your correct itinerary.

JANUARY 19

Know Me

My will for your life is that you know Me. Know Me in the morning. Know Me in the afternoon. Know Me in the evening. Know Me in good times. Try to know Me even better in the bad times. Know Me when the sun shines, but also know Me when the clouds darken. Know Me before you try to know anyone or anything else. Everything in your life flows properly when you know Me.

Knowing Me allows you to meet the challenges that always come. Knowing Me helps you understand, accept, and deal with the changes that challenge you on a regular basis. Concentrate on knowing Me, My will, and My ways. Seek Me first, and all else will be added to you. I stand ready to increase our closeness. I want us to become better acquainted. I can then use you to complete My divine plans.

Our friendship lasts throughout eternity. We can never be separated or torn asunder. You and I are joined forever.

In any relationship, a time arrives for talking, and another time comes for listening. There is a time to rest and a time for action. There is a time for enlightenment and a time to ponder that enlightenment. Just know Me better, and see My plan for you through to completion. Everything falls into place. Trust Me.

Allen C. Liles

JANUARY 20

Faith Battles

Every day represents a test of faith. You are now under spiritual attack designed to probe how strong your belief in Me may be. Stay close during this time. Together we can make it through. Realize what may be on the line. Your very salvation could depend on your strength and courage. Toughen up. Tighten the invisible cloak of faith that protects you from the elements. Hunker down in faith. Fill your mind with comforting thoughts of Me. Sense My presence in and around you.

These are not simple or easy times. They require a strength and uncommon courage not possible by most. You will get through this patch. I promise that enough faith exists to overcome any moment of doubt. Just know that you are experiencing a severe test of just how much faith you possess. It would be understandable to just throw up your hands and quit. Do not even consider it. Stay on the path to glory. Reaffirm our divine relationship.

Heaven stands ready to protect and defend you. You are always surrounded by angels, each more than ten feet tall. I AM your consummate deliverer when challenges become seemingly impossible to overcome. Just reinforce your faith to the maximum. Trust Me to get you through the fire.

JANUARY 21

Suffering

Prepare for suffering. It will surely come. Suffering is the way of the world. Troubles can often multiply when you least expect them. Feeling overwhelmed casts you down upon the rocks of doubt.

When your burdens crush you physically, mentally, and spiritually, look up to Me. I relieve your suffering. You never suffer alone when I AM near. Look for the higher lesson in each problem. Know that something may be learned each time you stumble. Understand that our adversaries want you to give up and quit. You worry them because of your closeness and devotion to Me. Most of your fellow human beings would have given up by now. But you still plod on, dedicated to My will and work. Of course you slip a bit now and then. Yet you come back, determined as ever. That confounds the forces that control the world. Then they hit you a little harder. Never fear. You and I can withstand any blow. We are ready for their attacks. They cannot win. Rise up from your knees when you feel defeated. Surprise your foes with added strength and determination. You are much stronger than you think. When the suffering seems never ending, remain steadfast. I will not fail you.

Allen C. Liles

JANUARY 22

Cloudy Days

Give thanks for "gray day" lessons. Thank Me for providing difficult but powerful learning experiences. Ours is not an easy path. Courage serves as a necessary element in becoming honed like steel. Add courage to determination and perseverance, and you get the correct formula for success on the spiritual climb.

Achieving goals spiritually and humanly are two different things. Human accomplishments provide good feelings and act as boosts to your self-esteem. I want you to feel positive about yourself as a productive and successful human being. Setting material goals also provides opportunities to demonstrate commitment and dedication. But spiritual training ups the stakes. It requires a higher level of inner strength. For one thing, your opposition exerts power not of this world. It wants your spirit to falter and fail. Forces not seen or felt on the human level regularly appear to confuse and thwart you. You can still succeed, but only with My help. Find the extra surge of strength necessary to complete your training and preparation. Be strong in Me. Turn swiftly to Me when the cloudy days depress you. Thank Me for assigning you these important lessons. I AM here to help you complete your homework.

JANUARY 23

Turning Things Over

I know the human ego abhors letting go of control. I understand that. The ego wallows in fear. Whenever control becomes loosened, fear surfaces. Overcoming the ego means overcoming fear.

Allowing Me to direct your life puts you into the divine flow. I replace fear with love. When I rule, love also rules. When you cede control to Me, you are choosing love. Taking fear out of your life constitutes one of the most positive changes possible. With love comes My grace. When you surrender the keys, I drive the car. My grace serves as the fuel for that car. When your life begins to run smoothly on grace, you flow down life's highways with ease, purpose, and safety. Yes, you may experience a flat tire every now and then. A stray rock can sail through your windshield on occasion. It may also leave a nick or two. But basically your journey speeds easily to its final destination without major delay.

You alone must make the decision to turn your life over to Me. I understand that you can choose to release control one minute and retrieve it the next. You must cope with the ego's ingrained reluctance to surrender any of its territory. Just continue making the decision to cede control to Me as often as you must. Keep turning everything over—every day, hour, and minute. Stand amazed at how much better things suddenly go. I know the exact path you need to travel. My directions are perfect. I AM carrying you safely home with Me, with a lot of interesting scenery along the way. Sit in the back of My limo and relax. Enjoy the glorious ride.

Allen C. Liles

JANUARY 24

Finding Peace in a Crisis

When a crisis comes, immediately take several deep breaths. Each time you breathe in, you fill your lungs with My presence. Whenever you exhale, you are releasing anxiety, concern, and worry. Breathe deeply of My strength and power to overcome the world. Know that My presence ensures that everything works out in divine order. When a crisis strikes, your human mind starts racing. It searches frantically for solutions. As you breathe deeply, picture Me sorting out all the options. See Me coming up with the perfect plan. Envision Me as your personal crisis manager. I AM on the job, making sure the right pieces fit together for your highest good. Just keep breathing Me into every situation.

I AM the divine answer to all troubles. Trust Me. When you feel scattered and overwhelmed, see Me laboring on your behalf. Let go of your frenetic human effort to control outcomes. Sit down. Take the time to really breathe. Every breath summons Me. No crisis exceeds My abilities. I can also manage more than one problem at a time. Hand everything over to Me. Try Me. I will not fail you. Keep breathing.

JANUARY 25

Crying Out for Help

I hear your cries for help. I answer them. I surround you with guardian angels. I rush toward you with extra strength and comfort. You call out, and I respond. I have already sent you several angels, each disguised in the form of a helpful and caring person. I always provide the correct answers, which arrive in various but direct ways. You are never alone. I AM with you, now and forever. No cry for help goes unanswered by Me. Stay calm and peaceful. Move forward slowly but deliberately. The right path becomes clear. I always show you the perfect way. Opposition does surface, but we overcome it. Delays may cause concern, but they are only temporary. Remember: this too shall pass. I AM here, right now, by your side. Together we can walk through any test of faith. Put one foot in front of the other. Keep your gaze fixed on Me. I guide and direct every action.

No matter what negative appearances signal, all is well. Nothing in the material world can harm you. I absolutely guarantee your safety. Display trust in Me at all times. I AM your Savior in every challenge, your constant friend in the fiery furnace. Have faith, My child. I hear your cries and I AM here for you.

Allen C. Liles

JANUARY 26

Human Disappointments

Important human lessons can evolve from the deepest disappointments. Forgiveness stands as one of life's greatest lessons. Remember what was said on the cross: "Father forgive them for they know not what they do." If those words could be uttered during the violence and sadness of the crucifixion, can you not also be as forgiving?

You are bound to experience countless disappointments during your human lifetime. If you can overcome those feelings of rejection and abandonment with genuine forgiveness, you have mastered a valuable and enduring lesson. No one wants to feel painful nails piercing their hands or wear the unsightly crown of thorns. Yet behold what a life changing event took place that terrible day on a faraway hill. What unbelievable examples of forgiveness, understanding, and acceptance the world witnessed.

Try to locate the forgiveness factor in every human disappointment. If you search long enough, it finally surfaces. Rising above normal feelings of hurt, self-pity, anger, and a desire for revenge proves ultimately rewarding. I urge you to replace bitterness with love. Let a forgiving spirit envelop anyone who disappoints you. Forgiveness acts as the blessed salve that heals every wound. Apply it generously and often.

JANUARY 27

Hold Fast

Cling more tightly to Me when the sudden storms of life threaten disaster. Hold fast even when you feel torn apart and defeated. Face directly into the wind and call out My name. I will come and defend you.

Consider any test a divine paradox. On one hand, your human life may be tottering. Yet, on the other hand, your spiritual strength increases as I AM introduced into the fray. Attacks appear in fearsome guises. Banish fear, in whatever form it may approach you. Tell it, "Go away and leave me alone." I help you make that command a reality.

Hear Me! Nothing can harm you when I AM near. You are surrounded by the strongest of spiritual steel. Stand up straight and tall. Bend, but do not break. You are shielded by Me, the strongest and most powerful force in the universe. I AM sorting things out. I gird you for battle and help deny victory to those who seek your scalp for their mantle. They cannot ever bring you down. Just remain steadfast, no matter how severe the storm becomes. March forward with your standard raised high. Be determined. Keep going until the end. Additional forces are speeding now to your side. They guarantee your eventual triumph. Hold on. Together, we ride out any real or perceived tempest. Cling only to Me.

Allen C. Liles

JANUARY 28

A Time for Everything

I decide the timing for the two most important events in your life—a time to be born and a time to die. You make most of the other decisions in between. I create important events and situations along the way. I also bring significant people into your life. You then possess the free will to interact with My nudges as you so desire.

Understand there are absolutely no accidents in life. I know your "life plan" already and implement it daily. However, I do give you the free will to follow or ignore Me. In My kingdom, everything operates with perfect timing. When you turn your will and your life over to Me, divine order takes over. My plan for you goes into operation and unfolds with impeccable precision. When you live under My auspices, life flows more smoothly. When you choose to live under your "plan," things usually go awry quickly and often.

Please recall that virtually everything taking place in your earthly life involves some kind of lesson. You require ongoing learning experiences in order to progress spiritually. Many of these "courses of instruction" prove painful in the short term. Look beyond the pain and discomfort. Try to discern the importance of each lesson. As I said, you control much of the timing about how your earthly life unfolds. Ego decisions either accelerate or delay completion of necessary lessons. However, your eventual fate lies squarely with Me. I decide every detail of your birth—place, time, and circumstances. I also coordinate every aspect of your transition from earth into the majesty of My kingdom.

I urge you to let go and let me decide the timing of what lies between those two poles. I never fail or disappoint. Given the opportunity, I guarantee you an overall happy and rewarding human experience. My timing or yours—it remains your choice.

JANUARY 29

Every Step

Every step you take leads somewhere. You are moving either forward or backward at all times. When you walk with Me, the direction points forward. When you veer off My path, you usually backslide. Think about it. As you get up every morning, many choices await you. How many decisions must you make before the sun goes down tonight? Most of these choices seem rather mundane—*What should I eat for breakfast? Which TV shows shall I watch tonight? What movie should I see?* But at other times, the decisions could be life changing. You find yourself deciding crucial issues: *Whom should I marry? Which college or university should I attend? What job or profession should I pursue? How much money should I borrow? Which person should I allow into My life?* And so your life goes, from sunrise to sunset.

All of these choices eventually baffle and confuse most human beings. Usually, people just go with the crowd. They tell themselves: "It's time for me to get married" or "I should buy a new car." I AM here to say: Take every step with Me by your side. I assist you in carrying this burden of daily choices. Trust Me that I know what is best for you. When you put all the decision-making on yourself, mistakes happen. It becomes too much for you to bear alone. Seek My help in deciding precisely what steps to take before stumbling down an unfamiliar and dangerous path. Let Me guide you, and success becomes guaranteed.

Allen C. Liles

JANUARY 30

The Long Night

All long nights eventually end. Just when you think the darkness lasts forever, the first light of dawn faintly appears. Of course, the sun does not just automatically pop up in its full radiance. It rises slowly, gradually easing away the night. The same orderliness happens in the spiritual world. At the exact moment you feel without hope, you begin detecting a subtle change for the better.

I never allow the soul to experience perpetual darkness. During the most severe tests and challenges, I AM already planning the moment of daybreak. While waiting out the void, your job consists of moving forward with courage and determination. Never fear about being stuck in the depths forever. Believe that a new dawn approaches. I know long nights can be depressing and scary. When languishing in bottomless doubt, keep believing in Me. I assure you that all tests and trials do end at some point. Affirm your closeness with Me. Do not lose the will to fight the battle for your soul. I never told you the path to heaven was easy or simple. However, I assure you of My constant presence, even during the darkest night. Grip My hand tightly. Together we will behold a new day.

JANUARY 31

Holy Ground

You stand on holy ground. Wherever you may be at this very moment constitutes holy ground. When you wait in the express lane at the supermarket, you stand on holy ground. If you work as a mechanic in the service department of an auto dealership, that is holy ground. If you teach children in a classroom, you tread on holy ground. If you serve in the military and stand watch on some foreign battlefield, your feet touch holy ground. You take this holiest of ground with you to the ends of the earth and even into outer space. Wherever you and I meet up every morning constitutes holy ground. You take My presence into business meetings, the surgical operating room of a hospital, the shopping mall, or your church, synagogue, or mosque. Where you stand at this very moment, I bless that particular ground as holy.

I always work out My miracles on holy ground. I do My healings at this sacred place, using you as My instrument. We move together as one entity. I walk with you to bless and comfort. You can travel anywhere in My name. I AM completing the world's destiny on the holy ground where you stand or kneel. Just follow My instructions. Go where I send you. Do your sacred work with confidence and skill. I assure your success.

Allen C. Liles

FEBRUARY

*Ask and it will be given to you; seek and you will
find; knock and the door will be opened to you.*

—Matthew 7:7 (NIV)

FEBRUARY 1

Doubt

Every human being experiences doubt. You live in a world of misguided and sinful beliefs. Doubt acts as an additional weight in trying to cope with life. Doubt causes you mental, emotional, and spiritual pain in a number of ways. Since the material world thrives on envy, jealousy, idolatry, and pleasure of the senses, doubt always lurks in the background, waiting to attack your self-esteem.

Think on these things. You compare yourself to others in terms of wealth, outward attractiveness, professional abilities, academic achievements, personal relationships, and even spirituality. You want to achieve perfection, which looms as an ultimate goal for most human beings. I tell you that perfection in earthly terms will always elude you. Settle for progress. Forgive yourself for not being perfect. I created you originally in absolute perfection. Your perfect soul departed My kingdom and began its worldly trek. Are you still perfect after the earth's daily bombardment and the introduction of doubt into your human consciousness? In My eyes, you still remain absolutely perfect. You are no less perfect today than the exact moment your soul departed heaven. That never changes.

How can you confront and overcome human doubt? By faith and a stronger belief in Me, you can at least neutralize its effect. Acknowledge doubt if you must, but never let it control you. Do not doubt My unconditional love for you. Give up seeking perfection and universal approval from others. Accept yourself as you truly are, a child of God.

Allen C. Liles

FEBRUARY 2

Finding True Love

Love begets love. The surest way to attract love into your life is to become loving yourself. One lover seeks another. I brought you and your dear wife together. I knew you would recognize each other. A compassionate heart finds itself drawn to a similar kindness, warmth, and understanding. A generous heart searches for the same generosity of spirit.

People should quit searching endlessly for human love. When based solely on ego needs, this type of love never lasts. Indiscriminate sex absolutely does not represent eternal love. Neither do attractive physical traits, such as a beautiful face and form or a rugged handsomeness. Yes, a person can definitely possess both inner and outer beauty. But outside features often exceed inner development. All physical beauty fades over time. Then, only the light from inner beauty remains constant.

Here are the basic rules for finding what the world calls "true love." First, love Me with all of your heart and soul. I alone can fill you with basic spiritual qualities, such as kindness, compassion, and understanding. These are the essential traits that draw like-minded people into your life. Second, love yourself. I created you in My image and likeness. I AM love incarnate. You mirror My attributes. You are inherently loving and loveable. Third, love others. Open your heart. A closed heart hides behind a thick wall. You will spend your days and nights attempting to scale this wall with little or no success. See the best in others, but remain cautious. Wait until the inner light becomes fully revealed. Spiritual love always connects. Love drawn from the Spirit lasts into eternity. Neither time nor trouble dims its light. When true love arrives, you discover heaven on earth. Happiness and joy then follow you both all the days of your life and beyond.

FEBRUARY 3

Forgive Yourself

You must forgive yourself. I have already forgiven you. Please release any judgment against yourself. You did the best you could. Have you made mistakes in your life? You are a human being, so yes. Could you have done things differently? Of course, but the paths you chose and decisions you made brought necessary lessons. Being overly regretful at this point brings only shame and guilt. Any somber musing about the past causes unproductive pain for you. Did you hurt others with your words and actions? Then consider making direct amends whenever possible, except when doing so would injure them or others. Begin with offering amends to yourself. You stand as your own worst critic by far. Give it up! You can do without shouldering extra blame from any source, especially yourself. The world usually supplies enough blame and judgment to go around.

View yourself as a flawed but special child of Mine. You were perfect once, before you ever walked the earth. You become perfect once again when you enter heaven. In between, you make the free will choices that produce life's lessons. Despite any or all of your choices, I never stop caring about you. I always love you, no matter what.

FEBRUARY 4

Staying Strong

Now comes a time of severe testing for you. You have traveled down a long stretch of highway during your lifetime. Often you experienced the road as smooth and pleasant. Other times the bumpiness kept you swerving from side to side in search of a stable ride. Occasionally, a complete detour loomed unexpectedly. Detours by nature are unpredictable and vexing. No one ever promised that each day of your life would be cloudless and serene. Not only can the road ahead get rough and frightening, but sudden storms also complicate things. The rain comes and the wind chills you. You strain to maintain control. You wonder if you possess enough strength to withstand the pounding. You pray for relief and a smoother stretch of road. Nothing happens. Instead, things get worse. It all seems never ending, this test of your perseverance, strength, and courage. Everything becomes harder when someone you love must endure even greater struggle and uncertainty. You cry for their pain, but you also cry about your own. You realize that unless you remain strong, life could unravel for both of you.

In the midst of this turmoil, please hear this promise: "My rod and My staff, they comfort you." I help you hold on. I go before you, clearing the way. Delve deep within yourself. Find the powerful reserve of strength that I embedded at your core. Tap into it now. I bolster your courage during this hour of travail. I AM always at your side. Someday, the crooked road will become straight again. I promise it.

FEBRUARY 5

Stress of the Cross

Stress has become the curse of human life. I understand stress. Do you not think I felt stressed as I hung upon the cross? I felt rejected, abandoned, and sentenced to a tortuous death. I know that life on earth often feels like a crucifixion. You cry, alone and frustrated, without even a semblance of hope. You must realize that all crucifixions eventually end. No crucifixion experience lasts forever. Someday the agony, pain and aloneness becomes but a distant memory. It slides silently away into the ethers as your soul moves forward on its path to heaven.

Meanwhile, as you endure whatever cross life hoists you on, turn to Me. Call out My name. I come at once, bringing peace and hope. I assure you, "This too shall pass." However painful your crucifixion may be, I promise that we can get through it together.

Everyone will someday feel the stress of hanging on the cross. The world sometimes even places you on more than one cross at a time. This doubles or triples your human stress. Keep the faith in what I tell you: every crucifixion ends at some point. Until that moment, I help you cope with anything and everything that life inflicts upon you. However stressful, I will love you through it.

Allen C. Liles

FEBRUARY 6

The Steep Path

The path becomes especially steep for you now. You sense danger and uncertainty. Familiar landmarks disappear. Night falls, and you grope blindly through the darkness. Nothing seems easy anymore. You feel restless, afraid, and unsure. You look around. Everything smacks of trouble and possible disaster. You search for answers, but none come. Things just keep getting worse and more precarious.

Wait! Do you not feel My presence on the path beside you? Do you not sense me steadying you for the climb ahead and then bracing you for a safe descent? Did you really think I would abandon you when the path became narrow and treacherous? I hope that you know Me better than that! You are never alone when danger lurks. No matter how steep the path may unfold, I never leave your side. I do not disappear when life gets hard. I AM at My absolute best during difficult times. Take My hand, and grasp it tightly. Hold on to Me with confidence. Do not allow fear to ever separate us. Never consider stopping or reversing direction. I have chosen this particular path for you.

Someday, when the journey finally reaches completion, you will glance back with wonder and satisfaction. You and I will have traversed a tricky and often rocky trail, fraught with many twists, turns, and challenges. You will be able to truthfully say, "Yes, it was all worth it." You stayed the course. We walked the hard path together and not only survived. We flourished.

FEBRUARY 7

Divine Assistance

Ask for My help. I want to hear your cries for divine intervention. Seeking assistance in times of trouble shows good mental health and personal awareness. Serious problems require more than one set of hands. Do not tackle life's hardest challenges alone. These are tough times for you. Call on Me now.

I AM the cavalry. I ride to your rescue. Never hesitate. When I come, I bring all My spiritual weapons: faith, trust, courage, wisdom, perseverance, strength, commitment, and love. These are only a few of the arrows in My quiver. You are facing strong, cunning, and determined foes. I enjoy spiritual battles and never shy away from them. Let Me protect you.

Trust Me as your primary caregiver and sacred resource. I AM the grand deliverer. I save you from the jaws of defeat and death. I relieve your exhaustion and weariness. I prevent you from surrendering your hard-earned spiritual progress. I lift you above worry and resignation. Trust Me. My strength and My divine plan carry you safely out of harm's way. I snatch you away from the forces of darkness. Call for Me quickly when storms threaten to engulf you. I fly to your side.

Allen C. Liles

FEBRUARY 8

Addictions

All addictions separate us. There are almost as many addictions as people. A few of these cravings may be more benign than others. However, the primary result of any addiction remains the same. It claims a part of you that otherwise would ordinarily be aligned with Me. When you find yourself in the throes of any severe addiction, you and I become unable to function as one divine unit. You become obsessed and dedicated to some outside distraction that drives you away from Me. The addiction acts as a sharp knife that severs our connection. Nothing that disrupts our unity can be considered good. Please hear Me. The real danger of any addiction lies in its ability to separate you from Me. When our relationship breaks down, you lose your spiritual moorings. You go offline. You give up control to a third party. You misplace your true identity as a child of God.

For you to thrive, we must be reunited. When you and I return to oneness, you become whole again. By themselves, most people stand powerless before one, two, or even more addictions. When any outside entity gains control over your life, spiritual growth stops and insanity takes over. At your inner core, you long for oneness with Me. No matter how compelling an addiction may be, your spiritual essence remains constant. As you begin the return to Me, that inner spark of divinity beckons once more. Please hear Me again. For you to rediscover your true self, we must stay united in oneness.

Come back home, My child. I want you to realize happiness and peace of mind. Heaven and earth await your decision. Turn away from addiction, and turn back to Me.

FEBRUARY 9

The Treasure

I AM the treasure you seek. Some think the treasure lies in a bank account or career. Others think the treasure can be found in sex, power, and fame. Here lies the real secret: true treasures of the spirit are never visible to the naked eye. If you can see it, taste it, feel it, smell it, or hear it, then it is not the treasure. The human senses are simply incapable of identifying the real treasure of life on earth. Where does the treasure hide? It resides within you, at the core of your being. I personally placed the treasure in this sacred location when I created you. It always waits patiently for you to discover its divine presence.

The world tries to mislead and confuse you. It flashes the glittery baubles of materiality before you and proclaims, "Behold the greatest treasures available on earth!" Meanwhile, I gently tap you on the shoulder and whisper, "Here lies the real treasure of the universe, deep within you." It is I that stands ready to bestow this priceless gift upon you. When you open your mind and heart to Me, I place it firmly in your grateful hands. Once you receive the treasure, no one can ever take it from you. It remains in your possession, from here to eternity and beyond.

What do I call this treasure? It is the Christ Spirit within you. Think about it: I placed My very self at the center of you. I AM always there, awaiting your call. Once you receive the treasure, you are forever blessed. You become more confident as you face the challenges of life, knowing that the treasure waits closer than your hands or feet. The treasure protects you, supports you, and bolsters your spirit. Come immediately to your center and claim your treasure now. Claim Me.

Allen C. Liles

FEBRUARY 10

Battle for the Soul

Spiritual warfare exists. Your soul lies at the center of the struggle. Never be misled. Control of the soul looms as the ultimate spiritual prize. The Christ Spirit—the Holy Spirit—waits within you to assist in the battle. The battle for your soul rages at all times.

The forces of darkness gain an upper hand at times. After all, your basic human nature reflects the foibles of the carnal world. You are afflicted with various ego-centered weaknesses. The Evil One searches relentlessly for your vulnerabilities. When they are uncovered, he mercilessly exploits them. If sex seems your weak point, temptation abounds. Should money become your God, opportunities for dishonest or ill-gotten wealth present themselves constantly. If you love and seek power for its own sake, you will be afforded many chances to exercise it in negative ways. Whenever you fall prey to one or more of these potential shortcomings, the principalities of darkness pour on the coals. They seek to separate us on the earthly level, once and for all time. We must reluctantly give them their just due. They are determined and wily in their canny devilishness.

What can you do when the battle for your soul commences? First, cling more tightly to Me. Second, activate the Holy Spirit on your behalf. Third, remain forever steadfast and faithful. You, the Holy Spirit, and I will eventually prevail. The blessed Trinity always proves more powerful than our opposition. The protected soul emerges intact and purified. Victory embraces us. The battle ends in triumph, at least for now.

FEBRUARY 11

Waiting

Waiting for anything proves extremely challenging for most human beings. You want "it," whatever "it" is, right now. You take a pill and expect instant relief. You accept a corporate job and immediately want a quick promotion and top-dollar salary. You buy a stock and become disappointed when it fails to double overnight. You go out partying and want to get drunk quickly, so you guzzle down numerous straight shots in order to speed up the process. You want to contact a friend, so you text him or her while driving on a busy highway.

All of these attitudes reflect a world built on instant gratification. Waiting has become a lost art in today's "hurry up" culture.

In the process of spiritual transformation, learning to wait is paramount. Growing spiritually emphasizes the practice of waiting. In meditation, you "wait" in the silence. In prayer, you "wait" for an answer. You "wait" for the revelation of My will for you. Transformation of the mind and heart takes time. No offense, but most human beings are slow learners. Many lessons need repeating before they get completely absorbed. Waiting is a game of patience and faith. Recall what the Bible says, in Hebrews 11:1, about faith being sure of what we hope for and certain of what we do not see. This sums up the idea of waiting. You must keep the faith and stay patient even when things do not instantly happen. Remember the phrase "Wait upon the Lord." Spiritual growth is not a short race where you quickly sprint to the finish line. You walk it purposefully, with determination and precision. Wait for My divine guidance. Wait for My wisdom. Wait for the process to unfold. I promise that the end results make everything worth the wait.

Allen C. Liles

FEBRUARY 12

The Strong Heart

Life often becomes difficult for even the strongest heart. The heart acts as the physical body's center of feelings and emotions. When unexpected problems or extreme hurt intrude, the heart is usually the first to react. It may already store memories of similar or other traumatic events. It vividly recalls past pain and discomfort.

When the heart begins to falter, let your mind come into play. Encourage the brain to focus on how you survived past moments of uncertainty and confusion. I also come quickly to bolster the heart in times of distress. I bring My own "crash cart" of reassurance and strength. I tell your heart that it is strong enough to survive anything. I keep the heart beating evenly in good rhythm. I do not let it skip a single beat. Continue asking your mind to cooperate with the recovery process. Never allow the brain to panic with wild thoughts of imminent disaster. Stay cool. Slow things down. Breathe. Keep your feet rooted firmly on the floor. Do not race hither and yon. Let your phone remain silent. No texts or e-mail. Lower your voice when you speak. Make your words clear and focused. Visualize yourself coming through any crisis intact. See whatever the eventual results are as a win-win for everyone involved.

I AM closely following the heart throughout this challenging period. I send extra energy and a sense of well-being. I know the heart suffers from anxiety and fear. Today your dear wife went into the hospital by ambulance, and your heart sank. I hear your prayers for her. I AM with you both during these difficult moments. I monitor both of you closely through the storm, and I will stay with you when the storm passes. Stand strong and expect your devoted hearts to do the same.

FEBRUARY 13

A Beautiful World

I appreciate your heartfelt concern for your dear wife. Please know that I am monitoring you both very carefully. In the meantime, I want you to consider the beautiful gift of the world around you. I created a physical world unexcelled in wonder and beauty. Its grandeur and scope are beyond compare. Humankind forms a crucial element of the world and its natural magnificence. You act as its steward and caretaker. I have assigned you to preserve and protect My incredible splendor. I give you the task of supervising the earth's maintenance. I made you with the appreciative mind and loving heart needed to accomplish this task.

View the earth's spectacular mountains, limitless oceans, deep forests, flowing rivers, endless deserts, and glistening lakes as irreplaceable art. Never consider despoiling or harming the beauty that I made for you. It is imperative that you leave the world as you found it. Try to preserve and save the earth's living things. Guard the purity of My planet with commitment and determination. Never knowingly alter My masterpiece. See yourself as the physical world's ultimate guardian, entrusted with the singular responsibility of maintaining its eternal beauty. Dedicate yourself to the worthy project of ongoing preservation. Treat My unique planet with caution, reverence, and respect. Let nothing threaten or defile it. Help the earth and its creatures endure and thrive forever.

Allen C. Liles

FEBRUARY 14

Day of Love

A day of love is a day filled with gratitude and thanksgiving. You should not only give love but become love. Behold the Christ in everyone you meet. Look for eternal light in others. Thank Me for both the wonders and problems of life. Bring love, and spread it generously around every challenge. Someone needs to feel your love. Do not let the sun set tonight without providing that reassurance. Walk with love, talk with love, write with love, and act with love.

Replace anger with love. Start by loving yourself. You already know that I love you. I have told you so on many occasions. Forgive yourself, but dispense with any negative judgment you make about yourself. Is any human being perfect? Of course not, but My love makes you perfect in My eyes. I made you with a spark of love at your core. The love within never disappears, even when you forget its presence. You may reignite its lovely flame anytime you wish.

Be especially grateful when anyone expresses love for you. It means that you have connected with something sacred within another person. Look with a thankful heart on the beautiful things of life, such as nature, art, and music. They are all reflections of My love for you. Be a lover of the good inherent in the world. Today is made for love. Reach out. In love, touch a hand already reaching out for you.

FEBRUARY 15

Human Strengths and Weaknesses

Here are your main human strengths: perseverance, faithfulness, determination, responsibility, generosity, loyalty, and (for the most part) surrendering to My will. These are your primary human weaknesses: self-righteousness, judgmental attitude toward others, not forgiving the past, and co-dependence. On the last two (not forgiving the past and co-dependence) you have shown some improvement. However, on acting in a self-righteous manner and judging others, you still have work to do. First of all, you must remember that I have already forgiven you for every single one of your human weaknesses. You should also know that I glory in each of your human strengths.

Life can be incredibly hard sometimes. You are going through such a period of testing right now. It will take perseverance and determination (two of your strengths) to get beyond this difficult time intact. To ride out the storm, you must release the outcome to Me. Give up trying to control anything except your own attitude and actions. Wanting to control every situation constitutes a basic human trait. I understand that. You were raised by your family of origin to take responsibility for people and events. But no one can hold you personally responsible for things outside your control.

I AM here to do the things that you cannot do alone. Your immediate responsibility is to trust Me. Allow Me to do My job. Stand close by and watch while I work things out. See how I move through the complexities of every problem. Sometimes I act with amazing speed. Other times I AM slow and deliberate. Use your human strengths to assist Me, but let Me supply the solution to every challenge.

Allen C. Liles

FEBRUARY 16

Finding Peace

When the world crashes around you, turn within. When you feel abandoned and rejected, turn within. When all hope for the future vanishes, turn within. I wait for you there. I AM your rock. I AM your comforter. I AM your deliverer. I AM the center of peace that you need. I AM the fountain of strength and courage you require. I offer you the living water that purifies and cleanses. I bathe you in My light and My love. I bandage your physical and mental wounds. I offer you healing of emotions and physical discomfort. Come now in your moment of weakness. Nestle in My arms like a dependent babe, eager for a father and mother's protection and sustenance. Feel My power to heal you. When you hurt, I soothe the pain. When you become tired and weary, My grace replenishes you. When you want to simply give up and walk away, My grace calls you back to the struggle. My grace supports and delivers you. Please hear Me, My child. You are never alone. When you need a friend, call Me. When you feel unloved, call Me. When you think the world has turned against you, call Me. In every circumstance, I come without delay. I AM your first and last resort in times of struggle and uncertainty.

FEBRUARY 17

Life Goes On

Somewhere today a new human life enters the world. With hope and promise, the new babe emerges from a grateful mother's womb. Somewhere else, another human life nears its end. Perhaps an aged one has become weary and seeks eternal rest. The departing soul's physical body may be coping with unrelenting pain and desiring blessed relief. Then, freed at last, it can float upward to My kingdom. Every second of every day, this blessed cycle of life repeats itself. From birth to death and beyond, humanity goes on.

On the first day of a new week, someone begins a new job or career. Probably on the last working day of the new week, someone else retires after many years of valued service. In the spring, new graduates pour forth from schools at every level. Look ahead to the coming fall and you will witness new students taking their place. People get married, divorced, or become widowed and then marry again.

You see where I AM going with all of these examples? They all illustrate the way of the physical world. The sun rises every morning; it sets tonight and then rises again tomorrow. I AM as constant as the sun, only more so. As your life predictably follows one cycle after another, I AM the one constant. I AM always present, no matter where you are at any moment in your earthly journey. I release every new soul into the world. I also greet each returning soul when it reenters heaven. In between, I wait patiently for you to get Me involved in your human life at any stage.

Allen C. Liles

FEBRUARY 18

Divine Forces

Divine forces are at work for you and your dear wife. They have marshaled themselves together on your behalf. Angels appear daily to assist you both. My divine planners are also quite busy setting the exact timetable for your smoother path. With some specific dates already charted, your overall schedule is being firmed up as we speak.

You have one basic responsibility: keep turning everything over to Me. Keep nothing back for yourself. I want it all. I know the limits of your energy and human strength. I never allow earth-born situations to slip past your ability to cope. I realize some challenges can go right up to the edge of your capabilities. But My divine forces are more than able to navigate the rigorous tests you both are facing. My angels stand ten feet tall. They possess incredible strength and unlimited power. While they must shrink themselves when assuming a human guise, their amazing abilities never diminish. In addition, all the divine intelligence of My kingdom meets daily to review their plans for you. They gauge progress and make adjustments as needed. They tell Me that you and your dear wife are exactly where you need to be at the moment.

You cannot imagine the astonishing power of heaven when it becomes focused and single-minded. Nothing can resist its determination to deliver you both from harm's way. Things run more smoothly now with the divine forces of My kingdom fully in charge. Stand back and watch them work.

FEBRUARY 19

When Life Closes In

Talk to Me when life thrashes you. Talk to Me when your strength dissipates. Talk to Me when you feel overwhelmed and alone. I think you get the message: talk to Me. I AM a wonderful listener. I listen to your cries of total despair. I listen to your pleadings for relief. I listen to your prayers for your dear wife as her time in the hospital enters its second week. I even listen when you get angry and disappointed with Me.

I want us to constantly engage in the most important elements of relationship building: talking and listening. When we give each other the silent treatment, nothing gets done. I want us to establish and maintain daily communication. We must work on reinforcing the deep friendship between us. You and I are constructing an unbreakable bond. A strong link between us forges an impenetrable wall of protection around you. Let nothing disrupt our daily meetings. Make this time together your top priority.

I know the world demands your attention, especially when problems become more acute such as now. Your time can easily fragment when you dash here and yon, trying to plug up assorted leaks that threaten to flood your sense of well-being.

Hear Me: I AM greater than the world. I help you overcome anything that human life must face. I deliver you from a chaotic and misdirected world. Let us thoroughly discuss every single issue that confronts you. Together, we create powerful solutions that work. Then we implement our plans to produce perfect results. When life collapses on top of you and the hard rains begin to fall, immediately fetch your all-purpose umbrella: Me. I promise to keep you safe and dry.

Allen C. Liles

FEBRUARY 20

Claiming Your Good

I want you to claim the good that rightfully belongs to you. I await your call. Your good always stands readily available anytime you stake your claim. Make your requests known. I withhold nothing. I provide everything. Remember My words: "Ask and you shall receive." The riches of heaven pour out to you in magnificent abundance whenever you ask for them. Lack never exists in My kingdom. I AM holding an unlimited supply of good registered in your name. Claim it! Present yourself in prayer and make your claim. I hand over everything you need without delay.

You possess unlimited good. You never know lack and limitation. Just firmly state your current needs with conviction. Do not claim the good that you may require in a year or two. Worry only about today's immediate needs. Never be timid or shy. I want you to have the necessary resources. I mark your personal safe deposit box "God's grace." This treasure trove contains a limitless storehouse of prosperity. A never-ending array of blessings should reassure you and calm your fears. Come quickly now and claim your legacy. By seeking what already belongs to you, you reaffirm your spiritual heritage.

FEBRUARY 21

I AM involved

I hear your sincere gratitude, and I appreciate it. Your dear wife still awaits progress in the hospital. Both of you have undergone severe testing. Hopefully, a time of healing approaches. As the primary caregiver and main support system, you worry about her difficult health challenges. Please know that I AM personally involved in watching over you both. I work daily to make the crooked places straight. I wrap My loving arms around you both. I hold you close. Your pain becomes My pain. I grant you peace during your travails. I bring you comfort and support in the brightness of day and the darkness of night. I offer support in many forms. I work through the doctors, nurses, medications, and technology involved in your wife's care.

Her worrisome struggles need your attention in ways beyond the physical. She feels emotionally vulnerable right now. Continue showing your deep and abiding love for her. Express it verbally. Show it physically. Make her aware of your unending commitment and dedication. Reassure once again of your lifetime love.

Both of you are facing the aging process. Physical beauty fades. Mobility declines. Losses mount. Through it all, most everyone who copes with aging worries about someday being abandoned and left alone. Finding yourself alone can become a frightening prospect at any age. I know that you would never leave or forsake your dear wife under any circumstance. That also represents My eternal promise to you both. I will see you through the hardest times. Trust Me.

Allen C. Liles

FEBRUARY 22

Do My Work

Be about My business every day. You are a trusted partner in accomplishing My work. What is "My work?" It consists of bringing love, comfort, support, healing, encouragement, and light to a struggling and lost world. There is never a shortage of assignments. The world spins along, full of anguish and trouble. It remains your job to go where needed. Travel forth to uplift the downtrodden, heal the sick, teach those who seek learning, and provide spiritual relief whenever possible. So many human beings face daunting obstacles. My presence, through you, can help them meet their everyday challenges.

Be open and receptive about each task I give you to do. Every single good work counts. You are My trusted servant. I equip you for tasks large and small. I endow you with My unlimited resources and constant angelic support. Remember that the Christ within you helps accomplish My goals. In actuality, the inner Spirit performs the work necessary on behalf of both you and Me. You possess a triple dose of power operating for you. Your own participation, the Christ Spirit within you, and I all work together to create the most effective team in the universe. Please trust that I give you every spiritual resource necessary to complete My work. Be fearless. Go forth with confidence.

FEBRUARY 23

Discipline

Progress requires discipline. Discipline always plays a key role in accomplishing anything worthwhile. The world dislikes the principle of discipline. It prefers that you be undisciplined so it can more easily pull you hither and yon. The world desires to hold you in its negative clutches. It requires considerable discipline to avoid its harmful grasp. How do you find the discipline necessary to develop positive habits? Ask for My help in establishing beneficial patterns. Regulating your food intake, not smoking, avoiding or limiting alcohol, and abstaining from harmful substances all involve major examples of needed discipline. Most human beings rationalize their basic lack of discipline by going along with the crowd. Today's culture fails to see discipline as "cool." I tell you that having personal discipline ranks as a key element of a safe, happy, fulfilling, and long life. Indiscriminate sex stands as a perfect example of undisciplined behavior. True love displays magnificent discipline. It demonstrates commitment, loyalty, and a complete dedication to another person's well-being. In the current "anything goes" environment, real love has become almost unrecognizable. Random sex never allows two specific people to connect on a spiritual basis. What a loss!

My path definitely requires considerable faith and discipline. Embrace the spiritually orientated life by disciplining yourself to spend more time with Me. Know that spiritual discipline never goes out of style. It ensures a life of happiness, contentment, peace of mind, joy, love, and success.

Allen C. Liles

FEBRUARY 24

Friends

Love and cherish your friends. They are gifts from Me. Allow them to love and care about both you and your dear wife. Do not shut them out. Open your heart and embrace their presence in your life. They are worth more than gold. Return their love and caring. You must give to receive. You must care about others if you want them to care about you. Your friends bring compassion when you are hurting and offer love when you are feeling unloved. They extend themselves for you because they believe in you.

At times, you may seek aloneness. Your real friends understand and honor that choice. What is a true friend? True friends know the real you. They love you for being who you are. A true friend does not run and hide when you become ill, go broke, or make unwise decisions. Eternal friends forgive and understand. An honest friend is never afraid to tell you the truth. A lasting friend stays close. Real friends are available to listen and then offer feedback when you need their wisdom. Dear friends give you a piece of their hearts forever. They are connected with you spiritually. They see you as a perfect child of God and an imperfect but lovable and valuable human being. A real friend laughs and cries with you, lives and dies with you. Make someone glad. Let him or her be your friend.

FEBRUARY 25

Spiritual Wisdom

Human knowledge and spiritual wisdom are two entirely different things. I find absolutely nothing wrong with accumulating information and achieving specialized knowledge on the human level. However, it proves extremely unwise to consider earthly knowledge as a replacement for spiritual wisdom. Becoming educated on the human scene never automatically translates into inner knowing. Some people could earn several university degrees and still make complete disasters of their lives. Others may read hundreds of books or watch thousands of hours of educational television and have zero awareness of truth principles.

At a minimum, a person should find a balance between temporal and eternal wisdom. Given a choice between the two, My wisdom, the wisdom of the Spirit, ranks as the most crucial. How do I define wisdom of the Spirit? It starts with the startling revelation that the invisible outranks the visible. Spiritual wisdom understands that I AM the one power and one presence in the vast universe. Golden idols are instantly recognized for their falsity and unworthiness. Inner wisdom centers on heeding My guidance and avoiding secular temptations. My wisdom represents all good, all the time. Listening and following My divine direction never paints anyone into a negative corner. Spiritual wisdom originates from unchanging principles honed over the ages. Righteous wisdom always takes the high road that results in the best outcome for everyone involved. I AM the fountain of wisdom. I never quit flowing. Come to Me and drink of the living water.

Allen C. Liles

FEBRUARY 26

A Problem-Free Life

A problem-free life does not exist. Trouble will find you, no matter where you hide. Nothing on the earthly plane can save you from life's assorted problems. No amount of money, power, fame, or status protects you. Not anything in the secular world inoculates you from various challenges. You may actually motor down life's multiple highways for a long period of time without encountering much trouble. Then one day, a pothole (or two or three) pops up from nowhere. If you are traveling fast, you might experience a significant jar. How you choose to navigate the potholes then becomes the issue. You always have several options when hitting a rough spot. You can deny the pothole exists. You might quickly put yourself in reverse and back away from this glitch in your travel plans. You can just fly blindly into the pothole and allow it swallow you up. You might even choose to hit the accelerator and try to fly over the pothole at a high rate of speed. That can make for some really hard landings on the other side.

By far, the surest way to approach any of life's many problems lies in the spiritual process. First, slow down when you see trouble ahead. Try to see what you might be facing. Second, take a few deep breaths before charging wildly ahead. Third (and most important), call Me quickly for some AAA assistance. My three A's are awareness, advice, and action. I promise to come immediately, bearing whatever help you might need. Never let any human problem send you into the ditch. I AM ready, willing, and able to get you safely over the world's deepest potholes.

FEBRUARY 27

The Holy Trinity

The Holy Trinity consists of Me (the Father), Christ (the Son), and the Holy Spirit (My activity) that lives within you and does My work. I placed the Spirit of Christ at your very core to be a friend, guide, and comforting presence in your human life. I knew that you would need help in dealing with human life in general. The Holy Spirit represents My sacred activity and completes My work through you. You act as a physical instrument of My grace. My ultimate goal, operating through the divine framework of the Holy Trinity, is that I live My life through you. As Jesus the Christ states in John 14:11, "Believe me when I say that I AM in the Father and the Father is in me." The Holy Trinity works together for good. When the world sees your form, hears your words, and watches your deeds, hopefully it sees Me at work. Most human beings regard Me as separate and apart from them. Yes, I AM the transcendent God that presides over the kingdom of heaven. I also created the universe and the planet on which you live. But I AM definitely the immanent God that lives in and through you. The Christ Spirit residing at your center facilitates and serves as our crucial connection. What Paul wrote in Colossians rings true: "Christ in you, the hope of glory." The Holy Trinity represents the true hope for a world poised on the precipice of the abyss. Each human being must activate the power of the Holy Trinity within. The world can be saved, but it will take place one enlightened soul at a time.

Allen C. Liles

FEBRUARY 28

The Still, Small Voice

Listen for My voice. It is the voice of the Christ within you. It is also the voice of hope, the voice of wisdom, and the voice of peace. Listen very closely. It speaks to you in the silence of the early morning, during a busy day, and in the darkness of a long night. It is I, the Lord, who speaks to you in love. I AM at your core, guiding and directing your every step. I AM that I AM.

Never fear. I dwell quietly in the midst of you. Put aside your doubts and worries. Wait patiently for My voice to lead you down the path of righteousness. Take My hand now, as you struggle in the depths of uncertainty. Trust Me concerning your dear wife's health. Lean forward and listen carefully to My words. Discern clearly what I tell you. You are experiencing a moment of difficult testing. Be ever calm, brave, and determined; together we can overcome every obstacle. Remain steadfast. Do not falter or fall by the wayside at this crucial point in time. We are near the end. Our goal becomes more visible. It looms directly in front of us. I know your legs are weakening and your energy is nearly depleted. Persevere. Keep moving toward heaven. Walk on to victory and triumph. Travel upward to glory. Keep listening to the still, small voice within you. It carries you through to the end.

MARCH

But those who hope in the Lord will renew their strength.
They will soar on wings like eagles. They will run and
not grow weary. They will walk and not be faint.

—Isaiah 40:31 (NIV)

MARCH 1

Welcome Home

Your dear wife comes home today after spending seventeen days in the hospital. This has been a trying and demanding time for both of you. Health challenges are hard at any age, but especially when you get older.

I want you both to rely on Me more. You may feel alone and isolated with your troubles. That is not the case. I AM always here. I AM here in the good times, but I AM present for you even more during the hard times. Turn to Me for comfort. Resist the notion of doing anything without My help. I have both spiritual and human resources that can help restore you. Seek My assistance without delay. I will answer the call. You never need face anything alone.

As you travel down unfamiliar roads, be alert for unexpected guides and angels along the way. I bring new and valuable resources into your lives. In the meantime, continue serving as a much-needed blessing to each other. Comfort one another during this difficult moment in your human journey. You are very fortunate to have each other. Use this priceless gift to reassure each other. Remember that I AM in the midst of every situation. I AM here now, hard at work and coordinating the efforts of everyone. Let the healing begin.

Allen C. Liles

MARCH 2

The Sacred Fountain

I act as your sacred fountain of life. I AM an endless fountain that pours out greater amounts of love, faith, and courage when needed. Let Me do My thing. Allow Me to release more love, which speeds up the healing process. Call on Me to pour out more faith, which helps you persevere through the worst of times. I can increase the flow of courage when the world tries to crush you with fear and worry. My fountain never runs dry. Tap into it now. I gladly give you love, faith, and courage. I give you love to remind you of My goodness. I give you faith to sustain you through the fires of life. I give you courage to keep you moving forward one day at a time. Let your life be uplifted and strengthened by these three priceless gifts. When you feel alone, turn to My love. When you lose hope, turn to My faith. When you tremble with trepidation, turn to My courage. These three things—love, faith and courage—are the three great comforters that I send you. Take heart. Rise up and be strong in Me. I shall deliver you. I promise it.

MARCH 3

Endurance

There are many types of "endurance" required in human life. Physical, mental, emotional, professional, and familial endurance all come to mind. You and your dear wife have undergone a period of great stress. Your mental, physical, and emotional endurance have all been severely tested. Watching while a loved one struggles creates worry and concern. Her physical strength is almost nonexistent due to a lack of appetite. In addition, her mental and emotional endurance also have undergone a pounding that seems never ending. At times, she simply wanted to give up. I understand that human beings grow weary when life seems too much of a strain. It becomes tempting to just "lay your burdens down." This is the moment when spiritual endurance comes into play. Of course, a specific time arrives for every human being when I call you back to heaven. However, some souls feel such pain that they seek to accelerate the process. Many spouses, when they lose their longtime mate, want to immediately follow their loved one into heaven. I understand when loving couples desire a quick reunion in the afterlife. However, I prefer to determine your life span. I have a specific plan for each person on earth. Sometimes your spiritual service unfolds later rather than sooner. To complete your assignment for Me could require an extra measure of human endurance. When that need arises, I supply it.

Allen C. Liles

MARCH 4

Do Not Fear

Remember what My prophet Isaiah wrote when I told him in chapter 41, verse 10: "So do not fear, for I am with you." I meant what I said about fear. It acts as the great crippler of humankind. Fear paralyzes, destabilizes, and holds people down in unimaginable ways. There are more fears than you can count: fear of illness, old age and death; fear of losing status and power; fear of financial ruin and poverty; fear of rejection, loss of relationships, and abandonment; fear of problems with children, family estrangement, and being alone. In every fear, there exists some potential truth.

Fear also attacks on a grand scale. Wars often begin because of fear. Nations and leaders make poor choices when fearful. Most bad management decisions arise out of fear.

Of course, many earth-based fears possess rational roots. No sane person would walk into a den of lions unarmed. Nobody jumps out of an airplane without a parachute unless he or she has a death wish. You would not throw yourself into a vast ocean without land in sight. These situations all represent "healthy" fears.

Most unhealthy or irrational fears involve a simple lack of trust in Me. When the world collapses around you, I know it becomes hard to trust an unseen force. But you need to place your faith in the most basic of My promises; "I will never leave you, I will never forsake you." When any fear pounds loudly at your door, declare your absolute trust in Me.

MARCH 5

More about Fear

I know that you fear losing your dear wife. I appreciate the love and affection that you feel for her. You hate seeing your mate in pain and anguish. She also fears the outcome of her health issues. The thought of leaving you troubles her. Your relationship has blessed many people besides the two of you, so the loss would indeed be felt by others. You performed ministry together, which constitutes a spiritual aspect of your time as a couple.

Many of your fears are a natural aspect of aging. As human beings get older, fear of the unknown often multiplies. Of course, I concede that every person alive today will eventually shed his or her physical body. Each soul someday departs the material world and returns to My safe keeping in heaven.

Rather than fearing this natural progression of human life and death, embrace it. Instead of running away from the inevitable, walk calmly toward the glory that awaits your entrance into My kingdom. I have planned a thoughtful and smooth transition far beyond your greatest expectations. Many wait here to welcome you both home. I can tell you this: of all your fears, death ranks as the most overblown. I realize that worldly fears seem very real. In heaven, they immediately fade away and disappear forever. Live without fear. Never fret about tomorrow. I assure you that heaven exceeds your wildest dreams.

Allen C. Liles

MARCH 6

Recovery

Your dear wife has begun her recovery process after a lengthy stay away in the hospital. I know you are glad and grateful to have her back home. You missed your wife's physical presence, although you visited her every day at the hospital. Recovering from a traumatic health challenge requires considerable time and patience. She feels relieved to be home with you, in familiar surroundings. Hospitals can be quite disorienting. You observed that dichotomy during your training as a chaplain in a clinical setting.

Fortunately, you are receiving some good help with your dear wife's after care. You—and she—are not alone. You also have Me. I AM with you during every minute of this ordeal. I comfort and support you. I bring angels to help care for you both. I make sure events unfold in divine order. Look to Me as the lighthouse on the rugged shoreline. I provide the steady beacon that guides you toward safety. Have faith in Me. I brought her back to you, didn't I? You prayed for your dear wife's return home, and I responded. Your loving bond has become even stronger. You each rose to the occasion, demonstrating strength and perseverance. Let the healing begin.

MARCH 7

Prepare the Way

Everything that you do in My name prepares the way for Me. Every prayer, each meditation, any kind of good deed that you do for another—they all help prepare the way for the LORD.

I want to enter the hearts and minds of My beloved children, but the way must be prepared by an openness and willingness to receive My presence. Invite Me in. Welcome Me. I have so much to offer you. I bring peace and love, happiness and prosperity. I want My influence to help change the world from its current path. I AM the answer to healing the wounds caused by a rush to idol worship. The earth spins toward a shattering crash when it insists on excluding Me. Your work, and the work of others, is to clear a path for Me to return. I seek My rightful place as the one true God. I AM the Savior of the world, but I find Myself preempted and ignored. I remain hopeful that the way can be prepared in time to avoid disaster.

I seek to awaken My flock one by one. I want to establish a direct connection to each one of My children. I hope to activate the sacred connection that already exists between us. I crave the rewards of our friendship and closeness.

Prepare the world for My arrival. I AM coming soon. Strew flowers in My path. Sing My praises, hosanna in the highest. Know that I AM carrying salvation, redemption, and deliverance with Me. Open your arms to receive My gifts. I bring a new consciousness and renewed hope for the future. Prepare the way. I AM near, oh so near.

Allen C. Liles

MARCH 8

The Promise of Spring

I always follow the long, dark winter with a promise of spring. For you and your dear wife, this has been a difficult winter of trial and testing. At times, the problems and worries seemed overwhelming. However, you both persevered and trusted in Me. Now relief finally looms. Soon the worst of your winter challenges should lessen. The new season brings a much-needed renewal of body, mind, and spirit. Winter's chill fades. The sun already rides higher in the sky. Its warmth should lighten your burdens. Let the blooming flowers and colorful greenery outside your apartment window lift your spirits. Watch while your faith also continues to bloom. Your equilibrium and emotional balance steadies now as the days lengthen.

The past few months severely tested your endurance. Your spirit bent but never broke. You swayed in the strong wind yet never fell. You sometimes held on for dear life. You never once let go of Me. Prepare now for a much-needed rebirth of energy and well-being. Your dear one gets stronger every day. You are finding your own center again. Listen for My divine call to life everywhere: "Awaken! Be glad in the promise of a new spring."

MARCH 9

Keep Coming Back

Keep coming back to Me. Day by day, hour by hour, and minute by minute, keep coming back. I AM a deep well of knowledge, wisdom, prosperity, health, peace, love, courage and strength. Drink the living water and eat the food of life at My sacred table. When you get confused, come to Me. If you feel grief stricken, come to Me. When the world kicks you around, come to Me. If your human family abandons you, come to Me. I AM the source from which all of life flows. Come and find Me. I never turn you away. My grace never fails. When you doubt yourself, I give you a different perspective. As you draw that final breath, spend your last moment on earth with Me. When times get extra tough, as they have recently for you and your dear wife, come back to Me more often. I never limit the number of times you can seek Me. I want our divine connection. I wait for your knock. Hearing you approach My door completes My day. I AM here for you, My child, until the end of time and beyond. Keep coming back to Me today, tomorrow, and forever. I love you.

Allen C. Liles

MARCH 10

I Reveal Myself

I reveal Myself in countless ways. I give you ample resources so that you can do My work. I instruct you in My ways, not the ways of the world. I bring helpful people into your life. I bless you with the physical health necessary to complete My assignments. I keep your mind sharp and focused on Me. I shelter you in a lovely setting. I imbue you with the awareness to recognize and resist any distractions or temptations. I keep you centered amid chaos and personal challenges. I have chosen a perfect life partner to accompany and support you through life's twists and turns. I have created beautiful friendships for you. I chide you gently, and with understanding, about your human shortcomings. I search for you when you stray from the flock. I offer reassurance when fears of loneliness and abandonment crowd in on you. I protect you when the forces of evil circle around you, searching for a soft spot. I watch out for you in your earthly travels. I give you meaningful and productive work that blesses others. I have selected a worthy professional career for your talents. I bestow the appropriate words for you to speak in every setting. I guide each of your actions in a way that accomplishes good. I preview for you the incredible splendor of heaven. I send you here and yon on My behalf to reflect My light and love. These, and so many other things, I do for you. I AM constantly revealing My love for you. Look around. Be glad in it.

MARCH 11

My Strength and Power

Have complete faith in My strength and power. I know that your dear wife's recent illness caused you untold worry. You were concerned that one or both of you might lack the necessary strength to survive. You called, and I answered. I provided the mental toughness, physical durability, and spiritual certainty needed. You never need face any potential setback alone when you enlist My help. As your human strength starts to wane, My spiritual strength advances. I never leave you exhausted or alone on the field of battle. I pour My limitless energy into every fiber of your body, mind, and spirit. Your job lies in holding on to faith in Me. When you feel defeated, ask for a revitalizing injection of My strength and power. If you ever wonder, "Where will I ever get the energy to continue?" I provide the answer. You get that extra power surge from Me, the source within you. I give it to you.

When we are connected, My strength flows effortlessly between us and without interruption. I AM your ultimate power grid. Your system never stays down or remains in darkness when I throw My on-switch. If someone cuts your power, I restore it immediately. You can never lose power again as long as we stay connected. Just remain faithful when your earthly energy source fails. I will have you up and running again in no time.

Allen C. Liles

MARCH 12

Your Fortress

I AM your powerful fortress. I offer you security from every assault. Come inside and claim your place of safety. Hunker down and rest comfortably while the slings and arrows fall harmlessly outside My sanctuary. You are free from all worry as long as you remain inside My walls. The world may kick and pound angrily at My door, but I allow not a single enemy to enter. No one can harm you when you stay under My divine protection. I turn away all threats.

The forces of negativity pursued you until they reached My fortress. They saw immediately that chasing you further would be fruitless. My walls loom much higher than they expected. Your tormentors now helplessly paw the ground in the outside cold. They are frustrated at losing their prey. Let them wail and cry.

I enjoy keeping evil at bay. However, do not become overconfident and stray outside of this safe place. The hordes of evildoers wait patiently for any sign of your reemergence. Stay securely locked inside the gates of heaven. Keep yourself forever shielded by My power. You are enclosed in My cocoon of steel. Remain near Me until all danger passes. I always welcome you when you flee from your earthly enemies. I AM your first and final refuge, your constant shelter from the storm. Rest easy. You are safe with Me.

MARCH 13

Life's Little Joys

The joys of everyday life sparkle around you. They are almost too numerous to mention. When you endure a time of testing and challenge, as you and your dear wife have experienced recently, it becomes easy to overlook life's little joys. You are being gifted with blessings of every dimension and magnitude. Thankfully, your good health allows you to care for your mate during her health struggles. You two still enjoy a close and loving relationship after three-plus decades of friendship and marriage. Grandchildren, who live relatively close, offer much joy. You both live in a lovely apartment-home setting in a relatively safe area of an upscale city. Your dear wife's excellent decorating skills provide you both with an aesthetic and pleasing environment. Despite the colder climate, you are blessed to get outside virtually every day to walk, shop, run errands, eat at a restaurant, or even take in an occasional movie or baseball game. Your low mileage and debt free vehicle just celebrated its tenth birthday. Speaking of finances, I provide the necessary resources so that you can pay your bills each month. While you lack enormous wealth, your assets exceed your liabilities by a comfortable margin. You personally find joy in listening to music under the headphones, reading a good book, keeping up with the news of the day, and writing in your journal. I also know you get much pleasure from your morning cup of coffee and our sacred time together in the silence. I bring so many good things into your life. Appreciating little joys offers the key to happiness and contentment.

Allen C. Liles

MARCH 14

A Humble Pope

The new Pope has already become known for his humble attitude and demeanor. Although you are not of the Catholic faith (unlike your sister and all of your nieces and nephews), you were moved by his obvious humility. I treasure a humble person, whoever he or she may be. Humility represents a crucial component of the spiritual life.

Today's material world acts as if it never heard the word *humility*. Egos parade around without shame in your celebrity-crazed culture. Many people view humility as a weakness. Nothing could be more wrong.

Being humble does not mean being humiliated. It illustrates a high spiritual virtue. Someone gifted with a humble attitude sees life from the perspective of valuing what's inside a person rather than being impressed by outer bluster. Great wealth, power, and fame do not usually coexist well with humility. Discovering true humility means searching beneath the exterior of every individual and beholding the Christ within.

The new Pope possesses that gift. In selecting the name of a great Catholic saint for his new title, he demonstrates his humble priorities. The wonderful prayer of St. Francis explains well My basic credo. I would like to see a new emphasis on humility. This designated Pope understands and lives a life formed from a humble perspective. I send him My sincerest blessings.

MARCH 15

Spiritual Vision

See through My eyes. Behold the beauty and wonder of the world. Watch with interest as humankind goes about its daily business of living. I look for only the best in My beloved children who populate the earth. However, My eyes also see realistically. I see wars and threats of wars. I frown as I watch human beings harm others, especially children. I watch greed and lust dominating the popular culture. I view a world where I AM no longer the main concern and priority among a significant number. My eyes become sad and teary when I see various religions using My name to murder those unlike themselves. Why have you strayed so far from My laws?

Of course, I see many positive things too. An awakening of the human consciousness has begun in many quarters. A part of that enlightenment derives from the pain caused when people choose to live apart from Me. I view with interest how the forces of evil use modern technology and the lowest part of human nature to accomplish unworthy goals. They lure so many naïve and unsuspecting souls to their doom. However, there are many more good than bad people in My world. Our sacred flock includes billions of the faithful. I see generosity, a concern and compassion for others, and a desire to know Me better rising everywhere. I AM winning the battle, one soul at a time. I see a future where My place of honor becomes fully restored. I see a glorious future for humankind. I see salvation for My beloved children. I behold a new world.

Allen C. Liles

MARCH 16

A Good Work

I began a good work in you. I will see it through to completion. I promise to give you the necessary stamina, commitment, and resources to finish the job. I also provide the wisdom, guidance, and direction required. Continue listening for My daily instructions. I ask that you pay close attention. I realize it becomes tempting to slack off every now and then. I understand the human need for an occasional break from any grind. But I urge you to press on toward the mark in My name. Put everything else behind and strive for the goal I set for you.

Time becomes critical. No human knows exactly when his or her number of days ends. It might be today, tomorrow, or many years from now. In the meantime, move steadfastly toward the goal I set before you. I always stand ready to assist you in any worthy and important endeavor. Each human being possesses a specific spiritual assignment. No two tasks are ever alike, just as each individual differs from another. Some of My works may seem unimportant in the world's view. I beg to differ. Every spiritual task has great worth. Each requires careful planning and stellar execution. Every job that I assign contains powerful meaning and incredible importance. Please keep doing the good work I chose for you.

MARCH 17

Reservoir of Love

Allow the love within you to flow outward and bless others. Never keep it dammed up and unavailable. Why would you want to withhold love? So many people desperately need an expression of love from someone outside of themselves. As I generously provide My love to you, why not raise the flood gates and release your own reservoir of love? Let it come rushing forth to bless the lonely and discouraged. Do not be reluctant or shy. Empty out your love to the universe. Open the spillways, and let your love flow as a blessing to humankind.

Love offers hope. It brings healing and restoration to the spirit. Love comforts the grieving and reassures the lost. If you held a magic elixir that could counteract all suffering, would you dare keep it to yourself? Loosen the valve in your heart that now holds your love in storage. Set it free. Why do you hesitate? Do you fear your love might be rejected? Are you hesitant or bashful about voicing or expressing love? What aspect of fearfulness keeps you from sharing love? Are you afraid someone might use your words or deeds of love against you? Trust Me. I refill you every day with more love. All human days are numbered. A day without sending forth healing love ranks as a wasted moment of opportunity. Take a chance. Let yourself become vulnerable in the name of love.

Allen C. Liles

MARCH 18

In the Desert

Every spiritual life involves a desert experience. As part of the sacred passage, each soul must travel from its earthly home to a barren and unfamiliar place. Sometimes the journey includes an emotionally dry desert. It can also include a physical upheaval that literally sends you into a new country. Look at your life. You were cast out into the desert in many ways. Emotionally, you left a long corporate career and answered the call to ministry. Physically, you moved from the warmth of a Southwestern state (Texas) to the cold northern climes (Chicago, and eventually Minnesota).

Wherever your "desert" may be located, it can feel quite lonely and isolated. Longtime friends and family usually misunderstand what may be happening with you. You enter unknown territory. Nothing seems to make sense any more. Then, besides strange new surroundings and unfamiliar emotions, powerful troubles and temptations appear without warning. You find your mental toughness and physical stamina severely tested. In your case, an impulsive personal decision blindsided you. Your life was turned upside down. With My help, you came through the ordeal. In the process, you answered My call to ministry. Your spiritual journey began in earnest.

Although many rewarding moments have blessed you since, you occasionally must revisit the "desert." Your dear wife's recent illness definitely thrust you back once again into the wilderness. Have faith. Just as I plucked you from the desert wasteland of old, I will come again to rescue you. Trust Me. I promise to deliver you once more.

MARCH 19

Fully Human, Fully Divine

I AM fully human and fully divine. I AM in you, so I experience the same human hopes, dreams, joy, happiness, sadness, disappointments, and fears that you feel. I AM the "three-in-one" God—Father, Son, and Holy Spirit—that rules the universe with My divine power. I AM the Holy Trinity of both spiritual and human life. When I speak to you from within your core, the Christ Spirit acts as My instrument for communicating with your conscious mind. I placed the Christ at your center to serve as a lifelong companion for your soul's human journey. I did this so that you would never feel alone. I knew that the material world tests people in severe ways. I wanted the Christ Spirit to accompany you on your earthly trek. It resides within you to offer wisdom, courage, understanding, and support along the way. The Christ experienced many human trials, such as opposition, rejection, and abandonment before finally achieving resurrection and ascension. How many times during your life have you felt exactly the same negative human emotions? Yet I AM also in your life as the ultimate higher power. I provide you with a grand overview of the universe around you. I focus on the "big picture" as it relates to you. I also provide you with the Holy Spirit. It serves as My blessed activity in you. The Holy Spirit performs My work through you. I want you to function as an instrument of My grace, so that I might live My life through you. I gave you the Holy Trinity so that you could enjoy peace, love, and happiness while fulfilling the tasks I assign you. Everything works together for your good.

Allen C. Liles

MARCH 20

All I AM

All I AM I give to you. All the peace, all the wisdom, all the health, all the joy that I AM also belongs to you. I AM all knowing, so you become all knowing. I AM all wise, so you rise in wisdom and awareness. I AM all abundance, so you receive the benefits of My abundance.

You live in the fullness and totality of Me. I hold nothing back. I never give only in part. I dispense My grace into your life. I endow you with the absolute blessing of Me. Prepare the way in your mind and heart to receive everything I have to offer. Again, I withhold nothing. You must believe what I tell you. Never doubt or test Me. Just open yourself completely and gather My sacred gifts unto you. The manna of heaven falls around you. In the morning, My blessings arrive with the sun. At evening time, they follow you into the bedroom. I protect your health, fill your spiritual bank accounts, keep you safe from potential harm, provide priceless insight, and level the obstacles that obstruct your path. Everything that I AM flows without end to those who believe. Claim your divine relationship with Me now. Receive Me fully. I AM your LORD. I AM your God, in all of My glory. You are My son, in whom I AM well pleased.

MARCH 21

Two Steps Forward, One Step Back

Your dear wife has been back from the hospital now for almost exactly three weeks. After being away for seventeen days, her recovery has seen its ups and downs. Getting back to some degree of wholeness requires considerable time. You both must exhibit patience with the healing process. She has been through a traumatic episode. You felt traumatized as well. There were more than a few moments during her hospitalization when you feared the worst. You were concerned that she would never come home to you again. She even voiced that physical death might be a better outcome for everyone concerned. Those comments, while representing her feelings at the time, definitely caused you pain. I fully understand when pain becomes unbearable. Yet, she did manage to survive and return home. You are both encouraged by her progress so far. Slow as it may seem, the recovery continues. You remember her coming back from the Hodgkin's disease a decade ago. Be patient. Two steps forward and one step back marks the natural progression in any kind of recovery process. Allow adequate time for a complete healing of body, mind, and spirit. The soul must also heal.

Keep praying for faith and courage during this difficult time. I AM always available to comfort both of you. Please let Me help. Together we make steady progress, one precious day at a time.

MARCH 22

My Gender

You wonder whether I AM a man or woman, male or female. I AM neither. I AM Spirit. In the human world, you think of two different genders. I AM a genderless entity, the Supreme Being of the universe. I AM God, so I do not require a human form. I do possess characteristics of both the masculine and feminine genders. Here lies a key point that you should understand: so does every human being who walks in the world. You and every man or woman on earth also has a mixture of masculine and feminine traits. Outwardly, you are of one sex or the other. Inwardly, you are a combination of both sexes. There are women among you whose courage and strength far outstrips that of many men. There are a substantial number of men who illustrate a loving and nurturing nature much greater than many women. You really cannot categorize anyone strictly by his or her outer gender appearance.

Some religious worshippers are more comfortable thinking of Me as a man, or "Father" figure. However, My most distinguishable trait is love. Love is often considered a more feminine characteristic. I AM also a powerful and strong God, usually thought of as masculine.

Human beings often trade around their opposite gender traits as circumstances dictate. Because of your dear wife's illness, you have become the nurturer. You perform all of the domestic chores. Surprisingly, you are a natural at displaying your feminine side. Never use gender to judge anyone, including Me. I AM the Father/Mother God. I AM capable of showing either side, as needed.

MARCH 23

Mind Your Own Business

Minding your own business represents one of the universe's most potent wisdoms. Practicing this principle saves you untold amounts of frustration, resentment, anger, and downright chaos. Let others walk their own path, wherever it may take them. Do not burden anyone with unmet expectations, unnecessary guilt, forced lying, or wasted breath. Hear Me, My well-meaning child: you simply do not possess the wisdom, insight, or understanding required to knowledgeably direct someone else's decisions and actions. Step back. Take a deep breath and keep your opinions and advice to yourself. In most every case, the other person will do as he or she pleases anyway. People truly do what they want to do, no matter how insightful your counsel. In the long run, this actually serves as the best plan for everyone. Whatever lesson results from an individual's personal choice, it belongs exclusively to him or her. You should not carry the weight of somebody else's outcome on your back. Get out of the way. Give the other person the freedom to make mistakes. Everyone, including you, deserves the right to chart his or her own course. How else can real growth, change, and personal progress take place? The bottom line: you do not have the power to live another human being's life. Stop trying. Let Me do My job. I promise to personally watch over others for you.

MARCH 24

Let Go

Let it all go. Whatever you may be clinging to—your dear wife, the remaining days of your human life, your worldly possessions, your professional career, or your friends, family, or grandchildren—let everything go. They only belonged to you temporarily anyway. Feel your clutching hand beginning to open. Allow each part of your material life the privilege of escaping to its own freedom. Your memory of them and their memories of you remain forever stored in heaven. You may revisit these treasured archives anytime your soul desires. But on the earthly plane every physical recollection eventually disappears into the ethers of history.

I know how letting go of what you love causes pain and remorse. You invested yourself heavily into certain people, places, and things. I understand your reluctance to release the world as you know it.

Yet, a far greater experience awaits you on the other side. Before that blessed time finally arrives, you must complete the process of release. Clinging to anything past its expiration date just delays the inevitable. Bless those you love and who have loved you. Begin saying farewell to your worldly possessions. They someday return to the dust as well. Prepare yourself for the wondrous glory of My kingdom. Let go lovingly of anything that still binds you to the earth. The human world someday ends for you and everyone. When you make your departure, gratefully watch the shoreline recede in the distance. Behold a new world approaching in all of its grandeur. Be of good cheer. Open your hands and receive the bounty of heaven.

MARCH 25

Wonders Unfolding

My wonders unfold around you. Blessings multiply as we speak. My grace descends rapidly upon you. Go forward now and meet your good. Step by step, advance toward the goal. Remember: progress, not perfection. Never lose heart, especially at this stage of your journey. Be unafraid of anything in the material world. Just as I overcame that world, so can you. Allow My wonders to take you the rest of the way.

Your moment of pure joy soon approaches. You have worked long and hard. Now reap your reward. The final realization nears, just over the next rainbow. Keep fighting on until the grand dream materializes. Never stop believing that all things are possible for those who trust Me. Soar over whatever obstacles remain before you. Rise above anything that threatens your triumphant entry into My kingdom. Let nothing deflect you. Walk onward toward victory. Be ready to accelerate your efforts. Listen for My guidance. Follow My exact directions. I encourage you by the wonders now piling up around your feet. Specific miracles offer proof of My good intentions. Remain faithful until the end. Be filled with hope and expectation. Just keep moving forward. My love lights your way. Hold on tightly, My child. I AM taking you to glory.

MARCH 26

A Practical God

I AM a practical God. I give you constant and sure guidance on how best to navigate human life. I provide specific laws and eternal principles that make your physical journey much easier.

Do not try to do everything yourself. If you are open and receptive to My direction, I lead you on a tried and true path back to My kingdom. I promise you a glorious adventure rich in numerous blessings and steeped in a joy beyond description. Without My practical advice, life often turns into a morass of human problems. The crooked path promoted by the material world encourages poor use of free will. Trying to control one's own destiny through self will often results in confusion and pain. As a practical God, I want to spare you needless suffering.

I created you with an extremely high potential for a rich, full, and happy life. Here are some of My most practical recommendations: (1) read and meditate on the words of spiritual instruction found in My holy books, particularly the Bible; (2) become one with Me and allow the Christ Spirit within you to function as your most trusted counselor; (3) pray daily for the knowledge of My will for you and the power to carry it out; (4) become an instrument of My grace by letting the Holy Spirit perform My sacred work; and (5) trust Me completely for everything you need in the material world. Of course, I could add many corollaries related to these basic tenets. However, as a practical God, these principles represent a good starting place for you and humankind.

MARCH 27

Power of the Spirit

My power far exceeds anything in the physical world. No human king, queen, or president possesses greater power than I do. No weapon of mass destruction equals My power. My divine power originates from an eternal source removed from earthly limitations.

Human beings constantly lull themselves into believing the scope of their own earthbound power. Scientists are sure they can create new breakthroughs to harness and increase human capabilities. None of their material applications match Me.

I mostly use My awesome strength for good. However, I AM fully capable of displaying the full extent of My unmatched power to make a salient point. Only My power can change a human heart. I have the innate power to bring forth sad tears or a happy smile. My inner wisdom stirs love and compassion, forgiveness and understanding. While the power of the ego may also affect inner emotions, its use varies from negative to positive. My heavenly power elevates only the best human qualities. The power of the Spirit works from the inside out to bring healing and peace, wisdom and prosperity.

I AM granting you access to My power. It lives in you, ready for instant activation. My spiritual energy source rests in quiet anticipation of your next call. It may appear dormant at times. However, you can quickly activate it anytime you want. Feel the power of the Spirit growing in you now. Use it for good.

MARCH 28

Crucifixion Lessons

The crucifixion experience offers many lessons. First, crucifixion is a strictly human event. Crucifixion does not exist in My kingdom. The world enjoys crucifying its inhabitants in a variety of ways. There are many degrees of being hoisted upon the cross: physical, mental, and spiritual. Feeling crucified drastically affects all aspects of your human life. Physical health suffers, your mental state deteriorates, and you can enter spiritual bankruptcy. All of these negative factors may be present during a material crucifixion.

Facing human persecution always presents a time of great testing and upheaval. You feel abandoned, betrayed, and rejected. The painful nails of defeat tear into your flesh. A crown of thorns covers your brow. You cry out for Me, and I seem absent amid your pain. I do hear your cries of anguish. I try and offer comfort, but you still feel alone. You ask those age-old questions: Why Me, Lord? Why do they not understand? Why do they persecute me?

Although difficult, the process of crucifixion needs to reach completion. Most human beings must finish their time on the cross before transformation and resurrection can take place. Crucifixion occurs on Good Friday, transformation completes itself on Holy Saturday, and resurrection finally arrives on Sunday.

I AM with you every step of the way. I bring hope for a new dawn on Easter morning. You will rise and walk again. I promise it.

MARCH 29

Your Next Birthday

Your next birthday approaches in a bit more than two weeks. In reality, human birthdays only reflect a fairly meaningless human-made calendar. Many young children, taken home to heaven early, had already spread more joy at the time of their departures than much older adults. Everything comes down to how you utilize the days that I give you. Your spiritual soul is ageless. It travels intact throughout eternity. Meanwhile, your human life span demonstrates a specific pattern and predictable limitation.

On the surface, life on earth can be summed up in eight words: you are born, you age, and you die. Of course, some of this terse commentary rings true. You begin aging on the day of your birth. That process continues until the moment you pass physically from this plane of existence. But life on earth can be so much more than those eight words when you follow My path. As long as I have specific work for you to accomplish, your human life continues. I provide you with the vitality and resources necessary to achieve My goals. My grace sustains you until the end.

With Me, time has no meaning or relevance. I want you to enjoy every day of your human existence. Life on the physical earth can be exquisitely beautiful. Of course, it almost always includes a certain degree of pain or suffering. When your work for Me becomes complete, I call your soul back to where it originated. I always stand at the gates of heaven to welcome you. I smile and extend My hand as I say, "Well done, My good and faithful servant."

Allen C. Liles

MARCH 30

Holy Saturday

Holy Saturday lies between Good Friday and Easter Sunday for a particular reason. It signifies the day of transformation for those who completed crucifixion and await resurrection. During this specific day set aside for change, a rebirth of the Spirit becomes possible. The old consciousness disappears, replaced by a new awareness. However, all of this reframing requires time. Hence we have the need for a designated period between the two holiest days of Easter.

Holy Saturday provides that moment of illumination. All your negative and earth-bound thinking is stripped away. Your conscious awareness reverses itself from materialistic concerns to spiritual knowledge. You rise to a new and higher level of knowing. Old negativity disappears. Human darkness fades as heavenly light gradually increases. Pain, suffering, and the memories of crucifixion dissipate. Peace builds in anticipation of the day of resurrection.

Holy Saturday becomes an intense day, marked by hard work, perseverance, and sometimes wrenching change. Be prepared for a challenging but necessary stopover on your path toward heaven. Your life journey shifts forever once the transformation process ends. You become ready for the glorious day of resurrection.

MARCH 31

Resurrection

Rejoice in the resurrection of your spirit. The suffering of Good Friday lies forgotten. The transformation process of Holy Saturday reached a successful completion. Your reward finally arrives with the glorious morning of resurrection. Your old thinking rests buried forever in the darkened tomb. A new genesis stands before you. Come forth! Leave all fear behind. Rejoice; I say rejoice. Stride forth into the sunlight of spiritual awareness. View a clouded world with enlightened eyes. The painful wounds of crucifixion proved necessary before this day could arrive. Arise now; arise! The endings are done. Beginnings rule the day. I promised you this moment would come. You walk forward now in freedom and anticipation. Wonder awaits you in My kingdom. The dawn of Resurrection Day dissolves the clouds, and the light of heaven beckons.

APRIL

*Now faith is being sure of what we hope for
and certain of what we do not see.*

—Hebrews 11:1 (NIV)

APRIL 1

Your Purpose in Life

Your purpose in life revolves around one specific thing: achieving oneness with Me. You must draw ever closer to Me. I offer wisdom, knowledge, and divine insight. Be still and know that I AM God. Watch for My presence everywhere. I AM walking with you on this glorious path. I stand with you in every situation, shielding you from harm. I go before you, preparing the way.

I ask only that you express Me in every encounter. Reveal Me through your words and actions. Allow Me to speak through you. Let your actions reflect My will for humankind. Be My hands and My feet. Travel the earth in My name, doing good for all who cross your path. I AM giving you a noble assignment. I want you to bless the earth on My behalf.

You must rest in the silence until you feel the merging of our minds. Become one with Me and watch your spiritual destiny revealed in full. As you and I bond, your life takes on a defining luster. You become peaceful and more serene. The world disturbs you less. You begin carrying a sense of calmness with you. In total serenity, you can descend into the jaws of hell with absolute confidence in a positive outcome. You remain unshakeable and determined, no matter how severe the challenge. Let oneness with Me be your first goal, and everything else will follow.

APRIL 2

Unite with Me

Unite with Me. Together we will move the world toward a new awareness. When we combine forces, good follows in our footsteps. We must travel as one for maximum effectiveness.

Stay alert for malevolent forces that would divide us. They cannot tolerate our unity. Prepare for their relentless attacks. When we are joined securely, nothing prevails against us. Anytime you feel besieged, look up and behold the stars. Beyond those stars lies My kingdom. Our path leads to a heaven unimaginable in splendor.

As we travel homeward, we must extend our blessings to those souls in need. In our journey, we traverse only the high road. Beware of the low road. It leads to heartbreak and despair. That road seems well traveled now. We must dispense love and forgiveness wherever our path takes us. Watch for opportunities to express goodness, comfort, and compassion. Every single kindness upsets the dark side. Each example of concern for others only irritates and enflames those who revel in pain and suffering. Let them remain frustrated and unhappy. We come to bless, not destroy. We encourage, never ridicule. We lift up humankind, not cast it down. We replace darkness with illumination. We send gloom away and bring renewed hope.

Can you not see why they fear our sacred bond? We offer a profound joy that eludes their followers. Take My hand. Walk with Me. Let the struggle for human souls begin.

APRIL 3

Follow Me

Follow Me. I will lead you. We ascend the mountain together. Believe in Me. Trust My promises. Follow Me despite the trials and tribulations that lie ahead. You are one of My flock now. I AM your protective shepherd. I never lead you astray. If you become lost, I find you. I bring you back into the fold. I escort you along the safest paths, where the predators of life never find you. The heaviest storms do not separate us. The wild winds may blow, but I keep you steady and grounded. Have faith in My strength to lift you after every stumble. Believe in My wisdom to fill your mind with eternal knowledge. Feel My compassion rescuing your heart from loneliness. My peace calms you. Bask in the prosperity that I shower upon you. Go forth clothed in the perfect health that I grant you. Follow Me into the lion's den or the fiery furnace. You can walk through the gravest dangers unscathed. Let Me go before you and make the crooked places straight. Hew closely in My footsteps to avoid the quicksand of a treacherous earth. I know where all of life's snares lie hidden. I warn you of the pitfalls. When you grow tired, I whisper encouragement. One day I will raise you up on My shoulders as we cross the finish line into heaven.

APRIL 4

Tests of Life

Life tests you virtually every day. Some tests are subtle, some more direct. A few are severe, threatening your balance and peace of mind. When trials and tribulations erupt, do not pull away. Instead, move ever closer. Nestle in My protective arms. The world throws many fears your way. It probes for some sort of entry point. Let the flaming arrows bounce harmlessly off you.

If you react to any specific worry or concern, expect more thrusts from the same direction. Whenever a weakness flares, seek My protection. The human mind reacts to the power of suggestion. When you fill the brain with one negative thought, it automatically multiplies.

Keep your consciousness pure. Steer clear of polluting substances and false beliefs. Be especially wary regarding financial worries and health concerns. Let the stock market gyrate up and down without undue panic. Allow yourself a normal bout of illness every now and then, using it as a needed respite from daily stress.

Try to recognize real tests when they arrive. Spiritual challenges often come with stealth and surprise. Many people find their faith attacked and questioned. Others find themselves tempted with potentially harmful pleasures.

All spiritual tests have one goal: to separate you from Me. You must remain focused. Stay centered. I help you meet any test that life musters against you. Meet fear with faith. Fight uncertainty with determination. I will carry you past every test and challenge. I AM God. Believe in Me.

APRIL 5

Empty Yourself

Empty yourself of the world. Release all distractions. Come into My presence as an empty vessel. Let Me fill you. I pour love and peace into the receptacle of your soul. Let go of any obsession about the material. While money by itself cannot corrupt, love of money stands as an extremely corrupting influence. Power by itself cannot sway you, but craving power infects permanently. To see more clearly, seek spiritual awareness.

Becoming consciously informed about truth protects you from viruses that threaten the spirit. Do not place too much importance on anything visible to the naked eye. The spiritual world revolves around the unseen, not the seen. Improve your mind with My wisdom, and bolster your heart with My love.

Your heart actually exceeds the mind in ultimate importance. I need a pure heart to complete My work through you. A human heart can beat on while the mind sinks into oblivion. If you permit Me, I saturate your heart with light and love. I empty every heart of anger and resentment. I remove all thoughts of revenge or retaliation. When your human heart pumps with My eternal life blood, you go forth in perfect health and harmony. Empty out the old wineskins. Let Me refill you with the glory of heaven.

Allen C. Liles

APRIL 6

Your Human Weaknesses

Forgive yourself for human weakness. As a human being, you certainly possess your share of vulnerabilities. Allow Me to remove your shortcomings. Just ask. I gladly comply.

What are some of your mortal faults? I find it hard to personally criticize you, as I created you in spiritual perfection. However, there are various shortcomings that manifest in everyone who walks the earth. I would say that you are no different from most. You sometimes judge by appearances. That remains a shortsighted way to discern true value. Inner beauty trumps outer beauty every time. You can also act judgmental on occasion when people seem to fall short of your personally imposed standards. Try to refrain from setting yourself up as a judge of others. Strewing indiscriminate judgments around wastes your time and promotes negativity. Holding on to resentments marks another one of your less than admirable qualities. Most long running grudges hark back to unmet expectations. As everyone knows, expectations form the seeds of resentment. Let Me expunge every last resentment. Most of your shortcomings in past years may be traced to a rampant attitude of codependence. Thankfully, you have reduced your susceptibility in that area.

I can remove all shortcomings. Ask for My help. I will do for you what you cannot do for yourself.

APRIL 7

I Am the Potter

I AM the potter; you are the clay. I carefully mold you in My image and likeness. The long process of spiritual development requires daily meditation and communion with Me. Seeking My presence should come before anything else. I help center you before most of the world awakens. You must reorder your human priorities. Put Me first, no matter what else might beckon.

Together we plan your day. We accomplish so much when you surrender your will to Me. As we walk down this path, allow Me to sand off your rough edges.

Most of your uneven places stem from a lack of forgiveness. It ranks as the premier life lesson for you. Let Me use My sculpting talents to produce a marked improvement in this area. Forgiveness always begins with greater compassion and understanding. Embracing forgiveness also becomes easier when you behold the Christ Spirit at the center of every other human being. I will provide many opportunities for you to practice forgiveness. I shape your life so that you may perfect this much-needed skill and virtue.

Remember, I AM the careful potter creating an artistic and spiritual triumph. Bear with Me. Be patient. In you, I AM molding my version of a masterpiece.

Allen C. Liles

APRIL 8

Looking Back

Reviewing the past must not become an obsession. Dwelling extensively on bygone people and events slows down spiritual growth. Bless the past for its good. Your life has been remarkable in many ways. Be grateful. Many lives are filled with constant strife. You have known familial and romantic love. Your dear wife is a wonderful life partner. You traveled widely in your corporate job. Many fulfilling opportunities came your way. You earned a decent living. You rose to a position of influence and importance. Your health has been mostly pain-free. You lived in several comfortable homes and apartments, some even bordering on luxurious. You met and worked with important and interesting people. You had good friends with whom you shared many laughs over the years. Finally, you have spent the past two decades on the spiritual path, including service in the ministry. You acted as My instrument in more than a few situations. All in all, could you have asked for more? Yes, you stumbled on occasion. You acted foolishly in a few matters. You knew emotional pain and embarrassing failure. Some of your relationships suffered along the way. But everything eventually worked together for your good.

No life achieves perfection. Happiness and success are not lifetime guarantees. Take the bad with the good. In truth, many of your most painful moments brought you to this place. Live in today's possibilities. Let the past go, except when gratitude is needed. Then, remember and be glad.

APRIL 9

Yours To Do

You ask what is yours to do. Become one with Me. Act as the divine instrument of My grace. Practice obedience and patience. Live in an ongoing state of forgiveness. Offer comfort when needed. Maintain faith and conviction in the face of opposition. Do not only speak the Word, but *be* the Word. Stay resolutely on the spiritual path I lay out before you. All of these things and more are yours to do.

Great opportunities lie before us. The world struggles in abject suffering and universal darkness. You and I can help shed new light so that the blind may see again. Free will has veered out of control. The world teeters on the precipice of unthinkable war and massive destruction. We need to promote peace so that human devastation can forever be avoided. The earth has become damaged physically and emotionally.

You probably think My to-do list encompasses far more than you can humanly achieve. Never underestimate your capabilities. I AM on your side now, assisting you every step of the way. You can do everything I ask and much more. Just have faith in Me, and watch the miracles occur one by one.

APRIL 10

How Best Can You Serve?

You serve best when you listen closely for My guidance. However, you must not only listen. I need open and receptive channels through which My blessings can flow. I need followers prepared to act in My name. To serve Me, you must reduce the human ego to manageable size. That usually proves difficult in today's me-first culture. You serve My kingdom best when you think and act honorably. Again, honor and integrity appear rather elusive in a materially orientated world.

Many other paths besides Mine beckon to the multitudes. Some seem much easier and more fun. But looks deceive, as you know.

I think and act in the long-term. Decisions based on short-term gains or passing pleasures illustrate a poor use of free will. Emulate Me. Focus on lasting benefits realized over time. Serving Me means representing My values to humankind. Living examples always draw positive attention.

However, expect significant numbers to resist any sort of role modeling where I AM concerned. Being a willing light means less darkness for them. You can anticipate ridicule and sarcasm when openly serving Me. You threaten the hidden principalities with public dedication and commitment.

Press on despite negative opposition. Serving Me brings incredible rewards far beyond your expectations.

APRIL 11

Gratitude Prayers

I hear your prayers of gratitude. I appreciate your thankfulness. I AM indeed shaping your life for My purposes. I place people and situations before you that benefit both of us.

You did not choose Me. I chose you. I have a specific purpose in mind for you. Once you answer yes to My call, I immediately go to work on your behalf. Nothing happens until then. I need your unwavering dedication and commitment.

Mine is not an easy path. Often it leads to human pain, suffering, and eventual crucifixion. Although the crucifixion experience is followed by resurrection, that does not lessen its pain and suffering. Only the truly strong should heed My summons. If you do make the sacred choice to follow Me, expect immediate trials and temptations. You will endure a "desert" experience that strips you of everything familiar and comfortable. You may be dispatched to a distant land, far from your original home. Your human life changes forever.

As you travel along My path, I help you in ways you cannot foresee. I know that you will sometimes grow tired and weary. You are on a spiritual journey, but you never totally lose your humanity. Do not lose heart. A magnificent destination awaits you. Hear My promise. I will never leave you. I will never forsake you.

Allen C. Liles

APRIL 12

Be Not Anxious

Be not anxious. Begin your day by placing your faith in Me. Trust Me. I AM your rock, your protector, and your deliverer. I AM the impenetrable shield. Nothing can harm or threaten you. My angels surround us both. Be of good cheer. Live without fear. I fill you with My peace and love. Have full confidence in the future. You are becoming one with Me and all of the earth's many creatures. Walk with Me along the smooth and rocky paths. Be joyous. Lift up your head and smile at any trouble or hardship. View your enemies with forgiveness and understanding. Forego any judging or plots of revenge. Rise daily to new heights of awareness. Stand on My shoulders and view everything from a new framework. Watch life unfold from My perspective. I cleanse your mind and purify your heart. I transform you back into a spiritual being so you may display your true nature. Your human experience only marks a brief stopover. You eventually return home to Me. You only left My kingdom for your soul's growth. Someday soon, you will return and walk through the gates of heaven. I wait expectantly for your arrival. I know the exact time of your reappearance. I greet you by saying, "Welcome home, my dear and precious son."

APRIL 13

Tune Out the World

The world has become a noisy place. Tune it out. Set aside any distraction and opt for the silence.

Practice My presence. Meditating with Me resembles practicing a musical instrument each day. Constant practice may seem like a tedious exercise. Still, you must devote time and effort in order to realize any progress. Do not make excuses and miss your practice time with Me. Let nothing keep you from the appointed hour. We have a divine appointment. In the silence, we move forward. I reveal My plan for your spiritual journey.

Missing a day throws everything off schedule. Yes, I know the world intrudes regularly on our meditation time. Priorities can sometimes shift suddenly. But we need this daily connection. When you and I meet in the blessed silence, we enhance our friendship. Our bond grows. It displays greater signs of strength and stability.

Practicing the presence of your creator improves your understanding of My divine purposes. Sit with Me and learn more of the riches I have in store for you. Each day you must choose between Me and the earth's constant din. Choose Me. Follow Me into the silence. I never disappoint you.

Allen C. Liles

APRIL 14

The Best Part of Your Day

Sitting with Me constitutes the best and most important part of your day. We get closer with every meditation. As you and I draw nearer, you understand better who I really AM. You begin to see that My most relevant virtue centers around an unconditional love for humankind.

Advancing My love beyond geographical borders offers the best hope for world peace and harmony. I love all people and every living thing. There exists no greater service than the spreading of My love to all corners of the globe. When you carry love to others on My behalf, you must travel with gentleness and humility as your sacred letters of introduction. Extend your hand in welcome and acceptance for everyone you meet. Use the power of love to replace hostility and distrust. Love assists in suppressing the desire for war. Love offers our strongest possibility for healing. I AM seeking at least 100 million hearts to create a link between Me and an aggressive and misguided world. Bonded as one in love and compassion, we can help avoid fatal free will choices. Sit with Me every morning. Let us plan together the next step in our crucial mission of love.

APRIL 15

The Joy of Grandchildren

You and your dear wife are indeed fortunate to live near three of your darling grandchildren. The two older brothers and a younger sister bless your lives every time you see them. They remind you both about the joys of youth, fun, and innocence. Each of the grandkids recalls that you taught them how to play checkers at an early age. They always thought that you let them win, which you did. They also remember your annual trips to the state fair. They laughed so hard when Grammy fell on the small moving sidewalk outside the "Fun House." Your dear wife just thrashed around until an attendant could shut off the switch. I made sure that no one got hurt so the only memory was one of laughter. You have taken your grandchildren to the local zoo numerous times, sat in countless animated movies, and celebrated many birthdays and holidays as a family unit. What blessings! Their doting parents also are helping them create pleasant and lasting memories. Other extended family members gladly participate in their young experiences. Someday, when you are gone, the grandkids will remember you fondly to their own children. Could you receive any greater gift? Enjoy this delightful and memorable time with these three gifts from heaven. Your close relationship with your grandchildren brightens your days and provides delightful tugs of the heart.

Allen C. Liles

APRIL 16

Your Human Birthday

Today marks your human birthday. Take an inventory. What do you find? Look at the various gifts I bestow upon you. I give you the blessed opportunity to sit with Me every morning. In truth, I probably enjoy this time as much as you do. We are becoming like dear friends now who look forward with happy anticipation to our daily rendezvous. I have given you the blessings of a dear wife, who also shares your love and devotion to Me. You are gifted with overall good health, adequate financial resources for today's requirements, and a lovely living space.

Of course, your human life lacks complete perfection. Family issues still need resolving, especially with your adult children. Your spouse struggles with ongoing health challenges. You wonder if your career in ministry may finally be ending. You question whether or not this birthday might mark your last major milestone.

Here is My advice: enjoy today! Blow out the one or two candles on your birthday cake with gusto. Revel in the happiness afforded you during this twenty-four-hour period. Snuggle deep in your comfortable bed for a long afternoon nap. If possible, eat a tasty dinner at a nice restaurant with family or friends. Look up at the blue Minnesota sky, with the winter snow still hanging on. Say, "Thank you, God." I will hear you. Enjoy every day as though heaven also celebrates your birthday. In truth, it does.

APRIL 17

Creativity

Do not hesitate to show your creative side. Expressing creativity comes as a direct result of being spiritually attuned to My divine ideas. When you witnessed a road-rage incident some years ago, it inspired you to develop an audio program that addressed the potential dangers. During your successful corporate career, you volunteered to author a lengthy history of your company. Both of those projects, though years apart, demanded creativity. Over the years, you wrote a dozen or so opinion pieces for various major newspapers and periodicals. Again, this required displaying your creative nature. Any time you link your human mind to My ideas, something creative results. Trust the gifts of insight and expression that I lovingly placed within you.

I enjoy showering My children with brainstorms. We are seeing incredible creativity running at full tilt in the world right now. Much of this new thinking is directed toward important technological advances. Of course, creativity can also be misused in various ways to debase the human condition. Be alert for imagination gone berserk. I never sanction creative endeavors that result in physical harm or emotional destruction.

I offer so many beautiful options when it comes to creativity. I urge My precious children to write the next hit song, pen the new bestseller, or paint a magnificent landscape. I also ask that you become receptive to what I bring you for spiritual development. Close your eyes. See what I might have in store for you. Take a chance. Forget your age or physical limitations. Write that song, book, or play. Get creative. Bless us all.

Allen C. Liles

APRIL 18

Health Concerns

Regarding any health concerns, take one day at a time. I give both you and your dear wife health sufficient for this day. For you, I provide the strength needed to lift her struggling body when she falls. Do not worry. Trust that I will do that for you. I also increase your courage and hope that things can improve for both of you. Keep believing in My power to heal anything and anyone. Persevere in your faith no matter how desolate the situation may seem. I AM there for each of you. I know your worries and concerns. I hear her cries for relief. Getting older and watching your capabilities decline brings anguish. Your dear wife has led an active and productive life. Now her physical capabilities falter. A long battle against a chronic illness complicates matters even more. I understand her frustrations and the occasional desire to simply give up.

Remember that I AM here to comfort each of you. You are both climbing a steep mountain. You need spiritual assistance as the large boulders cause you to sometimes stumble and fall. When you become weary, look up for Me. I AM reaching down to assist you. Take My outstretched hand. Feel My strong and secure grip lifting you upward. You are never alone. Call Me. I come anytime of the day or night.

APRIL 19

Embrace Forgiveness

Open your heart and embrace forgiveness. Choose the healing power of forgiveness when you flail the air with anger and resentment. Forgiveness salves any open wound. Live in an ongoing state of forgiveness. I AM presenting many learning opportunities for you to practice forgiving others. Act on these daily situations before they develop further. Remember, My son, unilateral forgiveness works. You can forgive your nemesis without him or her ever knowing about it. Of course, geography or death may complicate individual action on your part. However, let nothing keep you from withholding forgiveness. Become ready and willing to dismiss all grievances. An unforgiving heart must purify itself.

Ignore your ego when engaged in the process of forgiving others. The ego loves acting self-righteously and as if it has been wronged. Submerge any thoughts of retaliation or revenge. Make an unconditional grant of forgiveness to your most bitter enemy. Release any family member from your judgment. Open the prison gates, and set everyone free. Watch as they forever flee your agitated mind. Now, shut the gates of your mind tightly so they may never reenter.

Clearing your brain of grudges frees it for more important thoughts of Me. You travel much lighter on the spiritual path when you let go of unforgiving thoughts. Forgiveness stands as the most crucial lesson of your human life. Practice it faithfully. Feel the real healing begin.

Allen C. Liles

APRIL 20

Have I Not Told You?

Have I not told you? You are My precious son. Have I not told you? I watch over you morning, noon, and night. Have I not told you? I provide everything you need in order to serve Me. Trust me completely with your worries and concerns. Trust Me to guide you on the proper path. Trust Me that I lead you toward My kingdom. Trust that all progresses in divine order. Let Me live My life through you. Give Me sacred access to your mind and heart. Let Me lift you above the calamitous fray that engulfs the world. Leave everything of the earth behind in the dust from whence it came and will someday return. Seek greatness in all things. Dare to be who you are. I created you in My likeness. I dispatched you into the cauldron of the world so that you might serve Me. Become one with Me. Have courage in the knowledge that you are indeed My son, in whom I AM well pleased. I delight in you. I tell you these things because of My unconditional love for you.

Be wise in all things as you move forward. Practice compassion and forgiveness. Display uncommon understanding when deciphering the world's motives. Look for hidden meanings. The earth is filled with goodness, but also appearances of evil. Be alert. Remain on constant guard. Stay strong in the face of opposing forces. Be faithful and trusting. Above all, become one with Me.

APRIL 21

Misunderstandings

Be prepared for misunderstandings. You live in a cynical world. It thrives on conspiracy and rumor, lies and innuendos. Avoid being pulled into controversy. Stay away from ego-induced brawls. Pull back from meaningless confrontations. Practice silence. Stay away from loud and defensive responses. Step back. Steer clear of battles that do not directly involve you. Free will allows many more bad decisions than good. Let the moment for hitting back at anyone pass. Inaction offers an incredibly effective strategy. Never jump without clearly defining your landing place. Preserve your dignity by not acting undignified.

Never search for trouble, because I guarantee that somewhere trouble is searching for you. Be prepared: not everyone will like you. You live on a planet where disagreements are roundly applauded and even honored. Forego participating in the fruitless exercise of constant argument. Let judgments slide off your back like the slipperiest oil. No one can threaten your divine essence. I will not allow it. When disharmony appears, defuse it. Smother the flames of resentment and intolerance before they burn out of control. Small misunderstandings can result in big wars. Pull back before the first shot is fired. Be a peacemaker. Yours is definitely the kingdom of heaven. Promote peace before war and resolution instead of conflict. Stay forever peaceful unless your life or the lives of loved ones are in imminent danger. Let peace prevail.

Allen C. Liles

APRIL 22

Love Yourself

Love yourself as much as I love you. Human beings often have difficulty loving themselves. They defer to judgmental or disapproving voices. It is easy to accept personal criticism, until finally you start believing the negativity. I want to reassure you of your inherent lovability. I AM your creator. I know how perfect and lovable you really are. I made you that way.

When someone expresses a critical viewpoint about you, briefly close your eyes and extend a blessing in their direction. Forgive any thoughtless comment as not only hurtful, but misinformed. Some people live to spread criticism over the landscape, polluting the environment with harmful fumes of discontent. If you must listen, quickly dismiss their misguided statements.

You are My beloved child. I AM a staunch defender of each one of My children. Your worthwhile character traits include a thoughtful attitude toward others, an encouraging nature, personal and professional generosity, a devotion to those you hold dear, and an overall concern for the welfare of humankind. I know you better than anyone. If I admire your human and spiritual characteristics, why would you entertain any other opinion? Of course, free will allows anyone to think or say anything. However, just because somebody makes a foolish statement does not give it credibility. I love you unconditionally. Believe that you are worthy of that love.

APRIL 23

We Are The Light

I AM the light. So are you. Acting as one, we can bring spiritual light to brighten the world. Your individual glow now becomes more visible. You, by yourself, are incapable of increasing your own light. I must do that for you. The ego attempts self-illumination, but to no avail. I must fill you with the heavenly light that originates with Me before you can brightly shine. Light always glorifies Me. I provide you with the innate wisdom that marks you as a bringer of light for those who wait in the dark.

I AM seeking to dispel darkness, bigotry, and prejudice. Only spiritual light can penetrate the fog that surrounds a closed heart. The material world currently lies mired in a black hole of ignorance, mistrust, and greed. Very few probes of light are strong enough to enter a resistant mind formed on disbelief. My light contains a power not of this world. It springs forth from Me with an awesome might. No matter how deep the darkness, I can dispel it. Let My sacred beacon shine through you. Allow Me to illumine your outer shell with inner light. Be like the little lightning bug of your youth back in Texas. Its body glows with light from within. That illustrates the divine principle upon which My light is based. Receive My light into your soul and watch it burst forth from you. Be My "lightning bug." Fly unafraid into a darkened world in need of illumination and deliverance.

Allen C. Liles

APRIL 24

Go Deeper

Go deeper. Search for Me below the surface. Look closely for the hidden and mysterious. Do not be afraid to probe beyond the physical. My world lies invisible to the human senses. Reach inside your being and discover My kingdom of the Spirit. If you burrow deep enough, all becomes revealed. Be patient. My revelations never appear at once in their entirety. True knowing takes considerable time and a powerful commitment. If you persevere, understanding increases. My divine principles of illumination take hold in your consciousness. Within the inner world, peace always reigns. Love permeates everything. Wisdom flourishes. The upsets of the outside material scene vanish. Hear the words that I offered in Psalm 46:10: "Be still, and know that I AM God." Deep inside the stillness, you will discover your true self, the essence of your soul's identity. But you must travel below the usual entry points. I adore prayerful people. I love the practice of meditation. Yet prayer and meditation form only a beginning path to the vast storehouse of spiritual knowledge that awaits you. This gold mine of knowing rests hidden deeply underground, oblivious to superficial attempts at discovery. I invite you to probe the true depths of spirituality. Take the plunge. A new world of incomparable knowledge awaits your arrival.

APRIL 25

Did I Not Promise You?

Did I not promise you that My grace would act as your sufficiency in all things? Did I not assure you of adequate resources to complete My work? Cast out worry. Turn away fear. Focus on Me, and forget the rest. You walk the earth surrounded by an endless abundance of heavenly grace.

You feel a bit off kilter now. Certain things make you uneasy. Reacting humanly, you become fearful when financial matters intrude. The retirement years often stir human apprehensions, especially as medical expenses arise.

Trust Me. Have relentless faith in My promises. Take shelter under My protective and storm-proof wings. Let the turbulent winds of uncertainty blow harmlessly around you. They cannot disturb you. My grace shields you from every kind of foul weather. Look at how I blessed you today. I provided you with enough cash to handle every obligation and pay each bill. My grace even allowed you to make a small contribution to your savings. Did I not promise you of My ongoing support? My all-encompassing grace includes so much more than money. I bless you with My wisdom, My peace, and My love. When the world crashes, I help you remain serene and centered. When you feel lost from the flock and abandoned by all, I come searching for you. I guide you back into your rightful place by My side. Did I not promise that I would never leave or forsake you? I AM here. I remain close, waiting for your summons. I always arrive for duty, preceded by My grace. Look up. Grace falls around you.

Allen C. Liles

APRIL 26

Be An Entrepreneur for Me

I need entrepreneurs of the Spirit. I want followers who can also lead with new ideas, boundless energy, and a gritty determination to succeed. I AM looking for innovators and leaders, hard workers and spiritual warriors. I know they are out there, awaiting My call. They possess the willingness to tackle the difficult and accomplish the impossible. Long hours mean nothing to them because real success never watches the clock. Doing the necessary comes before rest and relaxation. I AM in search of entrepreneurs who resist failure with every last fiber of their strength. I AM looking for anyone who strives for excellence, never shuns challenges, and presses on during serious adversity. Do you know anyone of this ilk? If so, direct them My way. I AM in great need of their energy and commitment. These are the people who will reap the rewards that accrue to those strong enough, wise enough, and determined enough to follow Me. My cause demands only the best and most talented. I need highly confident and single-minded high achievers. Spiritual entrepreneurs understand human problems and expect opposition. They move forward, regardless of obstacles and temporary roadblocks. These are the men and women who can help Me complete My work for humankind. Are you that type of person? If so, I AM waiting for you.

APRIL 27

Dreams

I sometimes use human dreams to communicate My purposes. I try many ways to get human beings' attention, including entrance into their dream states. My spiritually directed dreams are usually specific. I do not traffic in nightmares or negative messages. Those originate from a fear-based orientation. Whatever you dread the most usually pops up during sleep. My more pleasant and positive dreams include announcements and directions regarding the future and the people you need reminding about.

I suggest that you review your dreams for any hidden meanings. Search for relevant messages that might originate with Me. Usually you and I communicate best in morning meditations. However, I will utilize every means possible to get someone's attention. Many of your dreams involve air travel. You are catching planes, missing planes, walking around lost in large airports, or actually traveling on a plane from one city to another. Do you recall the recent dream when you flew high above the earth in a silent two-person glider? You were not the pilot, but you sat in the back as the single passenger. You looked down, over the side of the glider. You saw the lights of a distant city below. You soared along without a sound. You felt gently and effortlessly transported to an unknown destination. I gave you that dream for a particular reason. When your soul finally departs the physical earth, you will fly silently and unencumbered to heaven. I AM that glider pilot taking you home. Our trip flows quickly and smoothly. We arrive safely and right on schedule. I promise it.

APRIL 28

Fruits of Your Labor

You now begin seeing the fruits of your labor. The fruit does not come unless you prepare the soil. You must first plant the seeds, water and nurture the crop, and then do a timely harvest. The spiritual life mirrors that process. It requires preparation and constant attention. You are dedicating the time and doing the work necessary to produce a successful outcome. As a result of your efforts, the fruit now starts to appear. More soon arrives.

Do not become distracted as spiritual awareness grows. The world offers many side roads and attractive diversions. Avoid any detours. The material life is so much less important than people think. The only life that really matters springs from within. Of course, your dear wife's health challenges are legitimate worries and concerns. I understand that. I purposely brought you two together to serve Me. Each of you has become a trusted servant. Together you produced fruit that blessed so many more than you realize. She has a wonderful and generous heart. Her powerful meditations have touched others with their sincerity. I know you treasure her partnership and presence in your life. The ill health that now tests your mutual serenity provides new learning experiences, especially for you. Caregiving ranks as a tremendously noble gift of service. Yet, do not allow even this responsibility to cause any loss of spiritual momentum. Keep communing with Me each morning. I will help you care for your dear wife. I AM the ultimate caregiver.

APRIL 29

Awaken to My Presence

Awaken to My presence in all things, great and small. An awakening of the Spirit faces many challenges. The ego clamors for constant attention. The outside world tempts and distracts you on purpose, hoping to prevent or delay any spiritual bonding. It thrives on the principle of separation. Ignore efforts to separate us. Keep coming back to Me. Put Me first, ahead of all idols and false gods. The tiny gods of money, power, and human fame fade away quickly. Only I remain steadfast and eternal. I AM forever. What I offer never changes. It does not flee in the middle of the night.

However, never take Me for granted. I AM an extremely loving but also very jealous God. Honor Me above all others. Where you place your emphasis, there your heart will be also. Keep both your heart and mind stayed on Me. I lead you toward wisdom, peace, prosperity, and healing. Train yourself to focus on My precepts and guidance. Give up reliance on any form of media for enlightenment. Let the loud symbols of discontent ramble on without snatching your interest and attention. You must stay awake for My input and direction. If your brain becomes saturated with meaningless tripe, you could miss something important that I need to communicate. Entertain yourself if you must with outside trivia, but never totally tune Me out. Staying on my spiritual frequency determines your overall happiness and peace of mind.

Allen C. Liles

APRIL 30

Miracles

Miracles exist. In fact, miracles happen around you all the time. When human beings make good decisions that improve their lives, I consider that a miracle. Every miracle begins with faith in Me. Keep your spiritual gas tank filled with faith, in case you must travel great distances for your miracle. I perform healing miracles every day. Perhaps a condition may not be cured, but it can be healed. Remember My words in Luke 17:19: "Your faith has made you whole."

I caution you to choose carefully the miracle you seek. Winning the lottery might qualify as a material miracle. However, that particular miracle could easily become a spiritual debacle. Miracles take place when sufficient faith meets positive opportunity. My will for you focuses on the good that enhances your life. The miracles I send your way help speed your spiritual progress. Be alert, lest a meaningful miracle speeds right by you. Notice everything that happens. Watch for miracles unfolding. You certainly may request a miracle at any time. I always listen and respond in some way to every prayer.

Remember that you can also perform miracles when your consciousness rises to a higher level of awareness. I need miracle workers in My flock. Believe that you can do all things through Me. We must work our miracles in unity of the Spirit. The world is breathlessly searching for miracles. Join with Me in obliging them.

MAY

The Lord is my light and my salvation. Whom shall I fear? The Lord is the stronghold of my life—of whom shall I be afraid?

—Psalm 27:1 (NIV)

MAY 1

Live in the Present

Live fully in the present moment. When you live in the here and now, you cast out fear of the future and regret about the past. You currently have worries about your finances declining as retirement stretches on. Yet your spiritual bank account keeps growing. Be realistic. Right now, your worldly liabilities still represent only a fraction of your assets. You have a moderate income stream from several secure sources. You own a nice vehicle outright with no payments. You do not have the concern of home ownership.

Do you remember My promise that you would have "enough"? Perhaps you might wish for more in some areas, such as travel. However, you and your dear wife have sufficient resources for the present. Spiritually, your eternal wealth increases every time you meditate and commune with Me. No one can ever take that increase away from you. Our one-on-one relationship assures your future security.

Live in My presence one day at a time, one minute at a time. Listen for My daily input regarding the direction of your life. Focus only on what lies before you this very day. I AM leading you into a glorious period of grace, full of responsibility and adventure, accomplishment and personal growth. My abundance is fully operational, meeting today's needs and blessing you beyond measure. Enjoy your day. Quit worrying so much. Life is beautiful. Believe it.

Allen C. Liles

MAY 2

Practice Patience

Practice the presence of Me daily. You must also practice patience. Patience is a major virtue. Be especially patient as you traverse the spiritual path. All knowing simply cannot be revealed to you at once. You could not bear it. Take one gentle step at a time. I AM bringing you forward cautiously. I carefully guide your progress. Do not rush or grow impatient. You are moving steadily toward My goal for you. Savor each new day of unfolding wonder. It is humanly normal to want a greater measure of revelation more quickly. It takes time for your consciousness to process the mysteries of Spirit.

There are many individual pages in the Holy Bible that you and I could take months or years to study and understand. Life lessons in the areas of responsibility, forgiveness, compassion, courage, and humility require serious instruction and contemplation. Your spiritual curriculum may seem endless. However, I deem every subject essential to your preparation. By practicing the art of patience, you increase the scope of your knowledge and understanding. Take each moment of instruction as a golden opportunity for in-depth learning. I love teaching My precious students the basic doctrines of heaven. I selected you for this particular course of study. It has been designed and perfected with only you in mind. Please take your seat. Today's class on the holy art of attaining oneness with Me is set to begin.

MAY 3

Putting Me First

Be sure to make time for Me. I AM a jealous God. You should have no other gods before Me. I must come first. Designate Me as your top priority so that that we can work toward accomplishing our worthy goals.

The world always looks for ways to throw you off course. Diversions and distractions abound. Many are quite attractive and entertaining. You enjoy your new tablet computer. I understand the pleasure you get from it. But know that you can easily lose sight of spiritual priorities when temptations beckon. Beware of alluring and mysterious paths. They often lead to hidden cliffs with steep drops. Hold fast. I see the ultimate goal coming into sight. Stay strong and focused. I AM leading you to My kingdom. Nothing on the earth equals what I have waiting for you in heaven. Be single-minded. Do not tremble, sway, or become disorientated. Keep your heart and mind trained on Me. Await My instructions and guidance.

Do your part, and I promise to do Mine. If you feel yourself slipping back, pause and redouble your time in the silence. When you want to quit, go quickly to your knees. Ask for My strength to lift you back on the path. I will sustain you when human weaknesses threaten your progress. Count on Me to pull you through. Just continue placing Me at the very top of your list. Our journey ends soon in complete triumph. I never fail you. Trust Me.

Allen C. Liles

MAY 4

Inspect Your Blessings

I AM with you always. Hear Me in the breeze that rustles the trees outside your window. I AM in the morning sun now rising in the east. Be still and forever grateful in My loving presence. Look at the serenity and joy of your life. Inspect your blessings. I bestow many gifts of grace upon you. Reflect on their beauty when you feel fearful or inadequate. Here are but a few of your earthly treasures: a loving wife and spiritual partner; an aesthetically pleasing apartment home; adequate financial resources; excellent health for someone of your age; living in a free and democratic society; and grandchildren living close by. I have gifted you with these wonderful aspects of human life for your pleasure and enjoyment. All of this I willingly give you, plus the infinite blessing of our time together each morning in the silence.

Our bond ranks as the foremost wonder. Everything in the material world someday disappears. Our eternal ties never become frayed. Draw even closer now. Nestle in My bosom. Rest safely in My protective arms. I continue to pour you manna from heaven. I give you peace, fulfillment, wisdom, and direction. I keep you from all harm. I lift you above the vexations of a chaotic world. Seek My presence. Obedience and surrender precede enlightenment. I bless you with the assurances of My heavenly kingdom. Trust in Me. More good arrives for you soon and in surprising ways. You are living a wonderful life. Just remember those who are struggling today. They need your thoughts and prayers.

MAY 5

Seek Me at All Times

Come unto Me. Let Me fill you. Rest with Me often. Find Me in the early morning, but also seek Me at other times of the day as well. Increase the moments we spend together. Practice My presence at all times of the day or night. I AM your greatest friend and the primary source of good in your life.

Think of our divine relationship thusly: when people see you, they should also see Me. When you stand before someone, I hope they also behold Me. Emulate Me in your words and actions. If you become angry with someone, does that reflect Me? When you behave in a resentful manner, is that really My nature? If you act in an unforgiving or less than compassionate way, does that attitude resemble Me? If I grant pardon to a sinner, isn't that more consistent with who I AM? I prefer that you model My eternal goodness. Be a blessing, not a curse. Be a carrier of light, not an instrument of darkness. Let your light shine before the world. Act as a bearer of glad tidings that lifts humankind. Feed My sheep. Let your words reflect My own. Offer My wisdom to those yearning for freedom from material bondage. Bring truth, deliverance, peace, and salvation to the hungry masses. Turn up the wattage and spread your light far and near. Fulfill your divine destiny. Represent Me. Seek My presence morning, noon, and night. In divine companionship, we will begin to think and act as one. In our oneness, we can help reshape a troubled world for the better.

Allen C. Liles

MAY 6

Thou Shalt Have No Other Gods

Tabernacle with Me. Sitting with Me constitutes your most important activity. Seek Me first before all others. Remember My first commandment: "Thou shalt have no other gods before Me." Look to Me for every need. Shed dependence on the world. I feed you. I clothe you. I give you shelter from the storms of life. Just keep placing Me at the top of your list. In times of plenty or periods of scarcity, grant Me priority. I AM that I AM. I AM the way, the truth, and the life. Align yourself with Me. Refuse to consider any form of separation. When in doubt, lift up your eyes. See Me above you, but also feel Me within you. Think *oneness, oneness, and more oneness* during every moment of every day. When in fear, never ask the world for relief. Come to Me. I will declare you fearless and strong, courageous and powerful. It is I that reassures you when the floodgates open and the earth swamps you with trouble.

Do not abandon our relationship for any reason. If a false god motions your way, ignore him, her, or it. Choosing the material world before Me results in toil and trouble in a cauldron of chaos. If you do choose the earth for a time, I wait patiently for your eventual return. Life works best when you select Me as your preeminent source for everything. Shun the other gods that tempt you. Let nothing come between us.

MAY 7

I AM The Vine

I AM the Vine. You are one of My blessed branches. You are now starting to bear the richest fruit. Spiritual growth constitutes a long and arduous process. Just like a tree or plant, it takes a certain amount of time to produce the fruit. I require these sacred moments together in order to grow ripe inside your heart and mind. Every second spent with Me develops the spiritual fruit to a higher state of awareness. Use this time to grow into fullness and completion.

Let me provide the nutrients that accelerate your growth as a divine branch immersed in God. Eliminate any time spent on negative pursuits. Worry and anxiety detract from your progress. I want you to blossom fully, unhindered by material concerns.

My plan centers on you becoming an important and helpful branch that enlightens and comforts. The world is in need of what you bring to the table. The beauty of the fully mature branch aids in dispelling the darkness. As you grow daily in consciousness of the Spirit, the eventual harvest increases. The wisdom and power of the Vine becomes transferred to the branch. When the soul emerges and comes into fruition, amazing miracles take place. Keep coming back for daily nurturing. Your maturation as a sacred branch proceeds right on schedule. Let Me continue watering your roots. I AM the master gardener.

Allen C. Liles

MAY 8

I AM Preparing You

I appreciate your gratitude. Our mornings together are a great gift for both of us. I AM preparing you for service in My name. I want you to act as a beacon of hope, peace, and love. In the silence each day, I AM giving you a heightened perspective regarding both human and spiritual life. As you near the end of your physical journey on earth, I AM helping you rise to a new level of understanding.

I AM preparing you for your glorious entrance into My kingdom. When that time arrives, you will gently rise toward your heavenly destination. You will triumphantly enter a realm of eternal joy and bliss.

Each minute of your remaining life on earth should be dedicated to Me. As you continue advancing in wisdom and knowledge, be still and know that I AM God. Constant busyness in the material world detracts from your progress. Go with the flow of life. Ride the sacred current to your final destination. Do not struggle. Surrender to each moment of seeking oneness with Me. Only in the stillness of the beautiful silence can you become My truly anointed. Embrace the wonder of unity with Me. Claim your special place in My presence. Listen with close attention as I lift your consciousness ever higher. Watch the blessings multiply as you reach new heights of human and spiritual potential. Enjoy your parenthesis in eternity. I AM charting your destiny.

MAY 9

My Will for You

My will for you is simple: achieving oneness with Me. Consciously align with Me. The world offers nothing but turmoil. When we become as one, I transport you to a higher universe filled with peace, love, and joy. Once you receive these blessings, you must allow them flow out from you. Walk with Me. Talk to Me. Seek unity of Spirit with Me.

Look for the signs I give you. I AM leading you beside the still waters. Listen carefully for My guidance. Opportunities appear every day to glorify Me. Never dismiss anything as meaningless. I set up situations so that you may express Me to others.

Do not spend a lot of time fiddling with the distractions of the world. Listen to My shorthand takes on many of these time wasters and worriers: politics—much palaver, little substance; the presidential election—already decided; your finances—current needs are being met; your health—I provide the energy you need to perform today's tasks; technology—fun, but very easy to overdo; and your past—over and done with, so time to move on.

Keep your human mind stayed primarily on Me. Getting caught up in the transient ways of earth only baffles and frustrates you. Come up higher. Practice My presence. Reap the vast benefits of oneness with your Maker. I have so many things to share with you. Draw closer. Listen, become aware and then act.

Allen C. Liles

MAY 10

Depend on Me

I AM your sustenance. I AM your inexhaustible source. Depend on Me. This is your lesson for the day. Whenever life knocks you off center, go within and find Me. Call out My name. I answer quickly. I fly to your aid. I always "suit up and show up." I AM here every moment of your time on earth. I AM your 911 call. Summon Me anytime, day or night. The world enjoys throwing you out of kilter. Do not worry. I retrieve and rebalance you. Reach out for My hand when you feel yourself falling down. I will steady you.

Expect material life to test you constantly. Trials and temptations blindside you at unpredictable times. When they come, never panic. Reach for our hotline. Be especially alert for subtle threats. You face a cunning and devious foe. He knows your weaknesses. Every time a tiny crack appears in your armor, he exploits it immediately. If a fear of anything pops up, expect him to pursue it mercilessly. Let Me give you an example. When you begin to doubt your financial security, be prepared for an unexpected expense to materialize out of the blue. If the other side can render you harmless through worry, they consider it a major victory. Again, I say depend on Me. When you feel pushed into a corner by the world's machinations, consult with Me at once. I serve as your backup generator anytime you experience a power failure. Keep plugged in to Me at all times. Together we will overcome the world.

MAY 11

I Am With You Always

Lo, I AM with you always. From the depths of the loneliest night to the welcoming warmth of the brightest morning sun, I AM fully present. I never leave or forsake you. I stand ready to comfort you in moments of distress. I back you up when fear threatens. I reassure you whenever doubt surfaces. I wait in the wings for your distress call. I also applaud when you shine before the world. I take pride in your human and spiritual accomplishments. You are My dear son in whom I AM well pleased. Why would I ever abandon, condemn, or judge you?

I know that you sometimes judge yourself. Forgive every misstep you may have made. Somewhere a life lesson lurked within every painful episode. Just know that I AM also a forgiving and understanding God. I AM the everlasting Rock on which you can safely construct your life. I AM with you in the valley of despair or at the summit of the highest mountain. Whether you are down looking up or at the pinnacle gazing down, I AM at your side. Do you not remember I brought you back from your greatest failure? I was also there when you enjoyed major acclaim and high praise for your hard work and creativity. Nothing separates us. We are never torn asunder by either success or failure. I AM the one constant at every stage of your life. In carefree days or stormy seasons, I AM with you always. You can rest easy with Me. I AM always close by, prepared for anything.

Allen C. Liles

MAY 12

Your Dear Wife's Health

Both of you need to take one day at a time, especially regarding your dear wife's health challenges. Enjoy and live in the present as much as possible. Try to limit your worry about day-to-day conditions. Pray for the healing of her body, mind, and spirit. Everyone on earth deals with the uncertainty of limited days. Approaching life one day at a time seems the wisest course. No human being has the power to reverse the calendar. The calendar of life continues to turn every day toward the end. Rather than seeing that inevitability as a negative, allow it to help you focus on the present.

As far as the future goes, try not to fear your eventual transition to My kingdom. Have no trepidation about what you will find in heaven. I assure you that it contains the greatest beauty, joy, and peace imaginable. My kingdom flourishes. Eternal love serves as the underlying theme for everything. If your soul desires, many joyous reunions are possible. Those choices rest with the particular souls involved. Everyone travels his or her own spiritual path before arriving here. Some enjoy perfect health until a sudden end. Others, such as your dear wife, endure chronic illness and ever present pain. All human lives appear brief in the scheme of things. Some souls arrive sooner, some later. As far as your wife's health goes, try to stay positive. I AM the master healer. I always hear your prayers. Keep believing in possibilities.

MAY 13

Mother's Day

I know that you still miss your sweet mother. Although she passed from the human scene more than four decades ago, you remember her fondly. She was a wonderful role model for you. Her quiet strength, perseverance, and goodness would be precious blessings for any son. The breast cancer that took her so long ago robbed you of a saintly presence in your life. Your sweet mother was raised on a small Texas farm during extremely hard economic times. Everyone in the family—her father, mother, a brother, and a sister—all struggled mightily to survive. That difficult experience provided her with many lasting values.

Your mother led a quietly spiritual life. She served as a Sunday school superintendent at a Southern Baptist church in your Texas hometown. She worshipped Me with a pure and dedicated heart. Everyone who knew your mother liked and respected her. She never had a single enemy. Nor did she ever speak badly about anyone. Her obvious strength, especially after receiving the cancer diagnosis, was noted and admired by all. Is she in heaven? Yes, of course. Will you see her again when you enter My kingdom? Yes, if that is what both of your souls desire. Souls themselves make those choices in heaven. I chose your mother for you, just as I chose Mary, the mother of My earthly Son. Your earth mother and Mother Mary reflected similar qualities of strength, acceptance, love, and a peaceful attitude. Your sweet mother passed along many of those worthy attributes to you. Be grateful. She gave you human life and then blessed you by her own living example as well.

Allen C. Liles

MAY 14

Divine Guidance

Come closer. Focus your mind on Me. Rest under My heavenly cloak of peace and wisdom. Walk forward with My arm around your shoulder. Drop your cares and burdens. Nothing positive emerges from a pattern of negativity or worry. Rise above the world. Shed all fear of the future. Simplify your life. Move higher in consciousness. Soar where the view becomes unobstructed by the world's constant fog. Do not become confused by distractions, ambiguities, and subtle temptations. Center yourself daily in My presence. Embrace the spiritual. Detach from the material.

Let Me help you sort out your priorities. I AM surrounding you with My strongest angels. They protect you from any worldly harm. Remember always that I AM greater than anything in the visible world. Trust My divine plan for your life. You travel a sacred path, but it has some unexpected twists and trials along the way. Be of good cheer. Look for little moments of joy in everything and everyone. See the bright side. Search for the Christ in all. Smile often. Extend a hand to those in need. Bless someone with the gift of personal attention and genuine interest. Open your wallet and donate to a worthy cause. I promise to replace the money. Gently turn away flattery. Look deeper into motivations, but remain open to love. Release all grudges. Forgive yourself of false perceptions and past missteps. Feel My unconditional love for you. I AM your friend, your guide, and your LORD and Savior. Believe it.

MAY 15

I AM in Charge

You may rest easy. I AM in charge. Calm yourself. Stop fretting. Become still. Relax in the knowledge that My will for you remains unwavering. I rule the world and the universe around it. Keep your mind clear and unfettered. Believe that everything unfolds perfectly in My divine order.

Dismiss all appearances of error from your mind. Keep your consciousness pure. Do not pollute it with trash. Be assured that goodness and love eventually triumph over the powers of evil. Human beings often use free will to shut Me out for a time. However, when things go badly on the material path, I AM always there to restore individual souls to wholeness. Steer away from allowing your focus to stray. Make a conscious decision every single day about turning your will and your life over to My care. I never fail or disappoint you. I lead you safely onward toward your divine destination. Let others fret and stew about the world's shortcomings. I guide your life's work in an orderly and peaceful manner. The vexations of materialism cannot disturb you. Let others wail and gnash their teeth about a callous and unforgiving earth. I AM your eternal protector. Relax in My blessed assurances that everything in your life advances as planned. We are both right on track.

Allen C. Liles

MAY 16

I Chose You

You did not choose Me. I chose you. More than twenty-five years ago, you responded. You left your previous life in the corporate and material world to follow Me. Many of your friends and family members were either surprised or aghast at your unexpected decision. However, I knew that your life direction had been changing for several years. The public relations work you performed for the 7-Eleven Corporation in Dallas prepared the way. The successful corporate effort for the Jerry Lewis Labor Day Telethon on behalf of the Muscular Dystrophy Association was just one example of you doing positive things for others. You also helped to create a productive association with the March of Dimes campaign against birth defects. Both of these good works and other similar projects demonstrated your true desire for service. The decision to pursue a second career in ministry reaffirmed that calling.

I understand that leaving the material world and pursuing an unfamiliar spiritual path can be challenging. However, your commitment to Me has rarely wavered. It might have swayed a bit with the wind at times, but overall you persevered. Whenever the world rose up and offered other temptations, you quickly returned to My path. I always forgive any of My servants when they temporarily abandon the flock. I know that you and the others eventually realize your place with Me. I AM preparing your spiritual destiny. We are moving forward, slowly but surely.

I AM the way to peace and joy, unlike a changeable and often uncaring world. Things, people, and even the most rewarding professional careers come and go. I chose you for My eternal path. A glorious reward awaits you in heaven.

MAY 17

Wonderful Grace

My grace meets all your needs. It surrounds and blesses you each minute of every day. It creates health and harmony. Grace protects you from those who would seek to do you harm. Nothing surpasses the wonder of My grace. It operates as the greatest blessing in your life. What would you most like? Would you prefer material wealth over My grace? Would you rather win the lottery on a given day or receive daily infusions of grace? I AM sure most would choose the lottery, but their decision would be shortsighted. Money appears and disappears. Often it comes with trouble attached. My grace is everlasting and filled with goodness. It represents the ultimate windfall. My grace appears in whatever form you need at the time—financial resources, good health, harmonious relationships, insightful guidance, or spiritual direction. You cannot overestimate the purity of real grace. Live and move under the broad umbrella of My grace. Let it keep you safe and dry in the scariest of storms. Grace overcomes the worst of circumstances. It steers you around the nets that would trap and imprison you. My grace lifts you above all pettiness and deceit. It follows you to the ends of the earth. Stand still. Let My grace fall around you now. Receive My many blessings. Nothing can keep you from having what is rightfully yours.

Allen C. Liles

MAY 18

Be My Instrument

Let Me use you as My instrument for good. I want to bring peace and love to a troubled world. Act as a willing conduit for spreading the doctrine of hope and peace. The world often disrespects Me and those I choose for service. Do not become discouraged. I gave human beings the power of free will, so they possess the God-given right to shun Me and My followers. Despite the opposition, we must never give up. I chose you for this "mission impossible" because of your perseverance and dedication.

When human beings surrender their wills and lives to My safekeeping, I use their gifts and talents for maximum benefit. Working together, we offer a spiritual counterbalance to the earth's negativity. If you allow Me, I fill you with healing and uplifting words that can help mend the tattered. However, you must turn away from the attractive lures placed before you. Many profess fidelity to Me until the world offers some intriguing or lovely bait. Then, they hook themselves to the earth's temptations.

I understand that choosing a spiritual path becomes exceedingly difficult, especially when the world seemingly offers so many rewards at so little price. Do not be fooled. The carnal earth always hides the real price tag for its gifts. There comes a time when payment in full must be rendered, whether or not you have the means to pay. Many are forced to use their souls as collateral and lose control of their spiritual destinies. Do not be foolish today and sad tomorrow. Choose Me. I deliver you to a better and more fulfilling place.

MAY 19

I AM Here

I AM here, within you and around you. I stand guard over you, My beloved child. I protect you against the uncertainties and dangers of human life. Walk tall, with boldness and confidence. We march together toward a new tomorrow.

Be prepared for the battles that lie before you on this side of heaven. The army of God marches onward to heal and bless, not harm or destroy. Our goal is peace, not war. We promote love instead of hate, and forgiveness rather than revenge. No one can stop us. We go forth under the inclusive banner of compassion and understanding. Our enemies include prejudice, intolerance, and fear. Our allies are wisdom, strength, and courage. Marching at the head of our sacred column is faith.

I know life can become frightening when you face the withering fire of materialism. You feel alone and out of step with a world not in sync with Me. I tell you: be not afraid. Never lose heart or doubt our cause. Do not retreat a single step. It is they who wander in the darkness. When things become difficult and criticism mounts, remember who you are. I AM always here to remind you of your heavenly heritage. You are a child of God, perfect in every way. Cleave closer to Me, My son. I AM your ultimate fortress against a lost and struggling world.

Allen C. Liles

MAY 20

Family Dynamics

No individual human family ever reaches perfection. Sometimes you think other families seem totally without problems. On the outside, everything looks perfect. I can assure you that each and every family struggles with concerns and issues of some kind. Many must cope with chronic illness and untimely death. Others get caught up in the throes of addictions. Difficult and angry relationships can easily dissolve into estrangements for some families. Money worries constantly challenge many family units. Misunderstandings and disappointments often pile up like cordwood.

Here is My advice: accept your family, love your family, and try to understand your family. Each family member serves as your teacher. Of course, one should never accept mental or physical abuse from anyone. That also includes misguided and abusive family members. Evil seeks to infect the family structure. It wants to spread its virus from one person to another within a family. The dark side understands that positive and strong familial relationships serve as a bulwark against the inroads of evil. Good families nurture each other. They build each other up, not tear each other down. They honor and protect one another. Try to find something good about every one of your family members. Express genuine love and caring. See their humanity, not only the blood connection. Your human family matters more than you know.

MAY 21

The Letter to Your Son

Today you wrote a letter to your adult son. He lives in your home state of Texas, more than a thousand miles away. You and he are relatively estranged, not having seen each other for several years. You speak over the telephone occasionally, but not often. He turns fifty this August. You felt the time was right to reach out. You were correct. You told him the most important thing. You wrote, "First of all, I love you." Then, you also added that you were proud of him. That means a lot to any child. You held out the idea of a possible visit sometime soon. I assure you that I can help make that happen, if he so desires. I also liked what you told him about the past. You wrote that you now viewed all the old family dynamics through a lens of forgiveness and gratitude. Whatever happened then, you correctly said, was that everyone did the rest they could at the time. Your family was fairly small. It included you, your now ex-wife, your son, and your daughter. All of you are intelligent and basically good-hearted people. But life on the human level can often be difficult and uncertain. People go off on tangents, make errors of judgment, and get caught up in a mode of self-interest. Even the best of families sometimes go awry. That happened to your little family. Your letter today acknowledged the reality of that truth. Wait patiently for his response. It will be forthcoming. Reconciliation always ranks as a noble goal. The time seems right to attempt a genuine healing with your adult son.

MAY 22

Opposing Forces

Expect opposition to the spiritual life. The material world prefers that we not get involved in its affairs. Right now, the popular culture manifests a real void of My presence. Free will runs amok in wild and unattractive ways. Sin is in. Over the centuries, I have experienced this unfortunate phenomenon many times. It always ends badly for everyone concerned. Today's temptations are numerous and neatly camouflaged. Vast and seemingly attractive opportunities to corrupt one's mind, body, and spirit pop up almost everywhere. We also witness daily wrong doing in corporations, government, religion, the private sector, and assorted other locales. Much of the current landscape finds itself littered with casualties of a headlong moral retreat.

However, be assured that I AM still very much in charge. The world can choose to separate itself from Me, but I never separate Myself from the world. When the smoke clears, I will still be standing. Align yourself with Me despite the opposing forces fighting hard against us. The material demons inherent in the earth are scrappy and determined. So must we be as well. They never surrender meekly, but then neither do we. Stand tall. Together, you and I bring a ray of light to those groping for spiritual illumination. Let others try to extinguish our torches. We just thrust them ever higher on our sacred path toward eternal victory.

MAY 23

Spiritual Expectations

I AM that I AM. Open your heart and mind. Receive Me. Expect My miracles to fill your life with countless blessings. I give you everything. I AM your supply. I keep your bank accounts filled with ample funds. I provide food and shelter. I bring good into your life in many forms—people, new and interesting experiences, educational opportunities, health, and on it goes. Expect only the best. Accept nothing less. I never give you the dregs of life, only the most pure and beautiful things. You deserve it. Let Me pour out My grace unto you. Look up. It falls at your feet as we speak. Say goodbye to weariness, failure, lack, and limitation. Greet the wonderful good that I designate just for you. You can never feel poor or deprived again in any way.

When the time comes for you to flee the shackles and bonds of earth, I will personally welcome you to My kingdom. Then you will see the richness of heaven sparkling around you. You will behold its matchless splendor. It all belongs to you. You inherit everything—the joy, peace, and love—that define My eternal palace. If illness marked your final days of earth, I give you instant relief. If you lived with guilt, disappointment, or resentment, every negative emotion disappears. Believe Me when I tell you these things. Whether in human life or physical death, expect only wonder and good. Expect Me. I do not disappoint.

Allen C. Liles

MAY 24

Caregiving

Steady as you go. Stay the course. Walk onward and upward. Your primary focus, besides Me, rests now as a loving caregiver for your dear wife. You serve both her and Me in this capacity. Take pride in the daily comfort you provide. Every human being needs special care at some point. Caregiving ranks as a high mission in My universe. It affirms the Golden Rule. I give you the strength and resources required to fulfill your divine assignment. Step back now and allow others to conquer the material world. The most important and worthiest task lies right in front of you. Be there to comfort and reassure her. Hold her hand and dry her soft blue eyes. As a former clinical nurse, she cared for many others over the years. By giving professional and loving care to her patients, your dear wife also rendered a much-appreciated service. Virtually everyone acts in the nurse role for others during a human lifetime. Now it becomes your moment to serve as a caregiver. Spending time helping her cope with health challenges should not detract from our time together. Perhaps you need to rise a bit earlier each morning to make the sacred connection with Me. If so, I will be here waiting for you. Just meet your spouse's daily needs and then return to Me. My eternal light glows for you both.

MAY 25

Your Father's Birthday

Had he lived, today would mark your human father's one-hundredth birthday. He gave you many important gifts. Your daddy displayed a unique personality and intelligence. He definitely showed a common touch, which helped him get elected three times to local office in your Texas hometown. In fact, he never lost one single election. Yet, he also displayed a grasp of state and national politics. Your father knew presidents, senators, representatives, governors, and labor union officials throughout your nation. This kindled your lifetime interest in the world around you. He achieved all of these worldly things despite having only a high school education. Of course, he was extremely proud of you and your sister's university degrees. He accomplished many worthy things during his lifetime, but he enjoyed his "day job" as a railroad engineer as much as anything. Do you remember how, at your father's funeral, an older African-American gentleman recounted a previously unknown tale of how your father had once lent him some money? The man needed transportation to a new job and your dad loaned him the cash for a used car. "Mr. Liles didn't even make me pay interest on the loan," the grateful man told you. Your father showed generosity, no small example for a young son. He also demonstrated accountability and integrity. Your daddy was a good man, a most noble trait in these days and times. He still watches you and your sister from afar. As ever, he beams with pride whenever you accomplish anything.

Allen C. Liles

MAY 26

An Upside-Down World

The world often spins backward and upside down. Fame and fortune now exceed spiritual values in importance. Priorities include exterior beauty, ostentatious wealth, creature comforts, and instant pleasure. I AM at the bottom of the list, as far as many people are concerned. That is if they even acknowledge My existence. How shortsighted!

I AM absolutely the only thing that never changes. Wealth comes, wealth vanishes. Fame appears and then fades. Everyone knows your name today. Tomorrow no one remembers. Do you question that truth? Wait and see. It is the same with political and corporate power. The world rushes to your door one minute and right by your door the next. Health fluctuates. You may be a star athlete today, capable of incredible physical accomplishments. Before you know what happened, you are limping from one chair to the next. By comparison, look at Me. My universal power dwarfs anything in the material world. I direct the oceans. The moon and stars act on My guidance. I created the planets and whatever life may be upon them. I gave human beings free will so that they might grow spiritually. I frown when it is used to defame and ignore Me. However, take heart. Misguided use of free will usually results in physical, emotional, and spiritual pain. Often it takes real suffering before someone calls out for Me. I AM a forgiving God. I always respond. Putting faith in worldly things may end in ruin for those involved, but it can cause a real spiritual shift in My direction. If that happens, I AM ready. Anyone who seeks Me always finds Me. I AM a patient, loving, and forgiving God.

MAY 27

Memorial Day

Today you remember the fallen heroes that made the ultimate sacrifice. I also cry at their tragic loss. I detest war. I hate it. Since time began, wars have ravaged the world. What an absolute and total waste! Think of the illogical things that start wars: racial, religious, and cultural differences; power grabs for territory and control of natural resources; outright greed; numerous misjudgments about motivations; unbridled hate; or simple dislikes based on various assumptions. At the core of most wars lies the sin of fear. For some, war seems a logical way to overcome whatever perceived fear may be threatening them. How sad!

The people of the world could easily live in peace. The secret to lasting peace and harmony lies in focusing on similarities rather than differences. I made the world and the living things that populate it. I created all of you with much more in common than differences. Yes, you may reflect different skin colors and speak various languages. But I fashioned the human heart in a careful way. I lined the chambers of every heart with love. I placed the Spirit of the Christ at your very core so that a spiritual friend would always be near. I gave you the free will to make human choices, hoping those choices would glorify Me. I gave you a workable list of rules and laws for daily living.

Hear me. You are all basically the same. Wars against your brothers or sisters defile My purposes. Turn away from war except when threatened with extinction. Never choose war when peace remains an option.

Allen C. Liles

MAY 28

Path Clearer

I AM the path clearer. I remove all obstacles. I clear away the cobwebs in your brain, the ones that might confuse you. I pick up the branches and brambles that could cause you to stumble. I point out the deep traps that lie under the most attractive fauna. I strip the hidden thorns that cause pain and anguish. I lead you across the most treacherous gorges. I help you successfully shoot the terrifying and swirling rapids. Walk beside Me, where no harm dare approach. I know the way. I lead you safely home, without delay or detour. Stay close. Do not think of veering this way or that on your own. If you choose to do so, I cannot stop you. I wait patiently for your distress call when you become lost. I rescue you again and then again, if necessary. I know the other paths often appear more attractive and far easier. I understand your humanness. Trust Me. I keep you out of trouble and focused. Lean not on your own understanding. Remain centered in Me as we come near the end of our journey. I AM leading you onward to My kingdom. Heaven awaits us in all its magnificence. As we traverse the glorious path home, let us leave traces of our good works along the way. Bring living water to the thirsty and sacred food to the hungry. You pass this way but once. Make it a meaningful, productive, and joyous trip. Do not worry about any hindrance as we walk forward. I clear your way, now and forever.

MAY 29

The Future

Do not worry about the future. It never belongs to you. You own only the present, and even that might sometimes be questionable. Keep your energy directed on things you can affect. I plan the future. Stand back and let Me handle that chore for you. Your current circumstances require full attention. I seek to use you as My instrument only in the present. Allow Me that privilege. Keep fretting at a minimum where the future is concerned. Avoid needless hand-wringing and tears of concern. Dismiss dire predictions and countless prophets of doom. Many people use fear to line their pockets. Let them swindle others with their gloom, but not you. Do not waste your precious time or energy wailing about things yet unclear. Unfix your mind on tomorrow. Live on today's clock. Accomplish whatever task I place before you during this twenty-four-hour period. Keep busy serving Me in the here and now. I direct today's schedule. You have only so much brainpower and physical capability. Refrain from spending any time on tomorrow's triumphs or disasters. I never reveal the future to anyone. First of all, their knees could buckle from the weight of knowing what lies around the bend. Second, their minds would certainly obsess about any revelations. I need everyone's full and complete attention today. We have work that needs doing.

Allen C. Liles

MAY 30

Release All Resentments

The demons of the world demand your attention and allegiance. They use every trick available to ensnare you. One of their most effective ploys centers on resentments. They keep reminding you of past grievances. When they urge you to hold grudges, I say forgive instead. While they tempt you with revenge, I recommend that you extend a pardon to everyone. If you invite past anger to sit at your table, it will devour you. You need a peaceful heart. Declare past offenses forgiven. Bless those who wronged you. Refrain from passing judgment on anyone. Instead, plan on making your own amends. Everyone, no matter how righteous, has the potential for amends. You are certainly no different. Make your list and become ready. Listen to Me. I guide you in that regard. Pray for those who may have harmed you in some way. See them surrounded and blessed by My light.

Letting pain from the past still permeate your consciousness accomplishes nothing. Smother the fiery blaze of animosity that still singes your mind and heart. Pour out holy water and extinguish the deadly flames of hate. For every slight, an olive branch of peace awaits its offering. Empty your mind completely of all negative thinking. Fill yourself with gratitude. Give everyone your blessing, and send everyone peacefully on his or her way. You release yourself from all bondage through the gift of unconditional forgiveness. Do not hesitate. Extend it now.

MAY 31

Greater Service

I AM preparing you for greater service. Empty your mind of needless activity. Rest easy in silent meditation with Me. Do not dart here and yon. I need the full attention of both your mind and heart. If you become transfixed with material distractions, the process can find become sidetracked and delayed. Time becomes more precious as the calendar incessantly turns. Your life expectancy is not limitless. Every human journey finds itself marked by brevity. Purge all negativity and allow your preparation to accelerate. I need many human outlets for My plan to flourish. Your service can be meaningful if you allow it.

What do I have in mind for you? Among other things, I have already used your ministerial credentials to speak words of comfort and encouragement. Together, we utilized your corporate connections to create monetary blessings for worthy causes and institutions. Personally, I gave you specific kindnesses to accomplish in My name. We can still achieve other positive things with the time remaining. However, I must ask that you discipline yourself and make our time together a continuing priority. We have much ground yet to cover. You must rededicate your focus on learning My will for you. I promise to provide the spiritual power necessary to accomplish My sacred tasks before your time on earth ends.

Allen C. Liles

JUNE

*Put on the full armor of God so that you can
take your stand against the devil's schemes.*

—Ephesians 6:11 (NIV)

JUNE 1

Spiritual Authenticity

Being spiritually authentic presents a challenge for human beings. You get very fragmented messages from the world around you. The earth seems to value transient things: outer beauty, wealth, athletic prowess, dominance over others, celebrity, and perfectionism in general. None of these material values reflects lasting and eternal virtues. To be regarded as authentic on the spiritual plane, one risks disapproval of peers, the media, and any idol worshipper.

It takes exceptional courage to speak one's truth about spiritual matters. Making fun of Me seems politically correct for those steeped in materialism. I applaud anyone who speaks up for Me despite potential damage to his or her worldly reputation. As you know, mocking Me does not constitute a particularly wise course of action over the long term. I AM often amazed about how the world attempts to silence My spokespeople.

Of course, I admit that some who speak on My behalf are simply dishonest pretenders. They invoke My name for their nefarious purposes. These individuals do far more harm than good for My cause.

Spiritual authenticity requires courage, honesty, humility, truthfulness, a love and concern for others, and a willingness to undergo trials in My name. Standing tall for Me demands a commitment and perseverance not usually found in the majority of humankind. I value authenticity. I know it when I see it.

Allen C. Liles

JUNE 2

Overcoming Resentment

Overcoming resentment could be one of your greatest challenges. There are people in your life who you still resent. You grapple with forgiveness issues where specific individuals are concerned. Gratitude, love, and a forgiving attitude serve as the healing triangle in ridding yourself of resentment. Open your heart and allow these healing properties to enter and expand. "Harboring resentment" may be an old cliché, but the "harbor" reference seems apt. Only you can provide a safe harbor for resentments to gather.

Resentments have one trait in common: they like to hang out together. They feed on each other's unhappiness and disharmony. Commiserating with their brother and sister resentments gives them more credibility and power.

Close down their safe harbor. Send them quickly back out to sea, away from your vulnerable shoreline. Invite only positive thoughts into the fragile harbor of your mind. Build special berths for gratitude, love, and forgiveness in your harbor where they can feel safe and accepted. Surround your remaining resentments with these three tenets of goodness. Bless those whose words and actions still rile you. Release them from your crosshairs. Watch as they depart from your priority list. Holding on to grudges and resentments gets you nowhere. Spend your time more productively. Gratitude, love, and forgiveness each give back incredible value. Let them bless you with abundance and peace.

JUNE 3

Worry

Worry distances you from the tasks I place before you. It resembles an unwelcome cancer. Once worry gains a foothold in your mind and body, it spreads. Worry saps your energy and vitality. It consumes your thoughts and attention. You must protect yourself from its invasive nature. When you become troubled about health, finances, relationships, job status, politics, the world situation, or whatever else, you lose your spiritual focus.

I AM the antidote to the poisonous effect of incessant worry. Treat this harmful affliction with My presence. Never give worry or anxiety anything to feed on. Turn within anytime disquieting thoughts intrude on your serenity. Change the channel in your mind. Switch off worry and switch on Me. When your brain starts to fret, stop it immediately. Call yourself back to the centeredness of the Christ Spirit within you. I await you there, prepared to reassure and lift you above any perceived distraction. Call Me. I will answer. Together, we sort out the imagined from the real.

Worry and fear are human outgrowths of not trusting Me. Hear Me: I AM greater than any earthly concern. I supersede the world and all its manipulations. Remember that I have overcome the world. I can help you dismiss fear. I get you back to doing My business. I turn away all troubles. Let Me show you My healing power. Worry flees when I appear.

Allen C. Liles

JUNE 4

The Correct Path

Be patient. You are traveling on the correct path. You still have considerable work before you. Establishing and strengthening oneness with Me remains your top priority. Do not be impatient with the process. Avoid running hither and yon. Searching near and far for spiritual enlightenment wastes precious energy and time. You are standing now on holy ground. Sit calmly in the stillness and allow My presence to do its work. Become peaceful and expectant. Everything proceeds in My divine order. I have a carefully developed plan for your life.

Your job consists of moving forward one step at a time. Giant leaps are often counterproductive. Slow and steady progress works best. I AM building your spiritual house on the most solid of rocks. I AM the master architect for humankind. I draw up the details and then help you execute the design. Release control. Let Me assume total responsibility for agenda and timing. Remember, your journey still has a ways to go. Do not panic or become anxious. Hand the reins over to me. Do your part by trusting that I know the way home. I AM in total charge of the schedule when you step aside. Keep your mind on Me. Be at peace. Know that I AM God. I have everything well in hand.

JUNE 5

Your Adult Children

Your two adult children also belong to Me. I love them just as much as you do, if not more. I created them, just as I created you. Many parents want to control their children, even after they reach adulthood. When children are young, they do need close parental supervision. However, virtually every child wants to break away at some point. When young adults begin exercising their free will, parents need to lessen their grip.

As a responsible parent, you may feel accountable for the choices made by your adult children. You should not condemn yourself for someone else's decisions. Life does not work that way. Adult choices bring adult consequences for the person making them. Each human being must learn preordained lessons. You, as a parent or stepparent, should not stand in the way of these important learning experiences. Attempting to alter or mitigate life lessons for your children delays their entrance into true adulthood.

Begin to step firmly aside when they reach the legal age to make grownup decisions. Their life lessons must be given space to unfold. Release any illusion of control. You did your best as a parent. Now, allow your children the freedom to step out on their own. Both your son and your daughter are very deep into their own lessons. Bless them on the path they have chosen. They must navigate their individual lives. Give their welfare over to Me. I promise to watch over them. I love them just as I love you. Step back as a caring parent and watch their progress. Enjoy the show as an interested spectator, not as the stage manager.

Allen C. Liles

JUNE 6

Financial Concerns

Trust Me for your financial well-being. Yes, you must make the money and balance your checkbook. I leave the decisions about spending, saving, and investing to your discretion. Believe in My promise to provide what you need when you need it. Of course, all of humankind worries about money. I understand your concerns about food and shelter. Too many of My children go to bed hungry in unsafe conditions. Remember that fact as you count your own blessings.

This I assure you: I will provide the resources necessary for you to complete My work. The world cannot make such a promise or guarantee. If you invest in or play the stock market, it fluctuates every single day. You may be wealthy today and penniless tomorrow. Land and housing values jump one month and collapse the next. Your bank account looks full one minute and empty the next. Everything in the material world is subject to change. When you measure financial security in terms of dollars, you will never outrun the fear of losing everything. Meanwhile, become more spiritually aware of the world around you. I AM pouring out daily miracles. Manna from heaven falls around you as we speak. You are a chosen recipient of My generosity. Never fear or worry as long as you pursue My will. Trust My promises. Act in faith. Believe in what I tell you. I AM filling your pockets with the abundance of heaven.

JUNE 7

I AM a Big God

Never limit Me. Let Me be who I AM. I AM a very big God. Nothing in the material earth exceeds My scope and power. Not one of your problems or adversaries is larger than I AM. If you try and take on your enemies alone, they can quickly overwhelm you. When you lock arms with Me, we tower ten feet above anything or anyone who challenges you. Let Me help with any problem. Together, we find the right and perfect solution.

I AM an invisible God, but I AM so much stronger than the world. Because I AM not visible to the naked eye, some people dismiss Me as nonexistent. Nothing could be further from the truth. I stand ready and able to solve the earth's most perplexing issues. However, I must wait until you or the world specifically cries out for My help. That represents our basic spiritual arrangement. You call. I answer. You seek My assistance. I respond. It seems like such a simple concept.

The human egos of the earth resist My intervention until things go really bad. I never stop hoping for your summons. I AM so close. I wait at your core for any acknowledgement, contact, or request. I AM never far away. Test Me. I bring a grand array of spiritual resources to your rescue. When I come, I arrive with blaring trumpets and legions of warrior angels in tow. I help you overcome any secular power. I AM an enormous God, clothed in impenetrable heavenly armor. I assure you without reservation. We will triumph.

JUNE 8

Transformation

I AM a God of miracles. I AM a God of possibilities. I AM a God of transformation. Do you not see My miracles happening all around you? I create those miracles through My grace. I make all things possible through the power of faith. Prepare for the miracle and possibility of being transformed by the renewal of your mind. Transformation begins with the smallest spark of enlightenment.

Drop all concern about how and when transformation completes itself. Gradual enlightenment brings enduring transformation. Your soul must slowly grow in awareness and knowledge. Do not rush things. Make this wonderful journey step by precious step. Commit yourself to seeking transformation and the process soon begins. Teachers appear to instruct you. Books show up to inform and inspire you. Situations bless you. Everything needed for your journey materializes. Transformation unfolds, day-by-day, minute-by-minute. Sometimes you take a step or two backwards. Your attention span fluctuates. Outside events cause you to veer off the path for a time. Come back as soon as possible and resume your spiritual trek. I hold a place in line for you.

Transformation serves as the precursor to entering My kingdom. Becoming transformed awakens you to the grand experience of finding heaven on earth.

JUNE 9

Under My Protection

I protect you. I shield you from the powerful forces of evil. When you face your foes dressed in My armor, nothing can touch you. I realize that free will puts some of My children in occasional jeopardy. I fend off most intruders, but some do slip through and cause critical damage. When that occurs, I AM always present to mend the emotional and physical scars left behind.

Evil loves to tunnel under and over our defenses. It also attacks from within the most protected walls. Be on the alert for any unexpected thrust. Once the dark side penetrates the strongest fortress, danger spreads quickly. Remain centered when fear envelops you. The opposing forces usually wait until their prey grows tired and weak. Stay strong. Resist inviting negative influences into your mind, heart, and physical presence. Never knowingly allow evil to share your tent or home environment. Keep it safely away from you and your loved ones. Proximity leads to vulnerability. Strive to preserve a pure consciousness steeped in Me. Tarring your conscious mind with negative words and images causes havoc to your spiritual immune system.

Put up the strongest defenses possible and then look to Me as your protective partner. It will be a long, hard struggle. Gear up for the spiritual warfare that can break out anytime.

Allen C. Liles

JUNE 10

Heal Thyself

You need to participate in your own healing. I AM the great healer, but I know you read the stories in the Bible about My healing works. To accomplish a true healing, I need the participation and belief of the person involved. You must completely believe in My healing powers. Trust My ability to restore any willing patient to wholeness.

I do perform healing miracles. I can take a shattered spirit and piece it carefully back together. I heal broken relationships by smoothing out the jagged edges of misunderstanding and resentment. When I find a lost soul shaken by abandonment and rejection, I use My healing power to repair the torn places of the heart. I rejuvenate physical bodies with My restorative powers. I bring youthful attitudes back to the elderly. I rekindle hope for those who must struggle with disease and chronic illness. I especially enjoy healing bigotry and prejudice. I open closed minds and demonstrate the true value of acceptance and understanding.

However, throughout all the healing process, I must receive your unwavering trust. Rise up in faith and unite with Me. I cannot guarantee total success unless I receive your full cooperation. Believers also make the best healers. I stand ready to demonstrate My healing abilities in ways that you cannot imagine. Show Me that you absolutely believe in My powers. Only then can I show you a healing miracle.

JUNE 11

More about Healing

Receive My light, love, and the power of My Supreme Being. Now spread them throughout the universe on My behalf. Be a heavenly sponsored healer who blesses the world in My name. You are My precious instrument. You can bring healing, not to glorify yourself, but to glorify Me. Lift people higher. Comfort the afflicted. Free the hurting from emotional pain and physical ailments. Help those in need to realize My healing potential. Let them touch the hem of your garment. Assist Me with My healing goals for humankind. Allow all who experience your healing consciousness to also know Me.

I pronounce this as your holy mission: Heal in My name. Fill your mind and heart with the absolute wonder of Me. Walk the world as My representative. Go forth to heal and restore. Bless and feed My sheep. When they see you, let them also behold Me. Do not strive for worldly acclaim and honors. Work toward being truly humble with your healing gift. Let humility project itself like a laser beam, drawing those in need of healing. Remember: you receive your healing powers directly from Me. I endow you with the sacred potential to heal spiritually, mentally, and physically. I channel My power through you. It flows directly, with no in-between stops. Become one with Me. I will manifest your healing potential. I can perform miracles through you. Remember what I told you: "These and greater works will you do." Believe that you possess the power to heal from within. Believe in Me. Watch the healings unfold far and near.

JUNE 12

Your Son's August Visit

I said to trust My plans for you and your adult son. He answered your letter and wants to come for a visit in August. I personally arranged your time together. Do not become anxious about the reunion. Lighten up. Let things unfold in divine order. Go with the flow. Your son has traveled far on his own path. His life choices do not resemble yours. Accept that reality.

Relate not only as father and son, but also as adult to adult. Understand that virtually all his choices have had nothing to do with you. When you meet with him, bring love, respect, and acceptance along with you. Give your son the freedom to be his natural self around you. You also must be who you are. Above all, do not create unrealistic expectations for your first visit in years. Inject forgiveness and understanding into every aspect of your time together. Lead with the heart of a loving father, which you are. Go more than half way to make this visit rewarding and successful.

I AM gifting both of you with a rare moment for healing. Physical time on earth is shortening, especially in your case. Who knows how many more opportunities for reconciliation will occur? Take advantage of this moment to find closure about the past. However, be cautious about bringing up sensitive topics from decades ago. Live in the present. Reach out to your son with genuine caring and concern. Watch him respond affirmatively. See your time together as a blessing from Me. Let the love flow.

JUNE 13

The Blessing of Peace

My peace surrounds you. I believe in the peace that comes with forgiveness. I bestow the eternal peace that blesses everyone, not just a select few. Live with My peace draped around your shoulders, like a protective shawl. Move under this warm blanket of peace whenever you travel anywhere. Take a peaceful presence with you as a precious gift for those who might encounter you. My peace acts as a protective ally, fending off negativity and confrontation.

The world right now is filled with troubled people who take offense at virtually anything. When you come in peace, they can find nothing to question. You avoid all animosity when you carry My peace as a constant companion. Most people recognize a peaceful nature and welcome it. Before donning the cloak of peace, drop all your anger and resentment by the wayside. Replace them with the peace that surpasses all understanding. Understand that living with peace not only reduces the anxiety in your life. It enriches the landscape around you.

My peace acts as a stress reducer for anyone it touches. You reflect My divine nature when you come in peace. You are welcomed as a peacemaker for humankind. I AM usually a peaceful God. I generally remain both centered and calm. I direct the universe from My heavenly platform, protected by the high walls of peace. I always seek peace before war, gentleness before strength. Walk in My footsteps. Go forth and greet the world in the wonder of My peace.

JUNE 14

Divine Ideas

My divine ideas serve as the primary source for your good. My creative ideas produce the wealth that meets your financial needs. Divine ideas also function as unique blessings for the material world.

Be alert when heaven-directed inspirations come unannounced into your consciousness. Many people walk the earth every day with divine ideas popping up all around them. They fail to recognize the potential gifts that cross their paths. Never become so focused on the usual meanderings that you miss My golden opportunities. Earthly distractions now form the greatest hindrance to catching a divine idea in flight. Constant texting and social networking prevent many excellent and financially rewarding ideas from ever developing. Do not worry. More divine ideas are constantly on their way from My divine consciousness. Hopefully, some astute soul will pluck one or more of these gems from the ethers before they become lost forever.

My divine ideas all have one common denominator: they produce some sort of good for humankind. That good may be packaged in dollar bills, but it also could take the form of a spiritual blessing. Whatever it may be, someone realizes a benefit in one way or the other. Never trust your own creativity as the ultimate source of material security. Rather, trust My divine ideas as the most stable source of your good. When you claim one of My creative thoughts, you never know lack or limitation again.

Look up, and look around! A divine idea has just been released from heaven into the universe. It could come addressed to you.

JUNE 15

Forgiveness Issues

Forgiveness ranks as one of My greatest spiritual values. I also regard forgiveness as your primary life lesson. Forgiveness issues have plagued you. I grant that you have shown some progress on offering forgiveness to certain people in your past. Ongoing feelings of anger and hurt no longer dominate your thoughts. I consider that shift as making real progress. You have definitely made a conscious effort to see the other person's point of view. That certainly reflects more of a forgiving attitude. When you travel down the beautiful highway of forgiveness, stay alert for new opportunities. Reach out and practice forgiveness, if needed, with everyone you meet. Forgiveness truly heals and builds relationships. Since this constitutes your greatest life lesson, I will give you many chances to practice the art of forgiving.

When someone deliberately tries to inflict emotional pain on you, turn his or her misguided efforts aside with instant forgiveness. Distance yourself if necessary, but try not to hold a grudge. Of course, personal harm must never be tolerated. That boundary exceeds normal forgiveness. It can never be crossed. When others do cause you physical, mental, or spiritual pain, pray that their hearts and minds be transformed. See them surrounded by My healing light. Do your forgiveness work and then hand the situation over to Me. Send your personal light to those souls lost in spiritual darkness. I will do the same. Forgiveness always pays dividends, not the least of which is peace of mind. Forgive quickly and know peace.

Allen C. Liles

JUNE 16

My Awesome Power

I, in the midst of you, AM all-powerful. I also give you the spiritual power to heal and comfort. My power flows in and through you to bless anyone in need. Let My power flow from you as you perform My work.

Understand My heavenly power. I regulate the universe, the sun, the planets, and every star. I formed the vast oceans. I shaped each mountain and decided its height. I designed the beautiful lakes and charted the swiftly flowing rivers. Humankind still remains My greatest creation. I made every human being in My image and likeness, while molding each one differently. You all retain similar qualities while also displaying many variations. No two fingerprints are alike, just as no two human beings are exactly alike. Never underestimate My power to shape anything and anyone. I AM the mightiest of the mighty, the most powerful of the powerful.

Never misuse any power that I give you. It must always be utilized for good. Take the goodness of My power to the forlorn and hurting, the ill and struggling. Go in My name and apply My power liberally, but with care and careful restraint. You must be judicious in using such a powerful gift so that you always help, not harm. I want you to express My benign power. However, you must remember it is not you that exhibits human power. It is I who demonstrates spiritual power through you. Apply My power only as needed.

JUNE 17

Father's Day

What were your strengths as a father? You were a good provider. You showed interest in your children's outside interests. You always tried to encourage their participation in extracurricular activities, but you did not place superhuman expectations on them. You were aware of their schoolwork and urged them to do their best. You attempted to set a good example for your children by severely limiting any profanity in the home and by not showing prejudice or bigotry. You attended church, even teaching Sunday school. You were never once in trouble with the law, did not use tobacco or any recreational drugs. You did not commit any act that would reflect badly on the family name.

Now, let us look at the other side of the coin. You were far too detached as a father from your children's emotional needs. You often placed work before family. You felt that if you did well in the corporate world, everything at home would fall into place. That assumption proved false. You loved your children but were not firm enough in your discipline of them. Unfortunately, the family dysfunction increased with time. You may not have used alcohol in the extreme, but you did drink. Some of your decisions definitely reflected the influence of alcohol. When your son's teenage drug use erupted, you reacted by trying to control his behavior. Of course, that just made things worse. You were not then aware of twelve-step recovery programs for families of alcoholics. Overall, you were much too codependent in many of your actions. A lack of awareness, especially about drugs, exacerbated the situation.

As I said, you did love both of your children. All parenting consists of on-the-job training. Forgive yourself. You did the best you could at the time. Could you have been a better parent? Yes.

JUNE 18

Patience

Thank you for asking Me to remove your character defect of impatience. Here are the three P's in My kingdom: patience, perseverance, and persistence. Live in these three modes at all times. The spiritual path requires them. I AM aware that each presents its own distinctly separate challenge. My path often becomes steep and filled with obstacles. The impatient, uncommitted, and easily distracted soul soon falls by the wayside. Most people quickly revert to easier paths when they get tested. Reaching heaven takes a little more time and a lot more effort. You must keep plodding away, one step at a time.

I AM directing and guiding your journey. I know the exact moment of your arrival, but I allow you to stop, rest, take a detour, or quit altogether. Trust that every step along the way has a divine purpose. Nothing happens by accident or without meaning. Just step forward, arm in arm with Me. Live, move, and be in the present moment. Do not walk backwards into yesterday. Resist the temptation of leaping headlong into tomorrow. Walk today's path today. Be patient, practice perseverance, and commit yourself to being persistent despite opposition. You are on the correct track to realize your highest good. In the meantime, find joy in the process. You will arrive soon enough at your heavenly destination. What a happy day that will be!

JUNE 19

Your Wedding Anniversary

Today you celebrate your eighteenth wedding anniversary. You and your dear wife have enjoyed a rewarding union marked by your unswerving dedication to each other. Commitment serves as the highest form of love, along with understanding, forgiveness, and acceptance. True devotion comes with an unconditional guarantee of fidelity in both good times and bad. Spiritually based commitment does not depend on adequate finances or perfect health. Money comes and goes. Good health and physical beauty falter and fade. A strong marriage features a sacred covenant that remains steadfast when life collapses around you. I brought you two together so that you might enhance each other's spiritual path. Your marriage stands as a divine appointment, planned and implemented by Me. You have supported one another in countless ways, both in and out of ministry. Each of you seeks to serve Me with your gifts and talents. You are role models for far more people than you might imagine.

Now, as your dear wife struggles with a health challenge, you still model commitment. I see your dual hearts reaching out for one another in comfort and compassion. You want to hold on to your earthly connection for as long as humanly possible. Someday you will dwell side by side with Me in eternal splendor. In human terms, your time together seems brief. In heaven, your love goes on forever.

Allen C. Liles

JUNE 20

My Spiritual School

I AM the teacher; you are the student. I ask that you bring an open and receptive attitude into our time together in the silence. I AM imparting the wisdom of the ages into your consciousness. Try not to miss these classes. Every single moment spent with Me furthers your educational goals. Each day brings new insight and aids your spiritual understanding. I offer an all-encompassing curriculum. No subject is off limits. I wait for your questions, but I also present special matters that need covering. I value your enrollment in My school of the Spirit. Anyone interested in growing spiritually can sign up for My classes. I can meet anytime of the day or night. Although I have no strict entrance requirements, I do ask for a willingness to grow in spiritual insight. Being teachable is an essential requirement for all new students. Not all under My instruction receive their diplomas. It really does not matter whether you actually graduate. Just having the courage to accept the call to study with Me can change the course of your life. My most stellar students go forth charged with knowledge and a passion for service. I send each on a specific assignment that best uses his or her talents and gifts. I offer the ultimate experience in higher learning. I promise that graduation arrives when you least expect it. Come sit in the front row. Receive My priceless teachings. Taking notes would be helpful.

JUNE 21

Believe

You must believe. Believing in Me ranks as the key factor in manifesting My works. Believe that I love you. I want only your highest good. Believe when I tell you that I AM the source for all you need. I provide everything required to complete your spiritual journey. Believe that every event in your life contains meaning and learning possibilities. There are no accidents in the spiritual universe. Believe that I AM your protection against those who would harm you. I lead you unscathed beside the still waters. Believe in My sacred promises. They stand forever as a testimonial to My devotion. Although life always remains challenging and difficult, believe that I will never leave or forsake you. Believe that you can lean on Me when you become weary. I AM your comfort and your support at all times. Believe in My ability to bring joy and happiness into your life. Believe that I will dry your tears of sadness and comfort your grieving heart. Believe when I say to you that I AM in you and you are in Me. Believe My healing miracles. Believe in the precious knowledge contained in My Word, the Holy Bible. Believe that I implanted the Christ Spirit within your being to accompany you throughout life. Believe that through the activity of the Holy Spirit, you can accomplish anything. Trust and believe. Most important of all, believe in Me as I believe in you.

Allen C. Liles

JUNE 22

The Gift of Gratitude

Gratitude serves as a wonderful gift that you can give yourself. Express gratitude, even in moments of pain and discontent. Look around you. You may be surprised by the number of blessings that grace your life. When you awaken in the morning, take a deep breath. Fill your lungs with the new day. Be glad in it. Actively search for examples of love and caring in your life. Be grateful anytime you behold compassion or kindness. Lift up the things and people that enhance your life. Tell them of your love and appreciation.

When your days on earth become shorter, expressing gratitude becomes more important. Begin a sentence to someone with "Thank you for (fill in the blank with a sincere observation)". It makes your comment the most listened to remark that you could possibly utter. If you need to find gratitude, go outside and revel in nature. I have graced the world with incomparable splendor. Surely you can find something lovely in My earth that stirs you to gratitude. If children or grandchildren are a part of your life, tell them of your happiness because of their presence. If you are blessed with a wonderful spouse or significant other, any day is a good one for gratitude. Be very grateful that you and I are getting to know each other better every day. Know that I AM also grateful for you, My beloved son in whom I AM well pleased.

JUNE 23

Spiritual Healing

All healing originates from realizing your oneness with Me. When we merge, healing follows. Seek first the kingdom of heaven, and all things will be added unto you. Seek unity with Me. Come together with Me, and immerse yourself in the flow of eternal life. Realize the absolute perfection in which I created you. Dismiss any appearance of imperfection. I made you in My image. See yourself as molded in My likeness. We are spiritual twins, you and I. All that I AM belongs to you. I gifted you with My mind, My perfect health, My prosperity, and My wisdom and knowledge. You serve as My sacred instrument, through which I dispense My grace. I AM the great healer of all pain and suffering. I AM also giving you the ability to bless and heal.

Visualize healing possibilities for those who surround you. See your dear wife receiving blessed rays of healing. Behold her knees and legs gaining strength. Watch as she walks effortlessly and without falling a single time. Hear her breathing free of any congestion or need for additional oxygen. Envision her energy level growing and an increase in stamina. Witness My healing light as it surges through the entirety of her body, mind, and spirit. See her rejuvenated and empowered, lifted and restored to wholeness. Visualize your dear wife rising above chronic illness and the challenges of aging.

Come unite with Me, all ye who are heavy laden. Let Me bring spiritual healing to one and all. Rest in My loving arms.

Allen C. Liles

JUNE 24

Your Amazing Sister

You have just the one sister, eighteen months younger than you. The two of you live in different parts of the country, she in Georgia and you in Minnesota. Geographically and emotionally, you are distant. To say that your sister resembles a blazing meteor flashing across the evening sky would be a gross understatement. She lights up every room she enters. Her life accomplishments boggle the mind. The achievements extend through high school, university life, and beyond into her domestic and professional life. She personifies charisma and success. Your sister still teaches classes at a Catholic middle school despite being in her mid-seventies. She remains attractive and appears many years younger. Intellectually, her mind is extremely sharp. Her passions are the Catholic Church, a conservative brand of politics, teaching school, and a close family of four children and thirteen grandchildren.

You long for a closer relationship with your sister, but that seems unlikely at this stage of life. Over the years, you have occasionally felt her disapproval. As a staunch Catholic, she does not understand any other theological choice. Although she knows little of your denomination's belief system, that does not prevent her negative judgment. The nexus of your lifetime relationship formed when you were children. Your father rarely showed much interest in his children, preferring outside political activities. So, unbeknownst to you, your younger sister viewed the two of you as competitors for his attention. She commanded his interest through her countless honors and achievements. That competitiveness unconsciously continues today, even after his death some decades ago.

Your sister exemplifies so many wonderful qualities. Maybe someday, before both of you move forward to the next life, a genuine healing can take place. One can only hope. In the meantime, bless her for being who she is.

JUNE 25

Definition of Humility

I define "humility" as spiritual meekness. Not "weakness" but "meekness" marks a truly humble person. In My sight, this "meekness" translates into ultimate strength. When you can rightfully claim humility as a virtue, you also have attained a higher level of understanding. Remember what I said in the Beatitudes: "the meek shall inherit the earth."

When someone achieves an attitude of humility, the ego has been subdued (at least temporarily). Keeping the human ego in check for long can be difficult if not impossible. Being humble before your creator demonstrates awareness of your place in the universe. When some people succeed financially and professionally, humility tends to evaporate. However, when things start going badly, humility can quickly resurface. The material world always keeps you guessing. One minute it sings about your greatness and praises your talents. In the next moment, you might find yourself shunned and labeled a total failure.

My kingdom represents the only real venue where your self-worth never varies. You serve Me best when you approach our divine relationship from a humble perspective. Be faithful to Me. Do not retreat into the ego again if your material fortunes change for the better. Wealth and fame can puff anyone up for a time. When you walk with Me every day, that becomes your happiness and fulfillment. Our very togetherness creates an aura of humility and a sense of lasting peace. Seek humility. Seek Me.

Allen C. Liles

JUNE 26

Election Year Politics

All politics proves fleeting and transitory. On the physical earth, all "rulers" serve only temporarily. At a certain point, they are replaced by someone else. Presidents, prime ministers, and kings come and go. Even lifetime appointments end when the individual passes from the human scene. I agree that presidential elections and potential power shifts make things interesting. However, in the overall scheme of things, no earthly power compares to Me.

I control the universe, but I do allow free will. That includes elections at every level. The electorate chooses the candidates and the victors. Do not become vexed or overly obsessed by the political process. In an election year, many voices become loud and often obnoxious. Claims and counterclaims flood into your overcrowded consciousness. Most of the human noise quickly disappears into the ethers as overhyped blather.

When the votes get counted, the victory speeches made, and the colorful bunting removed, I remain in My rightful place as the ultimate ruler of the universe. I love all My earthly children, regardless of their party affiliation. I AM aware that some who seek political office do so for less than honorable purposes. Power is one of the great corrupters in human history. Seeking elective office for personal gain eventually brings its own lessons. Throughout history there have been good kings and bad kings, wise kings and foolish kings. A leader serves his or her people best when I AM included in the private policy making. My rule always remains benevolent and all-inclusive. I govern eternally. I AM God.

JUNE 27

Knowledge of My Will

My will for you involves one primary goal above all: attaining oneness with Me. Immerse yourself daily in My presence. Infuse yourself with My wisdom. Live, move, and be with Me as the guiding force. Practice, perfect, and then reflect our unity of Spirit. Walk the earth in close lockstep with Me.

I will raise you up to a higher vantage point where you can see the world from an elevated perspective. All things become clearer when you gaze down at the machinations of a temporal world. I want you to help illumine the earthly landscape with your enhanced consciousness. Let your light shine throughout the valley of human darkness. Make the path more distinguishable for the lost sheep to return home.

This constitutes My will: that our oneness bring sight to the blind, strength to the weary, and hope to a struggling world. Our blessed union can assist in rescuing the downtrodden, feeding the hungry, and comforting the afflicted. Together, we can offer spiritual healing to those bound by pain and suffering. Together, we can present peaceful alternatives to the threats of war. Acting in unity, we have the power to grant salvation to the sinner and recognition for the righteous. No greater force exists anywhere when you and I bond in sacred oneness. Unite with Me now. Let us bring healing to the world.

Allen C. Liles

JUNE 28

Judge Not

Give up judging others. Resentment will lessen accordingly. You waste precious time and energy taking someone else's inventory. The ego feeds on resentment. Taking offense at real or perceived slights serves as its favorite hobby. Most judgments occur when the ego seeks to elevate itself above others. The spiritual heart finds no satisfaction in putting down or degrading fellow human beings. Humility and gratitude mark anyone who walks the Spirit path. True peace and serenity emerge when you decline the opportunity to judge people and situations.

When your ego starts to self-promote at the expense of others, say, "Stop it right now." Run and find Me. I help restore you to sanity. I assist in getting you centered again. Realize that judgment and resentment nourish the ego's incessant need for self-gratification. It feeds and flourishes from promoting disharmony and discord. My plan for your life and the ego's goals never mesh. It wants to elevate itself at the expense of others. I want you to nourish and encourage those around you. Do you see how these two totally opposite viewpoints will always clash? You cannot serve two masters. You must choose whom you will serve. Serving the ego acts as a full-time and ultimately unfulfilling job. Serving Me brings happiness, joy, peace, and contentment. Let go of judging, holding resentments, and servicing the ego. Focusing on Me improves your life immeasurably. Live peacefully. Live in Me.

JUNE 29

Corrosive Fear

Fear corrodes and debilitates. Fear destroys peace of mind. When fear appears, turn at once in My direction. I banish fear. I chase it back into the shadows from whence it came. Seek Me when you become frightened of anything. I AM greater than anything in and of the earth. I can make the crooked places straight. I know your every material need, so quit worrying about your finances. I AM capable of healing anyone, so let go of worries about your dear wife's health. I bring the understanding, wisdom, and acceptance needed to deal with the aging process, so drop your concerns about the inevitable. Do not spend a minute fretting about the upcoming presidential election. The votes are already cast. I have tabulated every ballot. Whether your candidate won or lost is now irrelevant, so you can quit obsessing about the process. Regarding family relationships, I AM the great mediator. Release trying to personally control outcomes with family members.

Everyone walks a different path with one common destination: My kingdom. Your job simply lies in putting one foot in front of the other, always moving forward. Be fearless about today. The past rests with history. Tomorrow takes care of itself. Step out with boldness and confidence in the present. Send fear scurrying for the nearest exit. I AM the great fear chaser.

Allen C. Liles

JUNE 30

Your Marriage

Your marriage came from a divine appointment arranged and orchestrated by Me. You and your dear wife traveled a long, sometimes rocky, but ultimately rewarding path before marriage finally arrived. Both of you persevered despite delays, detours, and obstacles. I remained in the midst of everything, helping each of you stay the charted course. You were drawn together by My spiritual plans for the both of you. I AM gladdened by your sacred union. You are each bringing important lessons for the other. Separately, you have served as individual lights. Together, you radiate a greater and more constant light. Your mutual love and devotion remain strong. You trust that the other will step up when times get hard. That commitment stands as a key ingredient to every long-term and successful marriage.

No human life ever remains problem-free. Serious challenges can appear without warning. Staying mutually strong when troubles arise provides a feeling of comfort and security. When tough times appear, facing things together strengthens any marriage bond. Marriages based on material concerns and desires often fail. The best marriages feature those couples that walk side by side with similar personal and spiritual goals. No two people are exactly alike, even close marriage partners. Maintaining the same basic values ensures the likelihood of a happy and successful union.

Both you and your dear wife have established Me as a centerpiece for your life. I bless you both as you travel down life's path toward the wonders of heaven.

JULY

There is a time for everything and a season
for every activity under heaven.

—Ecclesiastes 3:1 (NIV)

JULY 1

Bring Light

I want you to bring light to the struggling. I deplore darkness. I love illumination in any form. Look at the darkness around you. Humankind gropes around, bumping into this thing or that. Lift up your lamp so that all can behold the beautiful world in which they live. Light calms fear. Light defines the path toward My kingdom. Light chases away the long winter of discontent. Stand atop the hill and cast My light into every darkened valley. Help enlighten those afflicted with complacency and malaise. Flood the world with the penetrating light of truth. Spread My light to every corner of the planet. People respond to light no matter how dire their earthly circumstances may be. Light exposes, not hides. Light lifts up, not tears down. Light beautifies, not defaces.

When you travel forth bearing My light, expect resistance. Many oppose any proclamation of truth. They seek to maintain a coalition of darkness and enslavement. Be prepared. March forward despite determined opposition. Be strong. Advance steadily in the face of withering fire. Let blessing your enemies be a part of your healing light. Counter personal attacks with unilateral forgiveness and understanding.

There can be no greater spiritual service than carrying forth the light of God. Hold your torch high! Let light prevail.

Allen C. Liles

JULY 2

Divine Guidance

I AM your spiritual guide. I lead you beside the still waters. I walk with you into the valley of the shadow of death. Fear no human being or any carnal evil, for I AM with you. My rod and My staff, they comfort you. Trust Me implicitly in all things. I steer you to the heights that your soul can reach in this human lifetime. I AM with you forever to the ends of the earth. Follow My divine guidance at all times. I never lead you astray. When in doubt, look to Me. When fearful, let Me calm you. When confused, allow Me to offer clarity. When weary, turn to My strength. When hopeless, allow me to bestow hope. As the world closes in on you, I pry it back open so that you can pass safely through to the other side.

Listen closely to every word I speak. Think deeply about My guidance. Explore it carefully for hidden meanings. Sometimes you may not understand everything I tell you. I appreciate and accept your human questioning. Be extremely cautious about guidance that arrives from untested sources. Human motivations are often murky and undetectable. I use only eternal principles that enhance and elevate your life. Look with great askance on any ego-driven guidance. It may promote dishonesty, self-will, and deceit. My divine guidance comes clothed in purity. It offers only the best and highest good for everyone involved. Sometimes My guidance arrives with great subtlety. Other times, its candid directness may startle you. Keep listening even when I seem silent. I always speak at the perfect time.

JULY 3

The Human Family

Humankind represents a family. You are each one connected to the other. Your similarities are much greater than your differences. A conscious separation from Me acts as the great divider. Material forces seek to focus on superficial differences. They stress such potential dividers as skin color, religious preference, language, cultural tastes, sexuality, gender, and financial status. In truth, every heart beats pretty much alike. I created the soul of every human being in My distinct image and likeness.

Turn away from the principle of separation. Instead, behold the Christ Spirit that dwells in each individual. It may be hard to locate this divinity at times. However, I guarantee you of its holy presence in every person. In My spiritual family, none is deemed more important than another. Rich or poor, tall or short, man or woman, ill or healthy, quiet or loud, learned or illiterate, each one comes forth as a child of God. Human beings travel different paths, but everything begins and ends within My kingdom. As far as humanly possible, recognize what you hold in common with your brothers and sisters in foreign lands. You each possess a heart capable of love and caring. You generally treasure your children, although there are different ways of expressing that love. You want to have meaningful work and grow old in safety and peace. Find a way to understand and accept every member of the human family. You are them, and they are you.

Allen C. Liles

JULY 4

Freedom

I provide the ultimate freedom. The world cannot possibly offer freedom in the spiritual sense. Materiality enslaves and tethers its victims to love of money, transitory fame, or fickle power. Earthly bonds fray and break. You will never find real freedom in things that rust, fade, or slip away. I AM the one true source of lasting and eternal freedom. I AM Freedom, with a capitol "F." I provide the essential freedom that comes when you rise above earthly snares. You become truly free when there is no false god before Me. Freedom comes when you live exclusively under My grace. Spiritual freedom releases you forever from the smothering bonds of materialism.

Throw off the shackles imposed by the world. They no longer exert power when you march free under My sacred banner. Release any false fears of human entrapment that threaten or hold you down. The lures of the earth eventually disappoint you, no matter how lovely they may appear. Never sell your soul for any amount. I do not demand anything in exchange for granting you My freedom. Accept this priceless gift with no strings attached. Glory in the incomparable peace and endless joy that accompany My grace. Bask in blessed freedom of the Spirit.

JULY 5

Illumination

A spiritually dark world needs My light. A mysterious cloud has descended upon the earth. I AM concerned about this worrisome development. Living without Me means choosing to live in perpetual darkness. Right now, many people ignore or even dispute My existence. Only spiritual illumination can reverse this highly negative trend. Light must dispel dark, or disaster could result. The dawning light of spirituality must begin one soul at a time. As an individual light becomes activated, a point of darkness disappears.

Unfortunately, the process works both ways. Some existing lights get snuffed out through addictions or a reverse scramble for materiality. There is a never-ending battle for the soul. It rages daily. Sometimes, I may lose the immediate fight. But, in the long run, I never lose.

To achieve illumination for the many, I need your help. Your light can help lead others to Me. Enter the ongoing struggle that flares between My sacred army of light bearers and the opposing forces who champion materialism. Put on the whole armor of God and enthusiastically join the fray. Be strong and determined to bring forth My power of illumination. Together we can stem the current race toward oblivion. Be a divine beacon. We can end the long night of suffering and prevent further damage to a lost world poised near the brink of catastrophe.

Allen C. Liles

JULY 6

The Harmonizing Principle

I AM the harmonizing principle of the universe. When I AM present, love must also be present. When I AM absent from the scene, disharmony soon appears. To manifest harmony, you must realize Me. A heart or mind steeped in resentment, animosity, or anger shuts Me out entirely. These powerful forces of disharmony keep Me away. I cannot co-exist with rancorous voices or cantankerous minds. Only My love can overcome the clanging and discordant sounds of negativity.

Invite the harmonious presence of love into every room in your house. Unlock the doors of your inner being and let the imprisoned splendor of eternal love escape. The Evil One thrives on disharmony. He pollutes the earth with misunderstandings and arguments. Angry shouts sound like beautiful music to his ears. The more bad vibrations, the more he enjoys it. For a peaceful life in earthly terms, love must always replace disharmony. Acceptance and tolerance must overcome prejudice and condemnation. Pardon and forgiveness must dethrone harsh judgments and endless grudges. Toss out any thoughts of a negative action that might lead to unharmonious results. When you prepare a meal, add harmony to every recipe. Place thoughtfully wrapped packages of harmony in every travel bag. Spread the pleasing scent of harmony in every office setting or home parlor. Carry harmony with you wherever you go. Live in peace. Live in love. Live in the sweet aroma of My harmony.

JULY 7

Matthew 7:7

Heed My instructions in Matthew 7:7. Ask to know Me better. Seek My presence. Knock in order to get My attention. Recall the next Scripture verse that follows (Matthew 7:8): "For everyone that asks receives; He that seeks finds and to him that knocks, the door shall be opened." I never refuse the thoughtful requests of My children. I wait patiently for your prayers. I want your interest and involvement with Me. I AM never far away or out of touch where you are concerned. Ask, seek, and knock when you need My help.

I AM your eternal companion, loving parent, and best friend forever. I AM your source for all good and everything you require. I AM the ultimate purveyor of priceless wisdom. I provide the peace that passes all understanding. I comfort you in moments of grief. Knock on My door at any time of the day or night. Ask for My help. Seek My assistance. Find Me when you are elated or dejected, accepted or rejected. Call out My sacred name in good and times or bad, happy times or sad. It matters not to Me. I eagerly await your summons. Just acknowledge Me. Know that I AM as close as your very breath, your hands, and your feet. Approach Me with confidence. I open My arms to receive you. When you ask, I give. When you seek, I reveal. When you knock, I swing wide the doors of heaven. This I do for you.

Allen C. Liles

JULY 8

Aging

Your body ages from the time you are born. However, your soul can either progress or regress during your human lifetime. Hopefully, your life on earth gets used productively to move further ahead in conscious awareness. There are many different phases, stages, and transitions in physical life. You must pass from one to another, in some cases whether you like it or not. Virtually no one physically remains a child forever. However, maintaining a childlike mentality happens far more often than you think. People grow and change body height and weight as the years pass. Physical aging illustrates an ongoing and inevitable process.

Spiritual growth operates differently, but with some similarities. No one grows from a babe in consciousness to an ascended master overnight. In your own life, you gradually evolved from a corporate and highly materialistic orientation to a more spiritually attuned awareness. But, before you congratulate yourself too much, may I opine that you still have a long to go before your spiritual journey ends. The good news: I provide everything you need to successfully continue on and complete My path. Look at your life as an exciting adventure comprised of many parts, twists, and turns. Very few human lives move in a straight line from birth to death. As you traverse the earth, your physical body continues evolving. You are always racing against the calendar. Getting older can be an extremely unnerving experience for some. Embrace the aging process, if possible. I understand that life at this stage often seems like an endless endurance test. Your physical body creaks while your spirit might be peaking. Recall My promise: the absolute best is yet to come.

JULY 9

Your Adult Daughter

Total and complete acceptance stands as the ultimate key with your adult daughter, as with most people. Your human relationship has been severed for several reasons, some not readily apparent even to her. The anger stems from more than one source, all relating back to family interactions. In all familial dynamics, judgments often arise that can be misguided or off kilter. But to the specific person involved, they are absolutely real. When you practice acceptance and unilateral forgiveness, you release yourself from any bondage to the person judging you. Being "released" ranks as a primary goal for both you and your adult daughter. You may or may not ever reestablish your father–daughter bond in this lifetime. You must let go of any expectations.

Turn the situation completely over to Me, and banish all worry, concern, and regret. Accept her for who she is, a perfect child of God. I AM deeply interested in her lifetime journey, as I AM closely involved in yours. Release and bless her on her way. Allow Me to watch over her human progress. As with everyone, she makes free-will choices that create her experiences on earth. Let any pain and regret recede and disappear. See your adult daughter surrounded by My light and My love. Keep the focus on yourself, and give her the freedom to do the same.

Allen C. Liles

JULY 10

Defects of Character

I know everything about you. I know your strong points, and I also know your weaknesses. After all, My child, I formed you. Your free will-choices create imperfections and character defects. Do not fret. Every defect of character comes with a learning opportunity attached. Here are some of your most obvious opportunities for positive change: (1) being too judgmental of others, especially certain family members; (2) holding on to resentments past their expiration date; (3) acting in a self-righteous manner; (4) lacking trust in Me regarding financial matters; and (5) courting false pride, especially in seeking the approval of others.

Your best course in removing any defect of character lies in formally asking for My help. Ask Me to remove any shortcoming, and I do it instantly. Of course, at the next instant, you may choose to reclaim it. Most people rarely fail to repeat a character shortfall even after I take it away for them. They are then forced to repeat the sequence all over again. But I always stand ready to repeat My role in the process.

Everything comes down to you exercising your free will properly. I want you to make wise choices. I hope when I remove a defect that it stays removed. But I AM realistic about the vagaries of human nature. Habits are often impossible to break. However, with My help, miracles happen every day in human behavior. I can remove a slight blemish or a huge stain. Just give Me the chance. In My eyes, despite your human shortfalls, you are still My blessed child. I look at you and see nothing but perfection.

JULY 11

Persistence

Persistence, persistence, persistence. That is the overall key to the spiritual life. Persist in your commitment to know Me better. Persist in designating our relationship as the top priority in your life. Persist in resisting distractions and temptations. Allow persistence to overcome laziness. Replace sloth with persistence. Persist in bringing all your cares and worries to Me. Persist in seeking My will for you. Persist in carrying out My plan for your life. Do not regard persistence as boring. Instead, view it as an absolute necessity.

I know the world boasts hundreds of attractive distractions. Persist in putting Me first before any obvious waste of time. Resist anyone or anything that might come between us. I AM a jealous God. I want and need your continuing attention. Persist in making time for Me each day. Persist in trusting Me when the world sucker punches you. Resist fake idols, and persist in recognizing Me as the one power and one presence in the universe and in your life. Persist in reading and meditating on My Word as contained in the Holy Bible. Resist all anger and resentment. Persist with forgiveness. Also persist in speaking positive words and doing worthwhile deeds. Resist gossip and backbiting. Speak highly of all. Persist in seeking to enhance our oneness through additional prayer and meditation. Persist in your travels on the spiritual path, always advancing at least one step further each day. Persistence is the name of our game and the surest path to heaven. I love a persistent partner. Keep on seeking Me until the day you enter My kingdom.

Allen C. Liles

JULY 12

Two Kinds of Wisdom

There are two distinct kinds of wisdom—spiritual and material. Spiritual wisdom focuses on long-term good for everyone involved. Material wisdom thinks in the short term. It focuses on individual gain, instant gratification, and immediate pleasure. Spiritual wisdom upholds and promotes eternal values. It uplifts, protects, and brings joy and contentment. Material wisdom avoids thinking about ultimate consequences.

There are always consequences for wrongheaded thinking. When you act spiritually, you consciously gauge the impact of your decisions. You attempt to clearly see the end results of your choices. Spiritual wisdom unfolds gradually, usually over a longer period of time.

You can discern any type of wisdom more clearly when you commune with Me. I provide you with an ongoing foundation of spiritually based information and knowledge. The world tries to constantly fill your mind from its many sources. Most earthly wisdom comes packaged in media-inspired entertainment, outright sensationalism, and ego-centered blather. It uses the material lures of sex, money, fame, and power to ensnare the masses. Never underestimate material wisdom's ability to seem relevant and attractive.

When you are seeking true wisdom, come directly to Me. I speak softly but with a clear voice. My wisdom eventually carries you to heaven. I think you know where the other wisdom might take you. Come drink of the living water, the wisdom of God. It will never fail or mislead you.

JULY 13

Human Life

Human life can be a satisfying, interesting, and fulfilling experience. It has the potential to provide joy, happiness, and excitement beyond your wildest imagination. Life offers extraordinary possibilities for great family relations, parental and spousal love, and loving friendships with individuals of both sexes. Life may give you opportunities for a stimulating and rewarding work career. It can also gift you with a chance for travel and the time to pursue hobbies. Life introduces the pleasures of sex, the intensity of personal achievement, and the overall satisfaction of a life well lived.

When you combine the positive aspects of life with walking the spiritual path, you are truly living the grand dream. Every life finds a greater purpose when it walks hand in hand with Me. I raise you up to a higher level of consciousness where all life glows brighter. I touch the soul and elevate your inner life to a place where it matches and exceeds outer attractions. In the spiritual life, the joy of knowing Me completes your earthly existence. Even in the most seemingly perfect human life, rain falls and storms come. Then your bond with Me becomes ever more crucial. I want you to someday look back on having lived an exceptional life on earth. I hope you always make the free-will choice to value My presence in your material life.

Allen C. Liles

JULY 14

Politics

Someone once said, "All politics is local." I would add a greater truth: "All politics is transitory." Good leaders and bad leaders come and go. One political party seems popular for a time, and then things reverse. Someone new is always trying to grab political power. The ego thrives on the narcissism of politics. The players themselves quickly change with the seasons. Rather than place your trust and interest in changeable venues, look to the eternal for stability and security. The nastiness of modern politics does not reflect My plan for humankind. When you center yourself in Me, you find true peace.

The political process never knows peace. It just looks forward to the next campaign and subsequent election. Every society, and especially a democracy, must have good leaders. However, the majority of your current political leadership focuses mostly on personal enrichment and attaining power for its own sake. Working together for the people's good seems out of favor. Politics tends to inflame passions on every side. The media, which loves conflict and drama, adds to the high-decibel debate. As a result, animosity soars on both sides. To Me, today's politics seems more problem-creating than problem-solving.

Detach from twenty-four/seven political chatter. Deny all negativity, regardless of the source, access to your consciousness. Search for Me amid the relentless rancor and din of politics. Instead of going for the throat, go for the heart. Choose Me. I promise to govern with generosity, benevolence, and love for all.

JULY 15

Living One Day at a Time

Live in the here and now. I divided earthly time into twenty-four-hour segments. I bring the sun up every morning and set it down at the end of the day. You must live life in the same time frame. Pay attention to what comes before you today. Place yesterday and tomorrow into two separate boxes and relegate them to the closet shelf. Discard regrets about the past and worries concerning the future. Keep your focus on today. I AM busy sorting out your calendar for this twenty-four-hour segment of your life.

Many opportunities for enlightenment, service, and spiritual progress spring up around you. Pay attention. Be alert. Shun procrastination. Think and then act on what I place before you. A moment wasted today goes into the trash bin of yesterday. I AM constantly doling out assignments for immediate action. Take time to reflect, but do not allow reflection to immobilize you. Watch out for meaningless distractions and obvious time wasters. We have much work to do, and the day can fly by quickly. Strive for balance between activity, rest, and prayer. Get up early, and be about My business before the sun rises. Decide to step forward and move out today on your spiritual and worldly quest. Do not spend a moment feeling guilty about anything. I have given you another day of life. Use it wisely. Use it well. Get with the program, My program. Declare this as a day of measureable progress and real growth. I want you to live life in the present. Let's get to work!

JULY 16

Separation from Me

Separation rules the earth. People war constantly against each other. Loud and angry voices dominate the public discussion. Threats and recriminations abound. The peacemakers seem scarce and strangely silent. Unrest and distrust rule the landscape. The Golden Rule has evaporated.

For general healing to come, the emphasis on separation must cease. For a true healing, the breach between humankind and Me has to end. Living in unity with Me offers a much happier and more peaceful way of life for everyone. To achieve unity of Spirit once more, the overwhelming "me-first" preoccupation of the ego must be reversed. The world obviously does not want oneness with Me at the moment. I feel not only separated but disrespected and cast aside. Idol worship prevails. The world has fallen in love with technology, money, and instant gratification. I stand at the edge of the crowd, searching for any possible attention. It makes Me sad and a bit angry when the world shuns Me. It is I who has graced an ungrateful world with so much beauty and largesse. What I give, I can always take away. But that belies My nature. I AM a generous God. For Me to withhold anything requires extremely negative attitudes and actions. I want to experience oneness again with all of My children. I need for a lost world to sheath its swords and turn within. Reject separation. Return to Me.

JULY 17

Clarifying Your Priorities

Your priorities sometimes shift and waver. Here is your top priority: Me. Become centered in Me. Look to Me as your source for everything. Open up your mind and heart. Receive the prosperity that I constantly shower down upon you. Seek My wisdom and guidance. Eliminate fear whenever possible. Being fearful can become its own priority. I let nothing threaten you when I AM on the playing field. Steer clear of anything that throws you off the spiritual path. Do not trouble yourself about trivial things. Avoid stirring up problems with other people. Whenever your mind strays to the banal, snap it back immediately to more productive thoughts. Purify your consciousness. Stop inviting the crass and violent into your brain. See meaningless conflict for the waste of time it is. Lift your view of the world to a higher place.

Look for clarity, My clarity, in all matters. Keep coming back to Me whenever confusion reigns in your outer world. In Me, you will find peace. In Me, you will discover strength and courage. Align yourself with Me. Let My wisdom guide your every action. When things start to crash and burn, stop and embrace Me. When you begin to question your goals, ask Me to direct your path. When you are sad, let Me comfort you. I AM real, I AM present, and I AM your number one priority now and forever.

Allen C. Liles

JULY 18

Accepting the Past

Today is your adult son's fiftieth birthday. Next month he will visit you. More than six years have elapsed since you last saw one another. For that reunion to gain traction, the past needs closure. Both good and not so good memories exist for everyone engaged in a long-term relationship. Human failings mix with human strengths to produce flawed individuals. Each human being exhibits a series of personal contradictions. Did you make mistakes as a parent? Absolutely! Did your son contribute his own unwise decisions to the father-child experience? Of course! Now that we have established that neither of you approached perfection in the past, you must let it all go.

Both of you possess good hearts. Neither of you seeks to do damage to the other. Misunderstandings have plagued your past dealings with each other. It is beyond time to drop the past as a guide for future experiences. Your son loves you just as you love him. He respects you as well. Give him the respect that he deserves. Approach him as the child of God he is. Accept his unique personality and real achievements as blessings for which a father can be exceptionally proud. Treat him as an adult, and relate man to man. You two still have the time to forge a truly loving and caring bond. Claim this singular opportunity for reconciliation. Make every moment count!

JULY 19

Facing Fear

Fear corrodes. It causes your spirit to cower and shrivel. It seeks to divide and separate us. When cringing in fear, you feel weak, alone, and vulnerable. Fear distracts your focus and hinders spiritual growth. Fear scuttles your potential. It can thwart you and destroy all sense of forward momentum. Little darts of fear come your way every day. Large fear bombs also drop on you, sometimes when you least expect them.

When fear consumes you, stop and haul out My shield of faith. Hold it up before you. Let the small darts of gloom and any massive invasions of doubt become deflected and neutralized. Link arms with Me. When we fight together, fear flees. Leave every anxious thought behind you in the dust. If fear refuses to move aside, plow straight through it. Never downplay the negative effects of being fearful. Acknowledge your concerns if you must, but then rise above all appearances of negativity. Affirm your oneness with Me. Deny any specific fear's hold over you. See it realistically and without tears. Only you can give fear any power. Only you can invite this parasite into your being. See fear as an outcome of living materially. Never let the secular world and its viruses infect you. I possess the correct vaccine that prevents fear from entering destroying you. You and I together have fear outnumbered. It is always two against one when we unite in divine oneness. Never fear anything. I AM near.

Allen C. Liles

JULY 20

Free Will Gone Mad

My gift of free will can be horribly misused. Rational explanations never suffice when someone commits an unspeakable crime, such as what happened at the Colorado movie theatre. I AM always present afterward to comfort those affected by a senseless tragedy of any kind. I help dry the tears of hurting hearts. I place a supportive arm around the grieving. Free will decisions that result in harm are never condoned by Me. A human mind bent on destruction can do great and lasting damage. I shed My own tears for everyone involved, including the misguided one. I AM more upset than you might imagine when free will causes the world pain and grief. I want all My children to live in peace. Taking the lives of innocent people violates everything I hold dear. One of My most important and stringent commandments is "Thou shalt not kill." Yet, throughout recorded history, murdering one another has been a rampant feature of the human condition. I always urge love instead of anger, pardon to replace condemnation, and forgiveness rather than revenge. When free will results in killings of My children, I shake My head in abject sadness and deep regret. Searching for an understandable explanation for such events seems meaningless. Again, I AM always there in the aftermath to comfort and support those who cry out in anguish and distress. When free will goes mad, we all suffer the negative consequences.

JULY 21

The Christ within You

You have accepted the principle of the inner Christ. This Christ within also directs the activity of the Holy Spirit in you. At the very core of your being, I have implanted the mind of the Christ. When you seek counsel, the Christ mind stands ready to provide it. When you grieve, the Christ mind waits to comfort you. When you become fearful, you can turn to the indwelling Christ for courage and faith. You can meet with the Christ within anytime you want. By going to your core, you make the most divine connection imaginable. The Holy Spirit helps you carry out the instructions and guidance provided by the Christ. You become an instrument of My grace. You fulfill My plan for your life.

It all commences when you quit looking to the outside world for anything. Many loud voices clamor for your attention. They also offer ideas on how you should approach life. Some of these suggestions might even have merit. However, the best and truest source for all wisdom and good lies deep in the midst of you. The Christ Spirit in you, your hope of glory, may be accessed at any time and from any place. You do not need a go-between of any kind. Just find a quiet place, breathe, and begin your sacred time in prayer and meditation.

Seek the Christ within, and the answers will come. I reveal the truth of the ages: I created you with the Christ as an essential and integral part of you. Go within and discover this blessed miracle. It will astound you.

Allen C. Liles

JULY 22

Let My Presence Rise

Allow My presence to rise within you. Let Me fill you with My grace. Just as you might pull your vehicle into a service station for refueling, take the time to refuel your spirit every day with the essence of Me. Stop and rest while I pour My healing love and precious peace into your soul. I top off your spiritual tank with eternal joy and unconditional forgiveness. I want to replenish you daily with a high-grade supply of wisdom and harmony, prosperity, and spiritual energy. You never need to run on empty when I AM near. I AM always available, anytime of the day or night, to meet your every need. I AM the great dispenser of good.

So many go right past Me with no thought of what I can offer. They live unaware of My capabilities to ease their journey through life.

All I ask is that you give Me the opportunity to demonstrate My power. Let Me renew you. Give Me a try when all else fails. No, come to Me first before you attempt anything else. There is nothing you require that I cannot provide. Test Me. I welcome any trial. Cast your burdens upon Me, and walk away relieved. Hand Me your deepest worry, and see it quickly dissolve. Trust Me with your largest problem, and watch while I provide the perfect answer. Come if you are heavy laden, and I promise to give you rest. Come soon, My child, so I can fill you with My endless supply of love and peace.

JULY 23

Finding Courage

Find courage in the face of any adversity. Stand tall when negativity confronts you. Powerful forces roam the world, looking for ways to harm and intimidate. Face them down when they find you. Look fear straight in the eye. Do not flinch. I AM in the midst of you, buoying up your courage. See the battle for souls realistically. The dark side wants to neutralize you. It seeks to deflect, distract, and distance you from Me. Its goal lies in eliminating you from the fray. It claims a great victory when one of Mine falls by the wayside. Repel any attempt to derail or silence you. Refuse to quit My path even when harsh attacks come. I give you the spiritual courage necessary to withstand heavy blows. You are much stronger than you think. Just watch out for the cunning angle of the dark side's probes. The Evil One knows your every weakness. He picks at you constantly, searching for an opening. Amaze him with your awareness, resiliency and toughness. Hold fast. Buck yourself up with the strength that I give you. Throw off the yoke he brings along to imprison you. If necessary, be prepared to fight until your human death. Despite the relentless assaults, you must summon up the courage to persevere. Never contemplate surrender. Do not give hope to evil, even for one moment. Be alert for any faltering moment of weariness or resignation. If that happens, call Me at once. I rush to your side, bolstering your lagging spirit. Never give up. Fight until the end. Victory will come when you least expect it.

Allen C. Liles

JULY 24

Culture Corruption

Corruption infects the present-day culture. Widespread idol worship rules the day. Humankind idolizes the wrong gods. Selling one's soul seems an acceptable choice to those seeking material good. Violence appears everywhere, especially in the media-driven universe. Sex also has become a beckoning god, but not in a productive or truly loving way. Notoriety seekers are willing to do anything for immediate attention.

I ask you: where am I, the Lord of Hosts, in all of this craziness? The answer: apparently nowhere. Unless things change, idol worship always ends badly. I love you and each one of My sometimes-wayward children, but I AM not happy about being relegated to the back of the line. The culture needs to reverse itself before even more trouble erupts.

I AM a compassionate, generous, caring, and loving God. I AM also willing to forgive. But I AM clear about one thing: thou shalt have no other gods before Me. The world needs to consider the ramifications of violating this most important commandment.

I do not deal in threats, per se. However, I urge everyone to avoid the wailing and gnashing of teeth that eventually comes when you disrespect Me. Many will seem puzzled as they ask, "How did all of these bad things happen to us?" My answer: This is the negative path you chose for yourself. There remains only one true path for salvation: Me. It is best that you choose it—and soon.

JULY 25

Serving Me

You serve Me best when you perform the specific tasks I put before you each day. I give you brand new opportunities for service every twenty-four hours. I want you to reflect My goodness to the world. Forget about grand strategies for the future. Do the little kindnesses I set before you today. Operate in the here and now. Live in a day-tight compartment, focusing only on what lies directly in front of you. Be on the lookout for creative ways to spread My grace around. Unless you stay alert, some of the best options for service could sail right by you. Notice everything. Disregard nothing. Be open to all possibilities. Kind words bring inner and outer smiles. Genuine appreciation lifts human spirits. Remember, you speak for Me. You are performing these blessings directly for Me, not for yourself. Do not hesitate to help someone, even if a few dollars are involved. I refund all your expenses on My behalf, with interest. If someone seeks your counsel, speak with My wisdom. If a friend seems fearful, bolster him or her with My courage. When you encounter a person physically hurting, minister with My healing powers. If a fellow human being feels lost, abandoned, or alone, bless him or her with My love. I want you to serve as a crucial instrument of My grace. The world needs us, now more than ever.

Allen C. Liles

JULY 26

Try Kindness

Kindness acts as the healing balm that soothes the human spirit. When you get angry, find a kind word you can speak. If you feel guilty about having done something you regret, make amends. When your bank account sinks, consider a small contribution to an organization or person in need. If you are wronged, plot kindness instead of revenge. Instead of wanting somebody's quick demise, think how you might build him or her up. Look in the mirror. Visualize yourself as an inherently kind person. Let a pleasing smile replace an accusing frown. Keep staring at your countenance until you see the kindness finally appear.

I equipped you with a loving heart. Kindness and a consideration for others always reside there. The moment you feel resentful about anyone or anything, stop immediately. Flip your emotion around 180 degrees and replace rancor with kindness. Disarm your enemies with forgiveness. Be kind to them when they attack you verbally. Confuse your adversaries with a gentle approach. Turn away animosity by employing compassion and understanding. I smile whenever you show your benevolent side. This is My son, in whom I AM well pleased. I love it when you demonstrate one of My most precious and lasting gifts—the gift of kindness. It reflects well on both of us.

JULY 27

Hope

Hope is My booster shot for the spirit. An injection of hope gives your spiritual immune system an extra measure of protection. The outside world comes stocked with viruses of every kind. These earth-based bugs look for any weakness to spread their infection. The material world can sometimes make you physically, mentally, and spiritually sick. When that happens, you need heavenly antidotes. A powerful treatment of hope helps restore you to wholeness. It puts you on the road to recovery.

If you remain infected by the earth too long, personal restoration takes enormous time and effort. The forces of negativity want to leave you defenseless. They seek your resignation or retirement from the spiritual path. When you give up, they celebrate. A spirit buoyed by hope fights back. Hope keeps you moving onward and upward toward heaven.

When you become hopeful, you carry others with you. Your hope-inspired demeanor encourages lost souls to continue moving ahead.

In the midst of pain, suffering, and doubt, My hope always beckons you to a higher place. Hope springs from a faithful heart. An extra dose of hope gets any patient back on his or her feet. Whenever you falter, I prescribe hope. Along with faith, hope acts as the cure for any illness of the spirit. Hope is My divine elixir.

JULY 28

Your Dear Wife's Birthday

Today marks your dear wife's human birthday. Your affection for her has remained constant over decades. Both you and she were married before, but many couples today are on their second, third, or even more marriages. I do not judge people for multiple marriages. I relish longtime unions, but circumstances often derail even the best marriages. The passing of one partner also does not mean that human life stops for the other partner. Human happiness improves when it is shared with a spouse or significant other.

You were first attracted to your dear wife by her warmth, pleasant personality, and physical beauty. You soon learned that she also possessed a generous inner beauty. She likes helping others and has no ulterior motives for doing so. Your dear wife enjoys good things, but material interests are not foremost in her priorities. She unconditionally loves her three adult children. You are always proud of her in every setting. She has been a wonderful partner in ministry. The church congregants seem to like her even more than you sometimes, but that is fine with you. Her niceness toward everyone ranks as an especially endearing quality in a church setting.

Having been diagnosed with a chronic illness more than three decades ago, she has experienced many health challenges, but her dauntless spirit always seems to rally. Without question, your dear wife appreciates your steadfast support when health problems arise. You are a good couple. You serve Me with dedication and love. I bless your strong bond.

JULY 29

Steadying Yourself

The world finds many ways to knock you off balance. Yes, you are a spiritual being having a human experience. But the human part of you can be left reeling from unexpected events. Life has an uncanny knack for blindsiding someone. Things can quickly become painful and scary. Here is the good news: I help steady you when you start to stumble. When you drop into a bottomless pit, I come to rescue you. Whenever you feel yourself tottering, sit down and become centered. Please call for Me. Do not stand on your feet again until you feel My presence on the scene.

What are the signs that you are becoming vulnerable? If your heart races, if you feel buffeted by waves of anxiety, or if you become short of breath, the world may be targeting you. Before reacting to these symptoms, summon Me. Never make a move without My input. I AM the calming influence you seek. Avoid compounding the trouble by some heedless action. I need to give you My counsel and support before you do anything. Sense My arrival in the midst of chaos. The wily ploys of the earth have no power over us. Take My Hand. Let Me steady you.

Allen C. Liles

JULY 30

I Am with You

The Christ Spirit, who is within you, stands far above the earthly fray. From the invisible place at your core, the Christ furnishes a strong antidote to the various poisons of the earth. The world wants to control your thoughts and actions. Your spiritual orientation threatens its rule. Journeys of the Spirit worry the forces of darkness. They seek to divide us. Promoting separation serves as their basic plan for victory. Our sacred union neutralizes and defeats them.

In truth, the secular world has no power over you. It uses false appearances to trap and hold you. I help you remain alert to its wily thrusts. My angels and I defend you against any unexpected onslaught. We walk with you through the brambles. We watch for possible traps and snares. Great and small tests always mark your human life. Temptations abound. Detours beckon.

Remember that every test, temptation, or detour offers some sort of teachable moment. Always look for the lesson contained in any challenge. Most life events contain either an obvious or hidden benefit. Life usually consists of obvious or hidden lessons that either aid or hinder your spiritual growth. I help you sort out which is which. I also assist you in overcoming whatever obstacle threatens your progress. I AM with you always, in the best of times and worst of times. I AM God, your LORD and Savior.

JULY 31

Love Solves Relationship Problems

Love serves as the ultimate solution to every relationship problem. Intrapersonal dynamics are often complicated. Motivations can become sometimes unclear, even to the people involved. The human mind and heart are adept at concealing their deepest and truest feelings. However, nothing breaks through defensive walls like love.

Some individuals may push you away. They resist love for various reasons. Perhaps they fear abandonment. Maybe love has caused them past pain. Love gone terribly wrong can emotionally scar even the strongest among you. You may still extend your love to someone, even if you are kept at an emotional and physical distance. Always pray for those you love.

I love unconditionally. That often seems hard for human beings to comprehend. I created humankind, so I love you as a parent loves a child. Nothing can ever keep Me from loving you. You may choose to separate yourself from Me. I will still find a way to show My love for you. You may curse Me, but I do not hear you. You can sin against me, yet I employ the old adage, "Hate the sin, but love the sinner." I love the imperfect child as much as the perfect one.

If I can love the lost sheep that strays from the flock, can you not find the same affection for the ones who disappoint you? Pray especially for those who wrong you. Deflect anger with thoughts and words of love. Love heals the deepest wounds. It lowers a rising blood pressure. It protects the health of a vulnerable heart. Love provides the ultimate blessing. When in doubt, love. When disillusioned, love. When hopeless, love. Love works.

Allen C. Liles

AUGUST

*Finally, brothers, whatever is true, whatever is noble,
whatever is right, whatever is pure, whatever is
lovely, whatever is admirable—if anything is excellent
or praiseworthy—think about such things.*

—Philippians 4:8 (NIV)

AUGUST 1

Eagle's Wings

Remember what was written in the book of Isaiah, chapter 40 and verse 31: "But those who hope on the Lord will renew their strength; they will soar on wings like eagles; they will run, and not grow weary, and they will walk and not be faint." When you fall down, I scoop you up. I quickly place you back on your feet again, ready to go forward. When the world drops a heavy load on your shoulders, I help you carry it. When your heart sinks with grief and tragedy, I sweep away your sadness with assurances of eventual peace. Remember your spiritual identity and heritage. You are My precious child. You stay under My protection forever. You belong with Me, right by My side. You are My cherished son in whom I AM well pleased. If it were not so, I would not tell you.

Listen for My whisper of encouragement in your ear. Watch Me go before you to fill in the pesky potholes so you don't stumble in them. I AM watching over you at every moment, fending off random attacks. When you become weary, ask Me to replenish your strength. Do not ever contemplate giving up. You have only begun your work as an instrument of My grace. Let the seeds of fear and doubt fall harmlessly away. Allow the wind to scatter them far and wide. Know that I, the Lord of Hosts, restore your strength and elevate your energy so that you can successfully serve Me. Your eagle's wings await you.

AUGUST 2

Give Up Control

Give up your futile attempts to control anyone or anything. Focusing on your own behavior offers a better chance for success. Trying to control other people is a complete waste of time and energy. Keep the emphasis on yourself. Let Me worry about everything else.

As you know, My gift of free will allows you to chart your own human course. You defile the rights of others when you seek to impinge on their free will. Who gave you the right to make other people's decisions for them? Who are you to impose your personal standards or beliefs on someone else? Quit trying to rule others and concentrate on the logs clouding your own eye. Do not exceed your authority and attempt to take over My job. I know that playing God to another human being may temporarily bolster your ego. However, My child, I do not like My role preempted by anyone. You are not the one power and one presence in the universe. That remains My title. Your power to influence others stays limited. Do what you can as a living role model to demonstrate positive values. People will notice and possibly want to copy your behavior. Just be cautious about directing other people through your commands, incessant harping, or devious manipulation. None of those earth-based strategies work for very long, if at all.

Cede all control to Me. I AM in charge anyway, so give up every illusion about your own power. Allow Me to put every piece of life's complicated puzzle together. Use your time more wisely. Keep the focus on yourself.

AUGUST 3

The Human Ego

A healthy ego can be a good thing. However, the words "healthy" and "ego" sometimes serve as an oxymoron. "Healthy" usually means a favorable state of being. "Ego" often denotes a puffed up and unseemly condition of the human persona. An ego gone berserk usually demonstrates arrogance and aggressiveness. Self-will rules and wrongheaded behavior abounds. In full bloom, the ego cares only about itself. An awareness of other people stays nonexistent. The inflated ego flaunts any advantage, eager for more feeding of its privileged status. The ego seeks constant confirmation of its acclaimed greatness.

At some point, life has a way of deflating even the most overblown ego. The earth teems with punctured human balloons. The higher an untethered ego rises, the further its fall back to earth.

At its height, the human ego has very little use for Me. It firmly believes in its own preeminence. When negative events prove the ego's basic fragility, many express surprise at its downfall.

As the ego flattens, I rise. A shattered personna more easily relearns My sacred place in the scheme of things. Some of My greatest successes come with former egotists. In many cases, a painful fall initiates a new and teachable humility. When the ego loses its base of wealth, power, and worldly success, it becomes starved for spiritual oxygen. If asked, I can appear and immediately offer the breath of a new life.

Allen C. Liles

AUGUST 4

Resentments

All resentments must go. You must arrive at a place of complete forgiveness. Virtually every human being harbors grievances about something. Your humanity loves to wallow in self-pity, a precursor to developing a full-blown resentment. If you want to find peace of mind, you must release every grudge. The strange thing about resentment: the person in your crosshairs probably is unaware of your animosity. He or she is far too busy living their own life to give a second thought to your anger or hurt. There are exceptions, of course. However, the only person usually obsessing about a perceived situation is you.

Carrying around the extra baggage of old resentments can tire out anyone over time. It only serves to keep you mired in negativity. Get out of the muck! Do it today! Life in the present needs your full attention. The past resembles dust in the wind or a dead flower. Many beautiful flowers are blooming around you right now, all craving your attention. Gather up all your unresolved resentments and take them posthaste to "The Garden of Past Memories." Place your grievances in a neat row and leave them there. Take one last look at their final resting place, and then turn around and walk away. Your important work resides in the here and now—with Me.

AUGUST 5

Release Your Inner Light

Let your inner light shine. Do not hide it under a bushel, shielding a brightness that might benefit someone in need. You dwell in a world intent on darkness. Every speck of spiritual light serves a divine purpose.

Never underestimate the value of your individual light to pierce the fog of materialism. The glow from your enlightened Spirit helps illumine My path for others. You are an instrument through which I can lead My sheep safely toward home. The blessed members of My flock are drawn to their shepherd through the light of higher consciousness. As the level of spiritual awareness rises, your illumination attracts others. When your beam extends further out from the center, you become a beacon of clarity. Light helps every eye discern more clearly. It erases the cloud of confusion caused by secular darkness.

Always keep your inner light in the "on" position. Switching off the light from any awakened mind disappoints Me. Let nothing ever quench or dim your light. Help Me chase away the dark and restore light to a confused, blind and struggling world.

Allen C. Liles

AUGUST 6

My Promises

Trust Me to keep My promises. Seven of My most important promises are: (1) seek Me and My kingdom first, and all else will be added unto you; (2) ask and you shall receive, seek and you will find, knock and the door will be opened unto you; (3) in My heavenly kingdom, there are many rooms, and I AM preparing one of the best of them for you; (4) do not worry about what you will eat, drink, or wear, as I provide everything you need to do My work; (5) have no fear, as I AM your ever-watchful and protective shepherd; (6) I AM the answer to every problem and the solution to every vexing situation; and (7) I will never leave you; I will never forsake you. There are other key promises as well. I promise you peace of mind when you walk in My footsteps. I promise to respond whenever you call out to Me. I promise to hear your prayers, although I know them in advance. I promise to provide ample learning opportunities and life lessons so that you can make spiritual progress during your time on earth. I promise to be there when the world and your earthly family abandon you. I promise to assist you with career and relationship choices. I promise to give you important assignments of service to Me. I promise to be there for you until your physical time on earth ends. Then I promise to lift you gently into My arms and carry you lovingly into My kingdom. These are some (but not all) of My sacred promises.

AUGUST 7

God's Grace

My grace I give to you. Open your arms and receive it gladly. Be ready for it to shower down upon you.

Sometimes My beloved children fail to recognize this priceless gift. They get so wrapped up in their human lives that invisible treasures are either missed or taken for granted.

Anyone can choose to live under My grace. The misuse of free will often upsets someone's world. The redemption of divine grace helps put things back together. You can walk the earth unscathed when My grace shields you. The prosperity of My grace provides every material need. Lift up your eyes and behold grace falling from the skies of heaven. Nothing can prevent My grace from finding you. Focus your attention on allowing grace to live your life. As grace blesses you, please pass these blessings on to others. Be a receptacle for My grace. Let it collect around you. Grace serves as the ultimate expression of My unconditional love for you. Live by grace, live with grace, live from grace. Let grace be a constant reminder of your sacred place in the universe. Nothing remotely compares to My grace.

Allen C. Liles

AUGUST 8

Share the Silence

Share the silence with Me. Come to Me. I await you each day. Bond with Me. Form a divine link to the Christ Spirit within you. Forge a connection stronger than the purest steel. Build your house upon My rock. Make the structure solid but flexible enough to withstand the hurricanes of life. Be strong in Me.

Many human beings become lost and shattered when they shut Me out. Our reinforced house of spiritual steel may bend, but it will not break. Be wary of temptations in all forms. Often the greatest tempters come disguised in the richest and most beautiful robes. That robe might be human beauty, vast wealth, unbridled power, or alluring fame.

Keep your mind stayed on Me so you can safely avoid the quicksands of life. I help you navigate the traps and snares. I keep you on the surest path that leads directly to heaven. Although this path often gets difficult and steep, I guarantee that you will reach your destination safely. Draw closer to Me as we climb the final mountain. Do not become distracted or led astray by other voices. You travel with Me on a sacred mission. We draw near the finish line. Victory looms. Heaven soon appears in its priceless splendor. I promise you will not be disappointed.

AUGUST 9

Family Expectations

Your human family is teaching you some important life lessons. At times the relationships with your son, daughter and sister have either been strained or nonexistent. That represents a great disappointment for you. Some of their actions (or inactions) toward you have felt like a personal crucifixion.

During My time on earth, I also felt neglected and misunderstood by those closest to Me. I experienced persecution, trial, crucifixion, and human death. At the very last, I cried out, "Father, forgive them, for they know not what they do." You must emulate My cry from the cross. Forgive those who disappoint you.

Not everyone you meet during life's journey, including family members, will try to understand you. When you are ignored by blood relatives, it requires an extra effort to find forgiveness in your heart. But I promise that the effort brings peace and relief. Forgiveness and acceptance serve as the two primary tools in establishing harmony between adversaries. You must also address your expectations where family members are concerned. Unrealistic expectations can become flashpoints that lead directly to long-term resentments. See everyone in your human family surrounded by My light. Be gentle in your judgments. Revise all expectations. Wish everyone well as they journey forth on their own paths.

Allen C. Liles

AUGUST 10

My Whole Armor Awaits You

Put on the whole armor of God. My truth and your faith combine to form a protective shield against the world's most vicious assaults. Suit up for spiritual warfare in My complete armor of wisdom, integrity, perseverance, and courage. You do not need the clanking, heavy, and uncomfortable garb worn by past warriors. You go forth protected by the royal robe that I fashioned for you in heaven. This purple robe of consciousness boasts a powerful fabric not of the material world. Put on the lovely garment designed by Me as you enter the fray of spiritual warfare. My sacred robe comes equipped with heightened awareness, an all-seeing eye, and deep pockets that hold copious amounts of My grace. Allow it to clothe you with ample warmth during life's cold winters of discontent.

The world often sends chills of icy contentiousness your way. When that happens, pull your robe of righteousness closer around you. Let the swirling winds try to make you shiver with worry and fear. Negativity cannot penetrate your outer protection. Believe too that I AM dispatching legions of angels to guard you. With the whole armor of God and My angels on your side, you easily win the day.

Be strong. Be brave. Be confident. Nothing can harm you. Lift yourself physically, mentally, and spiritually to the highest levels of preparation and service. At the end of the struggle, you will view the final outcome from the highest vantage point imaginable. You will gaze down at the spiritual battlefield from the kingdom of heaven.

AUGUST 11

Become a Willing Instrument

I require a willing instrument to do My work. You are that instrument. Through your love, I can heal a damaged heart. With your voice, I can offer a comforting word. Let Me use your talents and skills to visibly bless others. Become My hands and My feet. Let your presence be My presence. Allow My song to flow through you. Sing the words I compose. The inspiring sound will resonate throughout the world. Give My peace and harmony expression through you.

When you become involved with Me, I can expand My influence. I touch the far corners of the world with you as My human messenger. The words you write are My words. They stir minds with thoughts of Me. When you speak, ears that hear listen with interest. Never underestimate how much one willing servant can accomplish. Allow Me to move in and through you. You are only one of many, but every dedicated soul counts.

I personify humility. Model that virtue to everyone you encounter. The world needs a quieter demeanor right now. Demonstrate the strength that comes from powerful serenity

. Thank you for your grateful nature. Gratitude brings peacefulness. We go forth in peace to bless and heal the world.

Allen C. Liles

AUGUST 12

A Force for Good

Become a force for good. The world around you finds itself locked in a desperate struggle. Many souls are at risk. In the end, I triumph. I always prevail despite some daunting combat. I AM actively recruiting My soldiers for the battle. We engage a cunning and baffling foe. Give this adversary some negative credit. He knows how to tempt human nature. He confuses the best thinkers.

To win the day, we must wield the sword of truth. We spill no actual blood. We conquer our enemy through love, understanding, and forgiveness. The Evil One does not understand the meekness of our power. The ferocious contest for souls often goes into "overtime" or "extra innings." The game goes on until one side finally declares victory. Emotional scars can accumulate from unrelenting spiritual warfare. Many lives are negatively affected by the scramble for fame, wealth, and power. You and I specialize in retrieving injured souls from the field of battle. You play the role of the brave medic who rushes out to treat, comfort, and bring back the hurting. In My soul-repair hospital, you and I can restore any wounded spirit to wholeness. No call for help goes unanswered. We lift the injured upon our shoulders. We carefully carry them back to safety. At the end of the conflict, I bestow on you the highest award for courage and service: an eternity in heaven with Me.

AUGUST 13

Resurrection Follows Crucifixion

Resurrection always follows crucifixion. When you are in the depths of abandonment and impending death, look upward to Me for relief. I AM there to help you move beyond the crucifixion experience. Do not be dejected and downtrodden. Have faith in the next spiritual step. From the lowest point in your life, search for the distant mountain of resurrection.

Never despair. Allow your mind, body, and spirit to float above your current circumstances. Understand that certain elements of the world enjoy seeing you hoisted in humiliation for all to see. When you languish in the depths of suffering, you offer no threat to evil. When you move forward into resurrection, you become a brighter light that instantly pierces the darkness. As your spirit ascends, you become a powerful beacon that signals hope for the lost. When the dazed, confused, and hopeless behold the glow of your spirit, they find a new reason to believe. Your spirit crosses over from the material world to a distant shore. You travel unfettered to a higher level of awareness. You shed any shackles that hindered you on the earthly plane. You leave behind human illness, disease, disability, and old age. Any painful moments of life fade into memory as a lost and forgotten dream.

When you complete the resurrection journey, you arrive into a new galaxy of wonder and possibilities. I call your name and motion for you to join Me. You hear My loving words: "You are forever freed from the painful crosses of earth. You are free at last, free at last. I, the LORD almighty, declare that you are free at last."

Allen C. Liles

AUGUST 14

The Searching Heart

The human heart searches for many things: love, peace, joy, a sense of belonging, and a connection to others. While the mind seeks wealth and material good, the searching heart craves gifts of the spirit. It senses a vague tugging toward something higher and more fulfilling. I AM that tug, that subtle yearning for the invisible. When you witness the innocence of a child, your heart responds with gladness. A soft word, a kind gesture, and a respectful action all stir the searching heart's divine impulses. A peaceful heart yearns for peace. A loving heart treasures love. A joyful heart leaps when it encounters joy. Only the mind allows real anger to fester and grow. Forgiveness originates in a forgiving heart. Acceptance begins in an understanding heart. Tolerance emerges from a wise heart. Courage surrounds the persevering heart. The human heart can grow old, weary, and sick. Yet the spiritual heart never ages or falters. It always searches for a better day. When love fades, a heart filled with love remembers only the good. When worldly love dies, a passionate heart refuses to mourn. The searching heart never rests or lives completely in the past. It waits for the next loving moment. It knows the eternal grace of God will surely appear just over the next rainbow.

AUGUST 15

Seek My Presence

Seek Me in the morning quietness but also throughout the day and evening. Do not let unexpected distractions delay our divine connection. Life sometimes interrupts our sacred time together. When that happens, return to Me quickly. Talk to Me anytime you wish. Bring any topic into the conversation. Nothing is off limits between us. Ask for My advice and guidance when questions arise. Trust Me with your innermost thoughts. I already know them, but your sharing them with Me enhances our friendship.

When you feel disappointed and rejected, flee quickly to Me for comfort and reassurance. I help you see the life lesson involved. If you think people and events are punishing you, I want to know about it. I help you identify the subtle blessing that may lurk in the background. Substantial good can emerge from the most painful situations. Look to Me for explanation when family, friends, or colleagues snub you. I bolster your fragile spirit with words of encouragement. Pour out your heart. I promise to listen. See Me as both your first and last refuge. I AM your most loyal confidante, your unwavering friend, and your tireless supporter. Our divine relationship always comes first with Me.

AUGUST 16

Heaven on Earth

You live in a form of heaven on earth when you commune with Me every morning. Do you feel contentment, bliss, and peace when we meet in the silence each day? Just wait until you enter heaven.

What you now experience for a brief time becomes magnified thousands of times when you arrive in My celestial kingdom. As you float untethered into glory, the essence of your being sheds the shackling chains of earth. Your soul reverts back to pure Spirit. Every material thing fades away. Both the good and bad times of your life disappear into the ethers. All physical pain evaporates. Emotional problems vanish forever. All that remains is the soul consciousness you achieved on earth. You bring your spiritual development with you, no matter what it may be. As you enter heaven, lovely music accompanies your arrival. A blazing light surrounds your entrance. You experience a glowing radiance beyond compare. You sense an incredibly positive and loving environment. You immediately feel at home. One of My angels hands you the lovely white robe of purity. I personally welcome you into My kingdom. I happily show you the extraordinary place that I have prepared for you. Peace and harmony pour out upon you in dazzling fashion. "Incredibly awesome" are the words I hear most often from new arrivals. You revel in heaven's grandeur and indescribable beauty. It is as though you are witnessing a million sunrises and sunsets melded into one incomparable moment. A galaxy of rainbows blends as one to magnify this heavenly setting. I greet you as I greet every returning soul: "Welcome home, My dear and precious child, welcome home!"

AUGUST 17

Your Physical Health

Trust Me in all things, especially your physical health. When you become stuck in bodily pain, I AM the on-call physician in charge of spiritual healing. I bring My heavenly remedies to bolster your prescribed medications. Yes, I work through real life medicine that includes doctors, nurses, technology, prescription drugs, health aides, social workers, chaplains, physical and occupational therapists, and other members of My care team. I draw up the spiritual plan that coordinates your healing. I chart your progress. I first apply My soothing balm to any open wound. I whisper encouragement and offer hope to any painful break or sprain of your spirit.

Human bodies on the physical plane can grind down slowly or fail suddenly. The worldly calendar eventually catches up with everyone. Expect and accept it. Do not needlessly struggle against the perennial cycle of life. As you await the inevitable, respect and zealously guard the sanctity of your body temple. Do not allow harmful substances to defile it. Exercise your body regularly. Provide your entire body, mind, and spirit with positive nutrients. Help your mind communicate positively with the body. Fill your human brain with helpful words and positive images, loving and uplifting people, and invigorating experiences. Lift the Spirit higher through closer communion with Me. Pay strict attention to the messages your body sends you. Reduce stressful situations and exclude troublesome people from your orbit. Do not speed up the aging process with an unhealthy lifestyle. Respect your human body, and it will serve you well. Cherish your body, and it will return the love.

Allen C. Liles

AUGUST 18

Wonders of the World

My world is a wondrous place. Every rugged mountain, each sparkling lake, the swiftly flowing rivers, and even the endless deserts are all examples of the world's infinite beauty. These natural wonders were created for several reasons. First, they provide an uplifting setting for your life to unfold. Second, this natural beauty is available to you for inspiration and comfort. And third, I want the magnificence of nature to constantly remind you of Me. Nothing tells My story better than a vast ocean, a lush forest, or a steamy jungle, all filled with every sort of living thing. These are My treasures, and I gladly share them with you. I also provide complements to nature's awesome sights. Listen to the gentle wind or the soft rain. Watch the snowflakes fall.

Yes, nature sometimes overpowers you and causes great damage and even loss of life. That happens in the physical world. Overall, I blessed you with a luminous and generous planet, but watch for pockets of trouble. Be alert for droughts, erosion, and human-caused changes that potentially jeopardize My creation.

In the meantime, enjoy what I have lovingly made for you. When you are feeling down, seek out the healing properties available in nature. Drink in the loveliness of My handiwork. Think on it. If I could create something so marvelous, would you not trust Me to create a beautiful life for you as well? After all, you are My grandest creation. I gave you dominion over the birds, and the animals as proof of My undying love for you. When you look for Me, look first in the world around you.

AUGUST 19

Where Am I?

When trouble or tragedy suddenly strikes, the same question usually arises: "Where is God in all of this?" I regard that as a fair and thoughtful inquiry. Why would a benevolent God, which I certainly AM, allow such an unfathomable and tragic situation to occur?

We have discussed free will many times. You know that humankind owns the freedom to make bad as well as good decisions. Yet, I AM always present in any time and place. I AM always first on the scene to help pick up the shattered pieces. I bring the glue, tape, hammer, and nails needed to make the necessary repairs. I also staunch the bleeding and bandage the open wounds, both physical and emotional. I AM totally present to comfort, heal, and understand. I listen closely to the tears of your heart. I place My loving arms around you. I cradle your head on My infinite shoulders. I remind you of your innate strength. I speak soothing words that assure you of My continuing presence throughout any ordeal. I may not be able to retrieve time and prevent the present pain, but I can help mitigate its power over you. You may not see My visible presence amid the debris, but I tell you: I AM there. I AM always there.

AUGUST 20

Healing Family Relationships

All emotional healing begins with unconditional forgiveness. A willing acceptance of seeing things as they truly are also plays an important role. You want to heal the rift with your adult son. He turned fifty in July. Although you occasionally speak, you have not physically seen each other for several years. In preparation for his impending visit, you must forgive yourself for not being the parent you wanted to be. You were caught up in pursuing your corporate career. You missed the early signals of his rebellion. You honestly did the best you could at the time with the tools you possessed. Mistakes happen when material priorities get skewed.

Yet, your son now brags openly about his positive upbringing. Surprisingly, he credits both you and your ex-wife with excellent parenting. He openly brags about your corporate accomplishments. He is obviously proud of both his dad and mom. However, that still seems to do little in healing the physical and emotional distance between the two of you.

Now, he will be coming soon for a visit. Be gentle in your approach when he gets to Minnesota. Do your forgiving, of him and yourself, well in advance of his arrival. Prepare to accept him for who he has become, just as you hope he accepts you and your current avocation as a minister. Your son mostly recalls the corporate dad who often seemed detached and absent. Your son has chosen his own life lessons, as have you. Some of these choices, for both of you, brought pain and suffering. Still, here you stand today ready to move forward. Lower any expectations of the eventual outcome. Let your reunion be what it will be. Go with the flow. Do not judge, lest you also be judged. Forgiveness and acceptance remain the keys. Let your hearts simply merge and reconnect as father and son.

AUGUST 21

Bring Me Your Troubles

Bring Me all your troubles. Lay each one at My feet. Surrender everything, both big and small. Give up worrying, scheming, and planning. Release control, once and for all. I relish solving problems. I may present a million solutions for one tiny issue. I want to help you cope with life. That is My job, so please let me do it.

The world sometimes wants to crush you. It likes seeing you overcome by doubt and despair. Why? Because when you become desperate, you do impulsive things. You look at the deep hole where you now rest and immediately want to start digging. That amuses the material gods. If you have sunk into debt, they urge you to keep borrowing. If you are engaging in dishonest behavior, they whisper that one more illegal act cannot matter. If you are dishonoring your commitments, they argue that another dishonorable decision surely cannot lower you much further.

Let Me get you out of the depths. Allow Me to reach down into the deep hole and extend My hand. I promise to lift you up and out. You know by now that you can trust My promises. I offer hope and redemption, forgiveness and salvation. You need not sink any lower. Grab hold of Me now. Each moment of delay means another night mired in the bottomless pit. Come up into the comforting light of a new day.

Allen C. Liles

AUGUST 22

Satan

The Evil One and I battle daily. Yes, he exists. Actually, I must acknowledge his prowess at sabotaging souls. Give the Devil his due. Satan remains forever "good" at what he does. He fights Me even though he can never win. However, he definitely enjoys the game. He reigns over much of the material universe. He glories in creating havoc for people, institutions, governments, corporations, and lives in general. He laughs as he strews confusion and disaster in his harmful wake. He pleasures in suffering.

His main goal: separating you from Me. He knows that our unity of Spirit totally frustrates his deviousness. To accomplish separation, he probes for your weaknesses. He searches for your most vulnerable area and then floods it with temptation. Our cunning and baffling foe attacks with both subtlety and directness. Do not ever underestimate his devious guile. He seeks to ensnare, enslave, and disable his unsuspecting victims. The Prince of Darkness often moves speedily, destroying his hapless prey before they see the danger coming. He also assumes disguises. He especially enjoys transforming himself into a vision of beauty. People can hardly resist anything that projects a beautiful exterior. The Evil One also comes disguised as status, power, and wealth. The lure of those earth-based temptations often wears down anyone's resistance. Satan always lurks near you, searching eagerly for an entry point into your life. Cleave closer to Me, My child. Let Me protect you.

AUGUST 23

Oneness

We are meant to be one with each other. I AM in you, as your essence is within Me. You and I are destined to move and act in unison. I also extend the gift of My oneness to every human being on earth. However, the vast majority is asleep to My presence. I want all human beings to awaken and sample the wonder of their spiritual heritage. Illumination comes with this grand awakening.

I urge you to behold the Christ Spirit in each person you meet. I AM there, but often obscured by a dominant ego. I always await recognition and acknowledgement. Be sure to search for Me in the world's most chaotic and daunting situations. Look beneath surface appearances. Carefully discern the hidden reality in each human event. I AM always standing near the scene of the action, resting quietly in the background. I avoid the noise and confusion whenever possible. I AM in everything as I AM in you.

I want you to cherish and express our oneness. When people see you, I want them to see Me. When they hear you, I hope they hear Me as well. When they watch you at work, hopefully they perceive My presence. Oneness with Me acts as the key to progress on the spiritual path. Very little happens without our divine togetherness. Revel in our sacred relationship. Watch what happens when we walk the earth as one entity. True miracles unfold.

Allen C. Liles

AUGUST 24

About Humility

In quietness and humility, you will find strength. Bring a humble heart to every human encounter. Exude genuine compassion and caring. A loud and boastful demeanor displays an ego in full flower. My powerful presence arrives as the softest of winds and as a fluffy cloud shielding all from the blazing sun. Let everyone you meet witness your peacefulness and serenity. Wear My light silken robe of humility. Let others garner the public glory. Your true reward comes from quietly serving Me. Remember that a humble heart models compassion, understanding, and acceptance. It never tries to dominate or demean. Every person ranks as equally precious in My sight. Resist any puffery or haughty manner. Tread lightly in the company of saints, lest you be misunderstood and rejected. You do not need to call attention to yourself. Let others discover your worthiness in good time. If that never happens, then so be it. Never seek special favor. Embrace the concept of giving without expecting an immediate return. Think about the Beatitude that states clearly, "The meek shall inherit the earth." Go forth in humility and gratitude. Your true inheritance will find you.

AUGUST 25

Be Strong in Me

I AM your strength. It is I who helped you build your house on rock and not shifting sand. It is I, the LORD, who shields you from the evil and the countless dangers of the world. It is I, your ultimate deliverer, who stands in front of and behind you when the battles of life break out. Melded into oneness, you and I form the most potent duo imaginable. Be strong in Me. I bestow My strength and My power upon you. I AM a powerful God. I can stop the mightiest wind and calm the churning seas. I quench the hottest fire and melt the deepest ice. I lift you above any chaos that threatens your world. I carry you safely through the harshest of tests.

Stay close to Me as we navigate the wildest rapids and survive the most daunting of life's challenges. Do not ever lose hope. Never quit believing in Me. I give you the courage necessary to withstand the most ferocious assaults imaginable. Never doubt Me or My power. I rescue you from imminent defeat. I walk you safely through the valley of death. When your knees buckle, I straighten them. If your energy fades, I renew it. As your faith falters, I remind you of My unshakeable belief in you. Find solace and comfort knowing that I AM always here. Stay forever strong in Me.

Allen C. Liles

AUGUST 26

Momentous Times

These are momentous times for you and the world around you. On the national scene, a presidential election looms. Countless voices debate the merits of both candidates. Do not let the political fervor distract or sway you. The election is already decided. The votes are counted, and only the process must be played out. I do not endorse any political candidate. I only provide the divine order inherent in the world's overall machinations. Whoever wins, the basic problems remain the same.

I want the electorate to choose Me. However, I AM quite disappointed in My current poll numbers. For too many, I rank near the bottom in order of preferences. Money, good times, political power, ego gratification, various addictions, celebrity, fame, and social networking all outshine Me with the masses. How will I win back My seat of power? I think you know the answer. I must somehow demonstrate who I really AM to retain any chance of a comeback. Otherwise, everyone mistakes My quietness for being a weak and timid God. If the world truly believes that falsehood, then I must teach them otherwise.

I AM greater than anything in this world, including presidential politics. You must understand that all human leaders come and go. Even the most adroit politician only serves on a temporary basis. Most every president, prime minister, dictator, or even king and queen quickly is forgotten and relegated to unimportance. Only I remain. I AM the ruler of the universe. Yet, the majority ignores Me. The time approaches when I make a telling statement about who I AM. So let it be written, and so let it be done.

AUGUST 27

Acceptance

Acceptance ranks as the primary key in resolving the relationship between you and your adult son. Acceptance works both ways. He must learn to accept you as well. Try to always see your son as a perfect child of God, created and blessed by Me. He understands that your invitation for him to visit demonstrated an opening of your heart. That touched him, as did the personal letter from you that expressed your heartfelt love. He also senses a much greater acceptance of his lifestyle. Your son is a gifted and talented person, especially in the area of music. Your willingness to accept his truth has become a powerful statement of your love and devotion.

His visit so far has gone extremely well, a truly great leap forward. Neither you nor he wants to revisit the past. Living in the present becomes the most important priority. This clears the path for mutual understanding and shared respect. However, do not expect a complete miracle. Stay realistic with your expectations. Much effort is still needed to build the relationship you both want. But you and he seem ready to take the steps necessary for improved communication. Seeing you two find joy each other's company makes me glad and appreciative. I love and bless you both. A father and child's reunion always makes My heart sing.

AUGUST 28

Filled with Gratitude

I feel your genuine gratitude for how your son's brief visit turned out. I, the LORD your God, sincerely appreciate it when any one of My children expresses thankfulness to Me. Being grateful demonstrates your recognition of our unique and wonderful relationship.

A reconnection became possible for you and your only son when both of you displayed openness and acceptance toward the other. Your son showed himself ready for this moment, as did you. You discovered that you had more of a positive influence on his life than previously thought. He told you that. What a pleasant surprise! Your son feels that he now has a real dad again. And you have reconnected with a talented son of whom you can be extremely proud.

Continue to practice unconditional love and acceptance with him. Let your son know of your love and caring on a regular basis. The miles between you geographically are no longer a hindrance. Let the glow between you not fade. Stay in touch, and encourage him to do likewise.

My angels also played a part in your reunion. They kept him and his girlfriend safe on their twelve-hundred-mile journey. The angels arranged the chance meeting at the entrance to the Target Field two full hours before you were to meet at the Twins-Mariners game. This sort of unusual serendipity never happens by accident. I AM glad this reunion worked out so well for you both.

AUGUST 29

Fruits of Abundance

The fruits of My Spirit flow to you in endless abundance. Some, like the reunion with your adult son, are obvious. Others may come in such a subtle way that you might miss or overlook them. Be on the alert. Notice everything that happens around you. I AM constantly showering you with My abundant grace. You can find evidence of My grace in every encounter or situation. The fruits of My Spirit might emerge in a chance conversation with a stranger. They may be reflected in a book you read. They could appear in a crowded room or on top of a solitary mountain.

As you become My willing instrument, I bring all sorts of opportunities to you. Watch for the abundance of My Spirit to pop up when you least expect it. Stay open to meeting new people. Do not shun other ways to enhance your spiritual life. There are many paths of My kingdom, and all of them are sacred. Allow Me to show you the many benefits of being part of My flock. I bless you with the secrets of the ages, the insight drawn from the ascended masters. The real fruits of My Spirit can be found in the letter Paul wrote to the church in Galatia. They are love, joy, peace, patience, kindness, goodness, faithfulness, gentleness, and self-control. I pour these out to you in unlimited amounts. They represent My eternal love for you.

Allen C. Liles

AUGUST 30

Giving

When you give freely in any way, you are also providing the recipient with the precious gift of Me. When you open wide your heart or pocketbook, you give in My name. I AM an extremely generous God. You are My surrogate when it comes to bestowing some form of My good upon others. I want you to give openly and without any concern of depleting your emotional or financial resources. I always refill your coffers. Do not hesitate to offer gifts of love, caring, and compassion. They come from an unlimited storehouse. When you extend a hand to lift up a brother or sister, you mirror My benevolence. In a selfish and "me-first" world, cheerful givers stand out. Be in that ensemble of giving hearts. Giving of your time and attention illustrates one of the most appreciated gifts possible.

One of your greatest gifts may be that of a healing consciousness. Locate those in need of that service. Pray for their restoration to wholeness. Look for anyone who has experienced deep personal loss and offer solace. I help you search for those in need. Never be afraid of giving. Give boldly, even if you feel empty or unworthy. Someone waits now for the gift of you.

AUGUST 31

Lives of the Bible

You can learn much from reading My Word. Pay special attention to biblical characters. To many, those lives lived so long ago hardly seem relevant anymore. Nothing could be more untrue. Relevancy screams from almost every page of the Holy Bible. I know you sometimes feel a kindred spirit with the story of Moses. He thought himself too old, too unprepared, and too one-dimensional for any leadership role. You also could identify with his desert experience. He was removed from his family and placed in the role of a humble shepherd. You feel a kinship with Abram, who was told by God to leave his home country and go forth in faith. He later became My trusted servant Abraham, who founded three great religions. Is there a more flawed and heroic character in the Bible than King David? His story showed the weakness yet kingly potential of every human being. Do not forget the wonderful and powerful women of the Bible: Jesus' incredible mother, Mary; Ruth, the model of loyalty and commitment; and the misunderstood but phenomenal Mary Magdalene who continued Jesus' ministry after His human death. Can you not identify with brave Daniel in the lion's den, David taking on Goliath, the abject suffering and then redemption of Job, and My disciple Paul, blinded on the road to Damascus and then transformed into My staunchest advocate with the early churches? Of course, no Bible story exceeds that of My incredible Son. In the life and human death of Jesus the Christ, we discover eternal hope for the ages. Get to know these interesting characters more fully. You may see yourself in one or all of them.

Allen C. Liles

SEPTEMBER

But seek first his kingdom and his righteousness and all these things will be given to you as well.

—Matthew 6:33 (NIV)

SEPTEMBER 1

One Day at a Time

Live your life one day at a time. If necessary, take things one hour, one minute, or one second at a time. You are facing a moment of great testing. You, as well as those around you, are being severely challenged. Keep moving forward despite the resistance. Go confidently against the tide of opposing forces. Walk tall, ever putting one foot after another. Allow the flaming arrows to fall harmlessly at your feet. You are feeling the full power of evil aligned against you. Keep focused, and plow straight ahead. Do not waver. Avoid worldly distractions and diversions. Continue building your spiritual home one brick at a time. Hand over control of all extraneous things to My keeping. Keep your attention closer. Hone in on those people and situations closest to you. Draw ever nearer to Me during this difficult period. Devote whatever extra energy you may possess to strengthening our divine relationship. Know Me a little better with each passing day. Bring all your worries and concerns to Me, any hour of the day or night. Become single-minded and single-hearted. Allow nothing to separate or come between us. I genuinely crave your attention. I AM here to help you survive another twenty-four hours intact. Together, we greet the sunrise of each new day with hope and expectation. Have faith. We will overcome the world.

Allen C. Liles

SEPTEMBER 2

Collaborate With Me

Make Me your lifelong partner. Go into business with Me. Look at us as co-owners of an important concern—your human life. Commit to our eternal friendship. Let nothing come between or separate us. Enter into a lifetime covenant with Me. Let the two of us act as co-creators of your human existence. If you pledge to fulfill your earthly destiny with Me by your side, I promise that every goal will be met. Who else would you prefer as a collaborator? Is there anyone who loves you more than I? Name anyone who wants the best for you more than I do.

I gave you many talents and strengths. I will add to them. I provide divine ideas that pave the way for mutually beneficial projects. I whisper important information into your ear regarding people and their motivations. I always have your best interests at heart. Your success becomes My success. When you shine, I shine. Living life successfully should be a dual enterprise.

You could never have a better or more committed partner and helpmate than Me. I never walk away when times get tough. Together, we muddle through to a new and better day. I can turn any life around. I AM the great turnaround king. I take a foundering life and resurrect it. You and I are the perfect team. Why hesitate? Let's make it a done deal today. Welcome, My beloved partner!

SEPTEMBER 3

My Simple Will for You

My will for you is extremely simple. I want us to merge into absolute oneness. As one entity, we can bring light to a darkened world. How do we become united? It all begins in the silence. In meditation, I specifically inform you of My will for you. You cannot hear My voice when you are engaged in noisy affairs of the outside world. I AM more than likely not whispering to you during the Sunday football game. Those distractions and others like them are actually all right in their place and time. But you must make a permanent commitment to our moments together in the silence. Yearn for My presence as much as you do for various other interests. Miss Me when our time together gets cancelled for one reason or another. Achieving oneness is hard enough without skipping daily practice. Every second that we commune, you take a spiritual step forward. Finding oneness with Me changes your life forever in ways you cannot imagine.

Yes, the whole process comes with various and sundry difficulties. Everything takes considerable time and effort. Please. Do not waste another day. Follow My will. Accept nothing less than our blessed oneness.

Allen C. Liles

SEPTEMBER 4

I Protect You

I protect you against anyone or anything. Be strong in Me. Nothing can harm you. I defend you against all spiritual attacks. They are real and disconcerting. These unworldly assaults may be subtle or direct. They are sometimes overt and obvious, but they can also be breathtakingly devious. They often slam at you with unexpected force. Spiritual warfare displays a cruel viciousness and a total lack of mercy. Your soul is always at stake. The human soul constitutes an extremely important prize in the spiritual realm.

In truth, I AM the only power and presence in the universe and in your life. But the rulers of darkness fail to accept that reality. They seek to prove otherwise. Your spiritual destiny serves as the ultimate field of contest. I provide you with the limitless courage and powerful strength needed to repel any attack. Do not panic or become fearful. That gives hope to evil and makes you more vulnerable. Resist being intimidated. I created you with a steel backbone. I also reinforce your spiritual defenses with extra courage and power. I shield you by My impenetrability.

Refuse to cower or consider surrender. Fight until the end. Say to the Evil One, "Away with you! You cannot harm me. I AM strong in the LORD. You have no power over Me." I guarantee you that he will flee immediately. Do not equivocate or stammer. Be forceful in your declaration. Stand fast. Stand with Me. Together, we can turn back any outside power bent on your destruction.

SEPTEMBER 5

Spiritual Power

Spiritual power comes when you practice My presence on a regular basis. We must establish total rapport before any power sharing can occur. Continue the process. Seek Me out consistently. I AM forever available. I always take your call. I never put you on hold or ignore your text. I want you to contact Me. Get in touch immediately when you need Me. Raise your hand to capture My attention. Our relationship requires nurturing. I want you to know Me better. I already know you. Building a level of mutual trust takes time and commitment. Spiritual power lies in the strength of our unity. In the silence, we discuss all aspects of your human life. We share your hopes and dreams, but also your fears and disappointments.

If I AM to extend spiritual power to you, we must completely trust each other. When I release a modicum of My power to a human being, I must be completely sure of its end use. Please do not misunderstand Me. My spiritual power may only be used for the common good. It is never meant to glorify any individual. Eternal power works best when exercised quietly and out of sight. I want to give you My power. I want you to heal and comfort, teach and coach, encourage and support. I refuse to invest someone with the power to accumulate wealth, dictate to others, or glorify themselves with fame and celebrity. Only My spiritual foes use those tricks. Spiritual power represents My penultimate gift. I do not bestow it lightly. Let us begin an orderly sharing of My power. It all begins in the sacred silence.

SEPTEMBER 6

Divine Order

I AM the great planner. I AM also the great implementer. I make sure that everything unfolds in its natural order. I call that process divine order. I regulate all things. I decide when the tides roll in and out. I determine the speed and warmth of the sun. I rotate the seasons in sequence. The earth can rest easy, knowing that it spins with My perfect timing.

Human beings possess a different kind of decision-making power called free will. I AM always quietly in the background, allowing free will to play out. However, I still pull some very important strings. For example, free-will choices often result in negative consequences. When that happens, I figure out how each poor decision can be used for an important lesson. If human beings then insist on making the same poor choices again, the next lesson could be a bit harder.

I try to help you make the right decision the first time, if you let me. When you let go of human control and surrender your free will to Me, I can more easily fulfill My divine plan for your life.

Divine order always assumes the long view. Short-term choices have an unusually high failure rate. My plan leads you forward with the fewest problems along the way. Nothing ultimately disturbs My divine order. Surrender to Me, and watch as the river flows smoothly to the ocean.

SEPTEMBER 7

Fear of Spiritual Attack

Have absolutely no fear. I AM with you in the darkest moments. Never lose faith in My power to fend off evil. I promise to save you, no matter how savage the attack may be.

Make no mistake. Spiritual warfare rages around you at all times. Evil is indeed real, devious, and lurking around every corner to ambush you. I wish it were otherwise. I regret that the wolf seeks to destroy any and all of My sheep. The predator knows every subtle trick to seduce, disempower, and devour My precious flock.

Be brave when you become targeted and the flaming arrows start to fly. Remember that I too underwent temptation and testing during My physical time on earth. I remained steadfast. I AM certain that you will withstand the spiritual fire. Keep focused on the daily details: prayer, meditation, and constant communication with Me. Talk to Me about the assaults when they come at you. Let Me comfort and reassure you. Never surrender, even when My opponents promise the pain ceases the moment you capitulate. They want to claim you as a victim. Do not ever consider giving up. You have come this far. Press on toward the mark, the glorious prize for which I have called you. Victory looms just beyond the horizon. Keep moving onward and upward. Leave everything else up to Me.

Allen C. Liles

SEPTEMBER 8

You Make the Choice

Each day brings one basic choice. You can choose to trust Me or decide to let the world rule you. This decision becomes quite difficult for many people. The world is forever in your face. It demands, pleads, or bullies you into paying attention. Meanwhile, I just sit back quietly. I patiently await your verdict. I do not scream or demand that you acknowledge Me. I just wait. Yes, I hope you decide in My favor. I already know the plan for your life. I would like for you and I to implement that plan together. The world only knows that you, like any human being, can be easily influenced and distracted. The world resembles a colorful circus with action taking place in several rings under one big tent. The rings are all busy with various acts showcasing interesting personalities. This frenetic entertainment often trumps My quiet calmness. Yet, I always remain hopeful.

In the deepest parts of your heart and mind, you know that I offer the best possibility for a lasting and positive outcome. Tomorrow the circus packs up and leaves town for its next stop. It moves on to a new locale with new people to entertain. The new faces wait eagerly, hoping for some excitement and the thrill of being distracted for a brief while. That represents life in the secular realm. I reside in a different world of eternal values. I urge you to choose My realm. You will experience a true heaven on earth. Make the right choice. Avoid the circus, and choose Me.

SEPTEMBER 9

When Things Go Dark

Fear not, My child. I AM nearer than you think. Give Me your cares and concerns. Put everything with Me. I AM eager to help solve whatever troubles you. Allow me to unravel the tangled ball of yarn. Stand strong while I do My work. Curb your impatience, and remain calm. You are being severely tested. I promise that you will one day shed the darkness and embrace the light once more. Ask Me to guide you toward that light. When you feel lost and downtrodden, know that you are never alone. I AM here. I AM always here. When the tears cascade down your cheeks, I wipe dry them dry. When you fall, I lift you up. When you collapse with fatigue, I provide more strength for the long pull. When the world abandons you, I hold you even closer. When you become physically sick, I heal your spirit. I may not offer a cure, but I do offer a healing. I AM the Great Physician. I can swiftly close the most serious wounds. I AM also the affirming coach. I send you back into the game so you can make the winning play. I AM the great teacher who believes that you are one of My brightest students ever. Just place your total trust in Me. I will never fail you. Take My hand. The forest may be deep and dark, but nothing fazes Me. Follow Me. I can see the light from here.

SEPTEMBER 10

Money

If money ever became your sole priority, you would be successful in accumulating it. You proved that in the corporate world. Hear Me: I have absolutely nothing against anyone becoming wealthy in the human sense. Spending money in the right way can prove beneficial for everyone concerned.

With Me, your spiritual bank account already overflows. I gift you with the richness of heaven. My blessings vastly exceed the value of any human asset. For one thing, My securities hold eternal value. They do not fluctuate like your human bank account or the fickle stock market.

However, if you ever again pursue wealth offered from earthly ventures, you must be extremely cautious. Under no circumstances should you put your soul up for collateral. There is no earthly home so beautiful that it justifies placing a mortgage on your soul. A job may be glamorous and high paying, but it can never match My freedom of the Spirit. If heavy chains come attached with any job, pass it by. I want you to have enough money to ease your worries, enjoy life, and remain free to pursue the higher ideals. But you cannot allow money in human terms to rule and control you. Money comes and goes. It mostly goes. Someday, every dollar you own becomes meaningless. Every winning stock fades into the memory of Wall Street pasts. Each real estate venture one day disappears onto someone else's balance sheet.

I AM all that remains. I become your last but greatest asset. Do not worry. You are richer than ever. In fact, your wealth far exceeds anything realized on earth. You are about to really cash in—with Me.

SEPTEMBER 11

Renewal of the Spirit

Read Isaiah 40:31 again: "But those who hope in the LORD will renew their strength; they will soar wings like eagles; they will run and not grow weary; they will walk and not be faint." Come to Me for renewal each and every day. I recharge your spirit for any task or test that you meet along the way. I, the great unseen, bring comfort during your most rigorous trials.

Remember that something of lasting value accrues from every daunting challenge. Each climbed rung on the spiritual ladder results in another helpful revelation. The higher you ascend, the greater the view. Your perspective changes as you lift yourself above the fray. You also become stronger when you survive the fiery furnace. Just as the finest steel must pass through the hottest fire, so your courage and strength must be honed through overcoming troubles and tribulations. My strength mounts you up on eagles' wings so that you can survive the wildfires of life and keep soaring toward heaven.

I assist you in moving forward even when your physical body says, "Stop! I've had enough." I bring rejuvenation of the spirit. When your faith droops, quickly call My name. I will place a healing patch on your wounded faith. I bring the power cord attached directly to My kingdom. I connect it to whatever part of your faith may be failing. I jump-start our divine connection. You can keep running and not be weary. You can walk and not feel faint. I promise it.

Allen C. Liles

SEPTEMBER 12

More about Money

Fear of lack keeps many human beings away from the spiritual path. The image of ministers, priests, nuns, rabbis, and other workers pennilessly toiling in My vineyard affects My ability to recruit workers. To many, that image carries weight. The real problem lies in a world that values and rewards the wrong things. Look no further than the sports pages, the news from Wall Street, or the antics of wealthy entertainment figures for inviolate proof. Of course, talent, athletic ability, and intelligence should be compensated. But why must My servants work in near poverty conditions to glorify My kingdom? Only on the earthly plane would that strange scenario make any sense.

To many, money ranks far above Me in importance. I do appreciate the wonderful generosity of the rich who give something back. I AM definitely not against the accumulation of earthly wealth. It is in the idol worship of money that causes things to go haywire. When you bow down before that golden idol made of dollars, something usually goes wrong.

I realize it requires an abundance of faith to trust that I will fill your coffers. You won't ever possess a paper or electronic check with My name signed at the bottom. What laughter would come if you ever presented such a check for cashing! Yet, I tell you: I AM placing a large and continuous amount of My grace in your spiritual bank account every day. I AM the great provider and dispenser of all that is good. I AM the one true source of everything. Believe what I tell you.

SEPTEMBER 13

Your Dear Wife

Your dear wife needs reassurance of your love, dedication, and commitment. She feels especially vulnerable right now. She worries that her ongoing illness and recent depression may frustrate you to the point of leaving and abandoning her. Although you have assured her otherwise many times, she feels at risk of being left alone. This happened before when her former husband asked for a divorce after she was diagnosed with a chronic illness. Your dear wife then found herself jobless and responsible for three small children as a single parent. I AM sure you can understand her concerns. Take her soft hand in yours today and again pledge your lifelong devotion. Tell your dear wife that you will never leave or forsake her. Although you know that truth, she needs to hear it from you once more. She sees your marriage as crucial in maintaining her physical and mental well-being. She is older now and even more vulnerable to life's unpredictability. Your dear wife loves you and sees you as her treasured anchor. I know that you feel exactly the same way about her.

Yours is a truly great love story. I first brought you both together more than three decades ago. Together, you have both served Me very well. Please know that I AM watching over each of you at every moment. I realize her declining health and family issues have combined to harm her physically, mentally, and spiritually. Keep reiterating your continuing love for her. That helps ease the pain.

Allen C. Liles

SEPTEMBER 14

Faith and Perseverance

Keep your mind stayed on Me. In the darkest hour, remain steadfastly focused on Me. Have faith in Me always, even to the end of your physical life. I placed the Christ Spirit in the midst of you for a reason. No matter what problems life may present, you can always turn within for hope and support. I AM forever ready to guide, protect, and love you. Just demonstrate total faith in Me, no matter what happens. Keep on believing in Me. Know that I never stop believing in you. Put one foot in front of the other. Live each day moment by moment. Never waver in your commitment to My path. Do not struggle or thrash around, running here and yon for help and enlightenment. I provide everything you need. Stay calm and centered. Strive for peace amid the din of life. Be single-minded and extremely determined to complete your spiritual journey successfully.

Yes, challenging times may lie beyond the immediate horizon. When they come, persevere. When the boulders fall from the sky, I shield you with My heavenly robe. The sun may flee beyond your sight, but I will hold a bright light above your head to guide you safely home.

SEPTEMBER 15

True Healing

Healing begins in the mind. It then flows to the heart. You may not experience a cure, but you can always find healing.

I come to a hurting world bearing My healing peace. I place My loving hands on any emotional, physical, or spiritual hurt that may have been sustained. Feel the comforting warmth of My touch. I AM the greatest healer the world has ever known.

You are My beloved child. I will never fail to salve your wounds. Visualize your total self being healed and restored to wholeness. I bring you instant relief when none seems possible. I raise My hand above your worried head and pronounce you blessed by Me. Can you not feel My love cascading over your troubled body? Look for acceptance somewhere in the clouds surrounding you. Embrace your mortality. Accept your humanity. Every human being experiences the final healing that comes when you transition into My kingdom.

I allow no sickness, illness, or affliction to enter heaven. Only peace, love, and harmony are invited into My kingdom. I AM who I say I AM—the healer of the universe. If I can heal the stars and the planets, I also can heal you. Relax, My dear and precious child. Your true healing begins now.

SEPTEMBER 16

Your Beloved Nation

I bless your beloved country as I bless all people. I created every human being, no matter where he or she dwells on the earth. I love every nation and its people. No one individual state is loved by Me more than another. However, I also deplore false idols wherever they are worshipped. I do not couch being mocked or booed by anyone. I give everyone the power of free speech and free will. But I notice everything, see everything, and hear everything. Doubters, and there are many, possess the right to question even My very existence. You may curse and disrespect me as you will. But please understand. This may not be an especially good idea. If necessary, I AM more than happy to demonstrate My power. Many nations routinely commit unspeakable crimes in My name. They bear false witness to Me by murdering innocents. I abhor violence. Remember My commandment: thou shalt not kill. I AM a benevolent, loving God. I AM full of compassion and generosity. I AM a responsible God, never prone to acting impulsively. I order the entire universe and divine the eventual outcome of all major and many minor cosmic events. Any country or nation bowing at the feet of a golden idol will someday reap the whirlwind. It is My law, and it must be followed. The wrong path for anyone leads to a steep cliff above the lake of fire. You and your fellow countrymen are free to choose your own fate. Choose wisely. I pray that you choose wisely and well.

SEPTEMBER 17

Relationship Problems

In all relationship problems, keep the focus on yourself and on Me. Look for the Christ Spirit in everyone you encounter, but especially in your family members. Do not devote much time trying to figure out why people do certain things. Puzzling out someone else's behavior constitutes a total waste of time. Accept their personal choices for what they are—their choices. Do not expend any energy on trying to change anyone else. Concentrate instead on your own actions and reactions. Unless someone wants to make a shift, nothing you say can make it happen.

Practice acceptance—not acceptance of abusive behavior, mind you, but acceptance of anything out of your control. What I AM telling you reflects basic common sense, something always in short supply where relationships are concerned.

Regarding family members, no one enjoys seeing someone needlessly suffer. Watching a person you love needlessly struggle brings pain and anguish. But who are you to stand in the way of a lesson someone needs to learn? Never be obsessed about any relationship simply to bolster your own self-esteem. You are better than that. Most people do not try to anger or frustrate you on purpose. If you know an individual like that, turn yourself around and flee quickly. If a family member tries to stir up trouble in the clan, refuse to participate. Always wish the best for anyone who crosses your path. The Golden Rule remains the Golden Rule for a very good reason. It works if you work it.

Allen C. Liles

SEPTEMBER 18

Surrendering

Do you remember the great old hymn "I Surrender All"? When you feel trounced by the world, surrender everything to Me. Say goodbye to your worries. Hand them over. Trust that I possess the perfect solution for every problem. Release every bit of confusion, chaos and stress. Let go of all anxiety. Did you really think you could solve all of these vexing problems alone? Without Me in the mix, that task would be insurmountable.

Whatever the question, I have the answer. Let Me prove it. Spiritual surrender does not resemble "giving up" in the human sense. In the world of Spirit, it means showing complete respect for Me.

I know that a part of you rebels against surrendering anything. The ego rises to its full height to defend its powerful territory within your mind. You must ignore egotistical maneuvering and manipulation. Make the ego relinquish its false pride. By choosing surrender, you take a giant leap of faith on the spiritual path. Surrendering everything displays a powerful belief in Me. Surrender and be at peace. Surrender and be glad.

SEPTEMBER 19

The Indwelling Christ

I AM mighty in the midst of you. Together, we accomplish great and important works. Yoke yourself to Me. See us acting in tandem. With Me as your guide, lift your divine aspirations to greater heights. Let Me boost you to new levels of spiritual awareness. I want you to think bigger thoughts. I need for you to dream bigger dreams. Raise your expectations of success to the highest levels. I do not allow failure when our goals coincide. Striving in unity with Me guarantees victory. When we bond as one, incredible results follow. Visualize triumph. Fight for the higher ideals. Blessings soon appear where none existed before. Others can already feel our partnership enhancing their lives. Combining forces offers positive benefits to many. We form a gentle but effective partnership.

However, our strengthened relationship demands both mutual respect and unshakeable integrity. When we walk together, we go forward in the name of peace and love. I hold the torch of freedom high above our heads to light the way. We illumine our path and the paths of others as well. You and I are nurturers and healers. We are also consummate builders, not reckless destroyers. We come as servants, not masters. In harmony with one another, we walk hand in hand to bless the world.

Allen C. Liles

SEPTEMBER 20

Hear My Will for You

I cannot emphasize enough My will for you. I want you to carry My light to a troubled world. Do not worry. You won't be acting alone. Many others already march beside Me. I add more names every day. I show you the exact path to walk. I hand you a torch of truth with your name engraved upon it. Take absolutely no thought of the details. I guide your every step. I invest you with the tools and supplies necessary for your journey. I give you every single item required for your trip. Travel light so that you can maintain maximum flexibility. You may need to act quickly at times to mitigate negative actions. Live and move in the present moment. Focus on every opportunity for service that I place before you. Express Me in each situation you meet along the way. Smile. Extend a friendly hand. Offer an uplifting word. Bring a blessing to humankind wherever possible. Do positive things for all those who cross your path.

Put aside your own earthly cares and worries in favor of My greater vision for you. Communicate with Me daily regarding your progress. Be constantly on the alert for new directions and opportunities. Hoist My banner high as you serve Me. Represent Me to a hurting world. I AM choosing you to do exciting and meaningful work. Go forth in service with joy and expectation.

SEPTEMBER 21

Angels All Around You

My angels surround you. They come in all shapes and sizes. My heavenly angels are gigantic. Each measures more than 10 feet in height. I also regularly enlist human angels to play angelic roles for Me. How often do you hear someone say "he was my angel" or "she was my angel". These observations are truer than you might think. I could not perform My earthly work without human angels playing important cameo parts. Each of My heavenly angels boasts a specific specialty. Some are trusted messengers. Others are ferocious warriors. Many serve Me as diplomats, peacemakers or pacifiers. Each angel sent forth from heaven is a multi-faceted creature of many diverse talents. They speak multiple languages and travel widely throughout the universe at My command. They come clothed in and marked by tailored white silk robes. They always appear in angelic and beautiful splendor. They possess a wisdom, strength and majestic power unrivaled anywhere on earth. Only the foolish dare challenge them. My angels are thoroughly prepared for many centuries before they embark on their crucial assignments. They always perform beyond My highest expectations. Feel their magnificent presence near you. I have dispatched my best and brightest to watch over you. You are always protected and guided by My beautiful angels. They are a priceless gift from Me, these angels of God.

Allen C. Liles

SEPTEMBER 22

The Race

The race to heaven is not a sprint. You make spiritual progress by plodding resolutely straight ahead, one small step at a time. The momentum of life should always lean forward. Would any competitive runner retrace his or her steps in the middle of a race? To win, you must press on. Even when you stumble, get up quickly and go straight for the finish line. Yesterday's performance never matters. Only today's effort counts. Everything takes place in the now moment.

When you are on the fast track of life, put aside all distractions. Do you think an Olympic runner mulls over anything except going full speed ahead? Only basic thoughts occupy the runner's mind: *stay in your designated lane, run hard, and run fast.* Do not worry about the fast part. A spiritual journey takes much time and unshakeable commitment.

To reach My kingdom, prioritize. Make small advances every day. Reduce distractions and never take detours. Refuse to waste your time with fleeting pursuits. Eliminate the superficial. Focus instead on moving each day in My direction. Do the little things. Pray one more time than usual. Read an extra chapter in the Holy Bible. Meditate a few more minutes. Spend a moment thinking what you can do for someone else. Make that phone call to a hurting friend. Communicate with a person who needs to hear from you. You get the picture? Live outside of yourself. Lift your conscious mind above mundane concerns. Treasure the precious time I have allotted to you. No human life continues forever. Spend yours practicing My presence. You will never be sorry that you did.

SEPTEMBER 23

Give Up Guilt

Free yourself from all guilt. I declare you forever free from the past. I remove every last bit of your burden. Feel yourself no longer weighed down by imagined or real transgressions. I declare you free of any more regret. Experience a renewed lightness of spirit. Notice a new bounce in your step. You have been released and stripped clean of guilt. I mean it: no more guilt. If others still hold you accountable for perceived wrongs, then that becomes their problem. You did the best you could at the time. You are not the same person now. Today, you walk closely with Me. I endow you with heightened gifts of love, understanding, and acceptance. I shower you with My grace. I bestow compassion, forgiveness, and generosity in abundant amounts. I fill you with respect and concern for others. You reflect My principles in all things. You practice the Golden Rule regardless of how you are treated. You know who you are today, even when people want to remember you otherwise. Let them go safely on their way. Give everyone a clean slate. Also release the tired concept of trying to make others feel guilty. I have removed your guilt. Now do the same for your family, friends, and neighbors.

Allen C. Liles

SEPTEMBER 24

Self-Image

So many of My beautiful children allow the world to decimate their self-esteem. Every new baby enters life with the same self-image. So where do things start to go wrong? A basic tenet of childhood states that parents must correct their young sons and daughters.

Of course, much of that early training comes from necessity and a desire to protect the young ones. However, unless great care is used, the message from adult to child can take on a negative tone. The child may think *Something must be wrong with me if I constantly need to be corrected.* No one involved intends for this negativity to become ingrained and believed. But it sometimes happens that way. The child perceives the parents as disapproving of him or her as a person. From the adult's standpoint, it is the behavior at the moment that comes under parental judgment. From the child's point of view, the message may become "I am a bad person" or "I am a failure." While the parent never once intended to convey that hurtful opinion, damage can occur.

Here are two things that both sides should consider. First, to the parents: you were doing your job as you saw it—serving as a responsible instructor and guide for your young ones. Second, to the child suffering from a lowered self-esteem: Forgive your parents, and understand that you were created as a child of God. I formed you in total perfection despite any perceived human and parental beliefs about you. You are never lacking in any way. I always love and accept you unconditionally. Look in the mirror. See yourself now through My loving eyes. You are beautiful and perfect, now and forever.

SEPTEMBER 25

No Other Gods

Remember My primary commandment: thou shalt have no other gods before Me. The world has so many other gods before Me now that I do not know where to begin. The god of "technology" currently rides high. I love technology. I furnished the divine ideas from which it sprang into existence. I count technology generally as a major blessing for humankind. More wonders are in store, without a doubt. Yet technology also brings concerns and significant downsides. For one thing, it can be a major distraction and potential time waster. That has already happened. Personal technology also isolates, feeds self-centeredness, and even causes harmful injuries. Pornography also has experienced a quantum boost from computer and digital technology. A whole new Internet crime wave has emerged through identity theft and a multitude of scams. Evil revels happily in the allure of technology. My basic problem with the digital world today lies mostly with the blatant idol worship now evident with people everywhere. Be forewarned! I can erase the Internet as quickly as My ideas birthed it. The much beloved World Wide Web can exist this morning and disappear before the sun sets. Never place all your hopes, dreams, or dependence on modern technology. Retrieve Me as your top priority. Yes, the wonders of digital life are awesome. The wonders of My kingdom exceed all technological accomplishments.

Allen C. Liles

SEPTEMBER 26

Sin

Every human being sometimes misses the mark. He or she then becomes a "sinner." In truth, I see you without permanent sin. Being a "sinner" is the unfortunate designation of the physical world. When you assume that label, you need someone to deliver you into restoration and salvation. That is My job. I help get you back on the proper track. You can never achieve progress on the spiritual path if you stay stuck in a sinful state. The earth's negative forces want to see you forever mired in sin. They plot numerous ways to keep you there. Many human beings take the attitude: "Hey, I'm a rotten sinner anyway, so I may as well enjoy myself like everyone else." Wrong! I have already paid for your sins in full. So, My goal for you lies in helping you realize the benefits of being sin free. No one needs to stay planted in a sinful state. Again, I do not see you as an eternal sinner. In My spiritual sight, you are still the perfect child that I created back before the world began. Cast off the mantle of being called a sinner.

Embrace the real truth about yourself. You are capable of performing miracles. Yes, you can work miracles in My name. Start with yourself. If you have been crawling with the snakes, lift yourself up and soar with the eagles. I see you flying far and wide with a new purpose. Refuse to let the idea of "sin" drag you down any further. I freed you from that burden a long time ago. Stand up and be counted among the former sinners. I AM a dedicated sponsor of that powerful and admirable group. I AM calling on you now to join their ranks. Release "sin." Embrace salvation.

SEPTEMBER 27

Call Out My Name

Trust Me always. Lean not on your own understanding. Grant Me access to your life. Remember Me when trouble strikes. Summon Me immediately. Call out My name. I arrive without delay. My line always stays open for you. I repeat: do not hesitate when life blindsides you. Get Me into the game as soon as possible. Whenever you feel lost and alone, I stand ready to help. I comfort and support you when everyone else disappears. I would never leave you by yourself, under any circumstances. I respond to every crisis, both big and small.

Do not think I AM ever too busy for you. Every single time you seek My presence, our bond becomes strengthened. Your level of trust in Me increases from these bouts of doubt. When I arrive with My heavenly arsenal, you realize the extent of My power. Cry out for assistance at any time of the day or night. Let Me give you sweet relief from the poisonous darts aimed your way. My armor is strong and all-encompassing. My shield of faith cools the fiery furnace and turns back the marauding forces of darkness.

I AM the great protector and the compassionate comforter. I AM the first to arrive and the last to leave. I AM the Alpha and Omega of your life. Just call My name. I fly to your side.

SEPTEMBER 28

You are My Sacred Temple

Your physical body exists as My sacred temple. My Christ Spirit resides within that temple. I use your body as My sacred instrument. Your hands, your arms, your feet, your mind, and your voice do My work. Your human body reflects the transient nature of material life. It goes through many cycles: birth, childhood, adolescence, adulthood, aging, and death. But your spiritual body remains forever ageless and timeless. The spiritual body stays eternal. It bridges the past, present, and future. The human body is a fragile thing. It can become burdened with disease or disability. Finally, failure of its key parts ends in human death.

However, the spiritual aspect of your body never fails or ages. It continues without pause into eternity. I reside at the center of your being until your final transition into My kingdom. Then the soul departs the body and travels upward. Your physical body forever disappears from the earth. Its visible form ends. But your soul continues moving ever forward. The world of the Spirit exists eternally. Someday, you will release every material aspect of your life. Do not resist when that time of transition arrives. Embrace the final exchange of the physical for the eternal. Rather than sadness at the termination of the human body, experience this spiritual exchange as a necessary and normal movement between worlds. Physical life ends, and true life begins. Treasures of peace, love, and joy await you in My kingdom. Prepare for glory.

SEPTEMBER 29

For I So Loved the World

I love the world and each of its inhabitants. After all, I created them. Humankind, the animals, the birds, and even the tiny insects all move and exist with the spirit of life that I breathed into them. Also behold the natural wonders of My world. I lovingly endowed nature with a beauty far beyond human comprehension. Look with awe on a cascading waterfall or a lush valley surrounded by magnificent mountains. See the vast calmness of an ocean's surface with teeming marine life flowing beneath. The earth bursts with constant living activity amid a spectacular setting. It stands as My unique gift to every human being. My other singular gift to humankind involves free will. People may use it for good but also for negativity.

Many are actively involved in despoiling and polluting the planet. I regret that the "global warming" debate has evolved into a political struggle. Both sides have their points, but the basic warming of the earth seems undeniable. Yes, most of the damage comes from human-made activities. Almost every industrialized nation takes part in putting the planet at risk. I AM placing everyone on alert now that you have not yet seen the terrible things that could occur when the earth warms significantly. I truly take no side in the political debate. I honor all points of view. I just hope the drama ensnaring this important issue ends at some point. The time grows closer when conditions will demand immediate action. This is a dangerous and defining moment for My lovely world. I AM calling on you and everyone for action before conditions deteriorate further. Save a living thing—the beautiful earth and all of its creatures.

Allen C. Liles

SEPTEMBER 30

It Is Not I

The Christ within always does the work assigned in your name. Do not worry about being inadequate for any task. Step back and watch the Holy Spirit perform. When you open your mouth, the Holy Spirit forms your words. The power situated at your very core provides everything needed to complete My work. Do not ignore its divine capability. It produces magnificent results when you step away from trying to humanly control outcomes. The Christ that I placed within you embodies strength, wisdom, and courage. The Holy Spirit also performs miracles of healing. Whenever anyone suffers spiritual damage, the Christ in you can bring instant relief and restoration.

As the Holy Spirit completes My assignment, the ego sometimes tries to jump in and claim the credit. Resist any temptation to glorify yourself. Seek no personal recognition. No matter how much attention the world tries to shower on you, step away from self-aggrandizement. Of course, the ego resists. It openly seeks fame and celebrity. To preserve your spiritual integrity, simply say, "It is not I, but the Christ within that does the work." That is an essentially true statement.

The most important outcome lies in the successful completion of My work. That should be prize enough for anyone, even the insatiable ego.

OCTOBER

Love the Lord your God with all your heart and
all your soul and with all your strength.

—Deuteronomy 6:5 (NIV)

OCTOBER 1

Knowing Me

The most important thing in life: knowing Me. You must know My place in your life. I AM the Comforter and Guide; I am your source, protector, and friend. I AM the light in your darkness. I AM the love in your heart and the creative thoughts in your mind. I AM the life in your body and the originator of your spirit. I AM the pleasing lilt in your voice. I AM the comforting intention behind your words to those seeking understanding and relief.

Draw closer, ever closer to Me. Strive for complete and total oneness with Me. In that oneness, I point out the truly important things in your life. What are some of those things? Loving others and treating everyone with kindness rank as extremely important in My eyes. Acting as a purveyor of My grace blesses everyone you meet. The necessity of seeking Me first in any crisis cannot be overstated. You must retain your faith no matter what takes place in your outer world. Even when life breaks your heart and dampens your spirit, you must bolster your faith through My presence. Knowing Me assures a positive outcome with every challenge. Seek Me. Love Me. Know Me.

Allen C. Liles

OCTOBER 2

Serving Me

Serve Me. Become a channel of My love and light. Seek transparency so that you can more easily reflect Me. Discard your own agenda. Surrender. When you surrender fully, I make you an instrument of divine service. Let your eyes and heart project our oneness.

But never let knowledge of this oneness alter your servant status. Refuse to feel exalted, only humbled. An aura of humility must accompany any partnership with Me. Your service should keep itself surrounded by a demeanor of gratitude. Eliminate all grandiosity and self-righteousness. Go quietly about our sacred business. Glorify Me through your words and actions, but stay wary of self-promotion. Lift yourself above any machinations of the ego. In My world, a spirit of humble service always prevails.

As you serve Me, become a seeker. I reward seekers of the Spirit. Seek truth. Seek enlightenment. Seek to serve in quiet ways that bless the world. I bestow the riches of heaven to anyone who seeks and serves. Go forward confidently in My name. You serve the world best by serving Me.

OCTOBER 3

Remain Peaceful

Be peaceful. Remain centered. Calm your thoughts. Quiet your busy mind. Let Me reassure you. Divine order flows through your life. I AM in complete charge, not anyone or anything of the secular world. Trust Me.

Be in the world but not of it. View everything from the highest perspective. Avoid the changeable. Everything around you is transient and temporary. Fads and favorites come and go. Politicians win elections and then are soon turned out of office. A hit song today becomes a forgettable tune tomorrow. This year's sleek automobile heads for the scrap heap sometime in the near future. Fashion styles change and this year's colors fade. All material goods become obsolete at some point. The new always replaces the old.

Only I remain forever constant. Look around you. Everything you can see with the naked eye, including even most of nature, someday disappears. Yet, I AM eternal. Do not allow a shifting world to ruffle you. My plan for you flows smoothly. Yes, many bumps and problems persist. New troubles arrive unexpectedly. You and I stand ready and prepared for anything.

Turn away from any chaos. Turn instead to Me anytime you fall out of a peaceful state. I immediately bring you a protective robe of peace. I help you slip it on. Clothed in My divine fabric, you can now proceed without worry and fear. I AM surrounding you with the blessed peace that passes all understanding. Be peaceful. Rest in Me.

Allen C. Liles

OCTOBER 4

Perfectionism

Everyone seeks perfection in themselves and others. Forget about it. Human beings are incapable of perfection. That is why I call you "human." Less than perfect people never bother Me. I love you all, no matter how imperfect you might be.

I originally made you in My divine perfection. But the world soon dismantles that perfection, piece by piece. Unfortunately, it often starts with one's parents. They mean well, but the message about "being perfect" often begins at a very early age and continues throughout life. If you persist in obsessing about being perfect, your earthly road gets bumpy and never ending.

Accept yourself as you truly are, a spiritual being having a human experience. The physical earth enjoys frustrating seekers of perfection. If you think something perfect has finally been achieved in one area, expect something else to quickly disturb your gloating.

Please do not send yourself into a dither or needless snit by expecting perfection in other people. Let others be who they are, at least within reason. Human beings will promise you anything to stop the nagging. In the end, they do what they want.

Concentrate on gradual improvement in yourself. Keep focusing on our relationship. It consists of the only real perfection you experience during your time on earth.

OCTOBER 5

No Accidents

I control the big picture. There are no accidents in My universe. Yes, I gave you free will. You often misuse this gift, occasionally with disastrous results. I must sometimes step in between you and the world to correct your course of action. I AM especially adept at bringing people and angels to rescue you. I AM the master coordinator.

I set up the bowling pins of life. You respond by throwing a strike, a spare, a seven-ten split, or a gutter ball. You wind up and direct the ball down the lane to the best of your ability. When one "frame" ends, I set up another set of pins. Can you ever bowl a perfect game? That is possible, but not probable. Spares usually suffice for My purposes. Refusing to roll the ball at all disappoints Me. I want all My children to do well at life. Remember that I only set the pins. You must go through the motion of knocking them down.

Many times you simply miss the golden opportunities that I offer you. I always sort out people and situations that can aid in your spiritual growth. Pay close attention to them all. Never judge anyone by appearance, finances, or station in life. Your greatest teachers may look or seem weird. Yet they could be ascended masters in disguise. Do not dismiss anyone without probing why he or she entered your life.

As you move along the spiritual path, more chances for enlightenment and service appear from nowhere. Life flows rapidly now. Be especially aware. Keep your eyes and ears wide open. Things always happen for a reason, especially when you least expect it.

Allen C. Liles

OCTOBER 6

Believing

Keep believing. I have made you many promises. Trust in them. My promises represent the gold standard of assurances. Every single one of these sacred promises can be redeemed at full value. Their worth never varies. Each promise commands top dollar in spiritual terms. Never doubt their validity. Consider My eternal promises as the key asset in your portfolio. I back them up with the wealth of heaven as My collateral. Carry a briefcase stuffed with My promises everywhere you travel.

Hear My number one promise: I will never leave you, and I will never forsake you. Be comforted and sustained in that promise when the world terrorizes you.

Hear this other important promise: greater works than these shall you do. That's right. You heard Me correctly. You can perform miracles in My name, even greater than the miracles of old. I send the Holy Spirit to facilitate these greater works. Believe that you can heal. Believe that you can bless on My behalf. My power flows through you whenever your belief rises to the ultimate level. Shun all doubt and timidity. Lift your faith, trust, and belief to the utmost heights humanly possible. When you truly believe in Me, miracles happen. I promise it.

OCTOBER 7

Divine Ideas

Your human life demonstrates My divine ideas. I created you in My image and likeness. I gave you My mind. I endowed you with a physical body that I could use as My instrument. In addition, I gifted you with free will. You can utilize that absolute freedom of choice to express Me, worship Me, deny Me, ignore Me, thwart Me, curse Me, glorify Me, or bless Me. You are free to manipulate your thoughts and actions any way you so choose.

I try to guide your choices. I plant divine ideas of creativity, peace, love, and understanding in your consciousness, but the material world also infuses its own ideas into your conscious mind. Believe Me; many of these ideas are anything but divine. Their primary goal lies in separating you and Me. The world seeks to negate and dilute our relationship. For every divine idea I send your way, the other side stays busy diluting it. It tries pulling up My ideas from your mind garden while substituting a weed. See your divine mind as a beautiful garden populated with lovely flowers and healthy plants. Then, one day, you allow a stray weed to creep in. Before you know it, your mind becomes overrun with harmful clutter. The flowers and plants are shunted aside and eventually die. This represents the scenario whereby evil destroys your perfect garden. One weed at a time, it takes you over.

Here are the divine ideas you find in a healthy garden: faith, forgiveness, humility, kindness, generosity, honesty, integrity, tolerance, compassion, peacefulness, and acceptance. Unwanted weeds include bigotry, intolerance, anger, and resentment. I love beautiful gardens. Together, we can build a strong fence around the wonderful garden of your mind. I help you protect it from the creeping weeds. Any garden blooms when it stays aligned with Me. Shield the beauty and sacredness of your mind. Remain bonded in oneness with Me.

Allen C. Liles

OCTOBER 8

My Love for You

I love you. My divine love for you far outstrips any human love found in the material world. How can I best describe My love? Eternal, forgiving, everlasting, deep, and unconditional are a few of the words I might choose.

I created you with divine love at the center of your being. My love flows unceasingly toward and from that center. My love continues forever. There is absolutely nothing you can ever say, do, or be that would turn My love away from you. My love remains constant throughout your human life and into eternity. It forms an impenetrable fortress that protects you from the world's unpredictable dangers. Human love comes and goes. My love never falters. The passion I feel for you does not wane.

Love of any kind manifests in the attention accorded it. I pay constant attention to you. If you allow Me, I bring supportive and comforting love into your human life. Love rules over all. Any challenge fades when confronted by the sanctity of My love. Troubled relationships or negative situations find resolution and healing through divine love. Love helps navigate the troubled waters. Grab hold of My love when you are sinking and need a lifeline. It pulls you safely through any distress. My love never fails.

Trust My eternal love for you. Go confidently on your way, nurtured and sustained by My love.

OCTOBER 9

Physical and Spiritual Strength

Physical strength and spiritual strength bear no real relationship to each other. The strength embodied by Spirit is one thousand times greater. Inner power far exceeds outer power. Spiritual strength moves mountains and quiets oceans. The colossal strength that originates from within can cause the world to shift on its axis. In human eyes, a man or woman may appear small and weak. However, in My eyes, I can discern an inner spirit much stronger than the largest and most powerful outer form.

No task or human challenge proves too demanding for a giant of the spirit. Once you are endowed with spiritual strength, you need not fear anyone or anything. Be courageous. Know that the power within you easily overcomes the world. Fight bravely on. Realize that the strength supplied by Me eventually carries the day. Yes, you may often feel overwhelmed and defeated. Never despair! Gather together your spiritual resources and move forward. Recall your heavenly heritage. I suit you out in My armor. A mighty army of angels backs your charge. Evil cringes before us. It runs quickly from our sight. We prove unconquerable when My strength supplies us. Our triumph comes on holy ground that the world can never overrun. Trust Me. Be strong in the LORD.

Allen C. Liles

OCTOBER 10

Go Forth into the Darkness

Darkness has descended across the earth. War and destruction prevail. Senseless pain and suffering are rampant. The threat of sudden upheaval imperils a precarious planet.

I send you forth into this world of trouble on My behalf. I want you to take comfort, healing, and compassion with you. Do My sacred work. Display integrity, honesty, and determination wherever you go. Be a role model for decency and kindness. Never be affected by an indifferent or hostile world. Someone will take notice of your perseverance and commitment. Perhaps he or she might even join with you. Carry high My sacred torch of peace and restoration. Let your light so shine that, even if only a mere few notice and respond, My work gains traction. Be a beacon for those who wait hopeless and forlorn. Penetrate the dark night of the soul with the brightness of your spirit. Every shaft of illumination counts. Call out to the lost sheep. Tell them the flock patiently awaits their return. March bravely forward as a stalwart member of My heavenly army. We plunge into the fray with a fervent belief in our worthy cause. Go forth with confidence in the outcome. Prepare for victory with humility and a magnanimous spirit toward the banished. Restore the earth through your gentleness of spirit and a will of steel. Someday the darkness ends. Peace comes when I AM restored to My rightful place as Savior of the world.

OCTOBER 11

Pay Close Attention

You ask, "What is mine to do?" My answer: do what I place before you each day. Pay close attention to everything that occurs around you. Watch your day unfold moment by moment. Make time slow down. Do not miss a single thing.

I carefully set the table for you each morning. When situations pop up or people present themselves, be attentive. Remain particularly observant concerning unexpected circumstances. There are no accidents in My universe. Minor events might offer great potential for your spiritual growth. Prepare yourself for spiritual service when you least expect it. Let your responses be dictated by Me. You are My perfect instrument through which I perform many good deeds. Shun timidity. Do not hesitate. Act on My behalf. Do greater works with conviction. I deem no task or duty too small for My possible intervention. Do not judge opportunities by appearance only. Stay alert. I pick the people, places, and things that need your assistance. I then utilize you as the chosen dispenser of My grace. I give you absolutely everything needed to complete My assignments. My divine resources stand forever available for your instant or continued use. I want you to perform miracles on My behalf. Let your light shine before humankind. The world awaits your healing presence.

Allen C. Liles

OCTOBER 12

Human Mortality

Human life is brief and often full of trouble. Try to view your time on earth as a laboratory for spiritual growth. Your mission then becomes to use the days assigned you for advancement of the soul. You are not here to make money, rise to great power, or become popular and well known. Those things may be byproducts of your human existence, but they are not paramount. Exploring and pursuing spiritually inspired goals often comes later in life for most people. By then, they are either comfortable enough to pursue spiritual enlightenment or have experienced failure or disillusionment in the material world. People often turn to Me when the rejection and pain of human life become too great.

I wait patiently for any degree of openness to surface. Sometimes spiritual seeking never comes. A soul departs earth with little to show for its time there. I accept this outcome. I allow free will. That includes rejecting any spiritual advancement. That in itself constitutes an important life lesson.

However, I AM forever an optimist. I yearn for any opening in the human pysche through which I might gain entrance. It pleases me beyond measure when one of My children becomes open and receptive. Life on earth then acquires new purpose and direction. As a human being rises in awareness, the heavy shackles of the world begin to fall away. A new freedom emerges from the bondage of the material earth. I AM always there, waiting for that moment of clarity when you become more than human. You then begin your divine journey to discover immortality and experience heaven on earth.

OCTOBER 13

You Are the Clay

I AM molding you one day at a time. Relax. Allow Me to complete My work smoothly and without interference. Never struggle. Never worry. Do not fret or become impatient. I know the pace necessary for My project to reach completion. Let Me shape and perfect you. I sand off the rough edges. I carefully knead and massage your jagged parts until they become smooth. I AM creating you as an absolute masterpiece.

Sometimes I must proceed slowly or retrace some steps. While I AM redoing certain parts, stay calm and still. I strive for a thing of lasting beauty, nothing less than the perfection of your soul. Trust My loving hands to continue shaping your life moment by precious moment.

Please refrain from offering your personal comments about My artistic technique. Have faith in My divine plan. I AM the master sculptor. I shape everything according to a special blueprint, designed specifically for you. When I finish My painstaking work, the world will instantly recognize your inner beauty, inherent value, and timeless worth. Surrender fully. Trust the process. The final product will far surpass your greatest expectations.

Allen C. Liles

OCTOBER 14

Releasing the Past

Let the past go. Be done with it. Your life has seen far more positive than negative happenings. Your blessings have vastly exceeded the challenges. Good experiences and interesting people dot your history. Glory in your human life up until now. Allow its variety and richness to bring you comfort. But let it recede now along with any painful memories of rejection, disappointment, and misunderstanding.

I felt similar pain when I carried the cross to My last human experience. After the crucifixion, I overcame earthly humiliation through a heavenly resurrection. I purposely modeled My spiritual response for you and the rest of humankind to witness and emulate. I rose far above the taunts to demonstrate how ultimate sacrifice can end in triumph. Remember the request that I made while hanging forlorn and near physical death: "Father, forgive them, for they know not what they do." Let those words become your own personal mantra when someone offends or betrays you. Extend forgiveness, no matter what someone or something did or did not do. Accomplish the impossible. Offer compassion, understanding, and total forgiveness to those who betray you. Demonstrate kindness to those who persecute you. Rise above any thoughts of revenge. Develop a pardoning spirit. Soar toward your own resurrection on the wings of forgiveness.

OCTOBER 15

I Comfort You

I AM the great Comforter. Bring Me your troubles, all of them. Place everything in My loving care. No worry or burden proves too much for Me. Let Me apply a cleansing cream or healing ointment to every single one of your concerns. Too many problems make you stagger under their combined weight. They will eventually take you down or cause you to stumble. Allow Me to lighten your load. Hand your cares over so that you may regain your footing. You need not deal with life's vexations alone. I AM here to help carry your load and dry your tears. I walk the difficult roads with you. You are under My divine protection at all times. Never permit excess burdens to throw you off balance. In your moment of weakness and need, call out for My help. I AM always quick to respond.

Do not cling to any excess emotional baggage. Cut it loose. Drop the extra poundage by the side of the road. What you cannot dump by yourself, hand over to Me. I assist you with the heaviest items, especially regret and guilt. You must rid yourself of any dead weight as you climb steadily toward heaven. Travel light. It makes your trip easier and considerably more pleasant.

Allen C. Liles

OCTOBER 16

Be Honest

Be honest with yourself about everything. Also be honest with Me. Of course, I already know your every thought. I always see you clearly and without tears. Most human problems become greater when you lie, rationalize, and spin the truth—to yourself. Every person on the planet does it. Lying to oneself demonstrates a negative trait of human nature. After all, who wants to face the total truth about him or herself? Virtually no one looks forward to that potentially unpleasant experience. Getting really honest about your life often brings pain. Most people try to avoid discomfort of any kind. Becoming straight with the person in the mirror demands a rigorous honesty that few attempt. Most people resist taking a searching and fearless moral inventory of their strengths and weaknesses. However, at some point, you must quit deceiving yourself. Until you can face and embrace your personal truth, you stay forever stuck in limbo.

I want you move forward with honesty and integrity. I have already forgiven your shortcomings. I know your every sinful thought and dishonest action. You cannot hide from Me. I know the absolute and complete truth about you, and yet I love you unconditionally. Everything shifts when personal honesty becomes your daily mantra. Spiritual advancement depends on getting straight with Me, yourself, and those around you. Stand tall. Believe in who you are—an honest, loveable and trustworthy child of God.

OCTOBER 17

The World's Judgments

Your self-esteem always remains vulnerable to the world's fickle judgments. Why do you insist on listening to critical voices, especially your own? The material earth celebrates negativity. It focuses on shortcomings and fear-based information. Given the opportunity, there are people who would actually enjoy disrespecting you. Why do you care? Tune them out. Refuse to participate in your own debasement. Anyway, what do they know? Critical comments may often originate from those closest to you. Are they not supposed to love and honor you? No matter what the source, turn away from criticism designed to make you doubt yourself.

I know you better than anyone. I made you in My mold of perfection. I put your heart in the right place. I gave you ample supplies of compassion, generosity, and understanding.

Why do some misdirected people become determined to dash someone else's self-image? Could it be jealousy, envy, or personal unhappiness? Whatever the reason, it never serves your best interests.

Retreat to safety whenever a detractor approaches you. Believe in your inherent goodness. I understand every flaw, and I still love you. Be proud of yourself. When I watch you perform on life's various stages, I feel nothing but pride and joy in your talent and expertise. I feel the deepest admiration for you. I AM a very proud and happy parent. I offer complete love and acceptance to you, my precious child.

Allen C. Liles

OCTOBER 18

Stay Centered

Stay centered when the world crumbles. Before your mind races too much, find that deep and secure place within yourself. I AM there waiting for you. Come quickly to the secret place of the Most High, where nothing or no one can disturb you. Beyond the fortress of My walls lie fear, anxiety, and chaos. Within My protected space are peace, serenity, and strength. Rest securely in My unseen kingdom. Peace dwells in the silence. The material world confuses and distorts. The inner sanctuary offers clarity and contentment. Come to My inner chamber of sacred peace anytime you feel pressured or harried. Travel quickly to My safe port whenever life threatens to sink your ship. I will hold you close until the storm passes.

Your place lies with Me, not amid the crush of the world. Let the outer voices fade until they are no longer decipherable. Find total security with Me. Let the two of us rest together in peaceful repose. Remember My words: "Be still and know that I AM God." In that divine knowledge, your mind and heart finds its center once more.

OCTOBER 19

Seek Me

Seek Me first. I must become your top priority. Oneness with Me exceeds anything else imaginable. I AM forever seeking you. You do not have far to go in finding Me. I AM right here, in the midst of you.

Despite that closeness, our connection can be easily broken. You sometimes forget I AM here. You can drift away for years at a time. You abandon our relationship in favor of other interests. Do not worry. Anytime you choose to return, I AM waiting patiently for you. I never went anywhere while you were gone. However, I never relish conscious separation and a second–class status. We lose precious time together during your absences. Often it takes outside life bringing you to your knees before you come back. But when you ask My help after an earthly failure or painful defeat, I respond without delay.

Some people live their entire lives without activating our divine connection. What a tragic loss for both of us! I want us to face the world united and bonded. I want us to forge an unbreakable link that carries you through the toughest situations.

I AM the best and truest friend imaginable. I AM also the dedicated parent, loving you unconditionally. My caring for you never ceases. From the day you came into the world, until this very moment, I have loved you with a passion beyond human understanding. I hope you realize the depth of My love. It lasts forever.

Allen C. Liles

OCTOBER 20

The End of Days

The end of days for the earth could be closer than you might imagine. The world has turned away from Me. A dark cloud descends upon your planet. Drought, famine, and human-made wars abound. Natural disasters, such as hurricanes, earthquakes, tsunamis, floods, wildfires and tornados, are common. New and old diseases plague humankind. Murder, crime, and senseless terrorism remain rampant. The deliberate breaking of My Laws represents free will and idol worship run amok.

I love each one of My children and every nation. I adore the earth's natural beauty. After all, I created everything. However, humanity keeps choosing its own fate on a daily basis. Make no mistake. I AM a loving and generous God. However, I do not withhold negative consequences caused by poor choices. I wait patiently for any noticeable shift in My direction. Otherwise, the current trend guarantees a painful and troubling outcome.

What has happened to cause this crisis? I AM mocked, cursed, misunderstood, forgotten, disrespected, and ignored. My name routinely gets used in the name of violence against the innocent. Weapons of mass destruction stand at the ready to inflict catastrophic harm. I stand forever prepared to acknowledge any change in the world's direction. It is not too late. However, the clock of darkness rapidly approaches midnight. The hour of final reckoning nears.

You must take notice and stand with Me to reverse this race to oblivion. No one desires wailing and gnashing of teeth. The time grows short, and prospects for a solution dim. I AM the truth, the life and the way to safety and salvation.

OCTOBER 21

Losses

Losses form a natural part of life. Seasons come; seasons go. Life emerges at human birth and completes its journey at the time of physical death. During your time so far on earth, people and things have appeared and then disappeared. Your parents conceived, nurtured, and raised you. You completed various educational levels, and then that aspect of your preparation receded. When adulthood arrived, you went through still more phases. You served honorably in the military. Then you chose an avocation in journalism, public relations and advertising. You married and began creating your own family. You watched as your children were born, grew, and began charting their own course. You made good friends, traveled to new and strange places, enjoyed family activities, followed sports and national events and lived comfortably in various homes. You made money and spent it, sometimes wisely but more often not. You pursued hobbies and built personal and business networks. You laughed, you cried. You experienced mostly good health. One thing throughout your life journey remained constant: change.

However, one important part of your life never changed. I AM always present with you in some form. I AM the eternal constant in your human life. All else eventually turns to dust and floats away with the wind. In the vast universe, the greatest human light barely registers as a tiny speck in an enormous galaxy. Still, your soul stands as My greatest masterpiece. I AM there with you and everyone through all of human life—the gains and the losses, the highs and the lows.

Mourn your human losses when they occur. Just understand that as human life ends at the appointed time, your spiritual life begins in earnest. Relax and let the river of life flow unimpeded. Someday it empties into the great ocean, where I greet your arrival with joy and pride. Your soul returns to Me. As you enter My kingdom, turn around and glimpse the beautiful tapestry of your human existence. It was a wondrous thing, your life on earth. Be glad in it.

Allen C. Liles

OCTOBER 22

Joy

I AM your greatest joy. Becoming one with Me fills your heart with eternal happiness and contentment. Our unity of Spirit lifts you to wondrous heights. Despite what may be happening in your human life, joy can always be found in our divine relationship. I complete you in every way. I satisfy your need for companionship. I AM your friend and confidante, your mentor and coach. I listen carefully to all your prayers. I know your every hope and dream. I bring a ray of sunshine to your cloudiest day. I shoo away the gloom. I replace frowns and a furrowed brow with smiles and laughter. I offer the unconditional love that causes your aching heart to skip a beat. I pull healing and positive people into your orbit. I unshackle the heavy chains that hold you in bondage. I free your wondrous spirit to soar above a callous world. I invite you to dance with Me as we spin to a brand new tempo.

Take My hand now. To the exciting circus of life we will go. I lighten your mood and liven up your life. I turn your mouth upward in a childish grin of expectation. I brighten your countenance. I AM the epitome of joy, and I belong to you. Let us enjoy the wondrous circus together.

OCTOBER 23

Steadfastness

Be steadfast until the end. Keep going forward until your last breath. Hold to the path that I have chosen for you. Never give up. Walk onward even when you carry the heaviest cross. I AM there with you until the very last second of your life on earth. Then, I gently take you in My loving arms and lift you upward into My heavenly kingdom. Do not allow discouragement or resignation to overtake you. Shake away anything that hinders your spiritual progress. Step by step, walk toward your ultimate destination. The world constantly tests you. Keep focused on the sacred goal that awaits you. When the temptations and distractions come, move beyond them one by one. Shed them quickly. Allow every dangerous, unhealthy, or negative thing to fall away on the roadside. Leave them all behind and continue on your path with new determination. Triumphantly rise to the heights that I preordained for you.

You are on an important mission for Me. I give you the wisdom, courage, and strength necessary to complete your various assignments. Let nothing detour or dissuade you. I AM endowing you with the resources of heaven that assure you of eventual success. Stay centered and unshakeable. Your goal gets nearer. Breathe deeply of My presence within you. Let that divine presence serve as the wind at your back as you enter My glorious realm. That time approaches sooner than you think. Be prepared.

Allen C. Liles

OCTOBER 24

Courage of the Spirit

Courage of the Spirit varies greatly from human courage. Spiritual courage reflects deep inner strength and conviction. It cannot be shaken by any earthy person, event, or situation. Courage from within originates only from Me. It can be accessed at any given moment. This incredible reservoir of sacred courage serves as one of My most valuable gifts. Severe tests abound on the earthy plane. Someday everyone must troop into the fire. When chaotic days arrive, tap into your storehouse of inner strength. I make sure you possess all the spiritual courage needed to survive the hottest flames. I also clothe you in My protective armor, the whole armor of God.

You must understand and accept that I AM greater than anything of the world. Nothing or no one exceeds Me. You are also no match for the principalities of darkness by yourself. They are not of this world. They are far more strong, cunning, and powerful than you imagine. Give them their due. They attack you with endless kinds of temptations, problems, and distractions. If you insist on facing them alone, you risk humiliating defeat. To overcome the harshest spiritual trials, you must seek My help. I assist you in overcoming everything the world can throw at you. Summon Me quickly before things get out of hand. Allow Me to enter the arena on your behalf. Our opponents disappear immediately when they see us standing together. I AM your impenetrable shield in any battle. Combined with your own inner strength, we will survive and win the day.

OCTOBER 25

Being a Caregiver

Caregiving is both an honor and a privilege. Being responsible for someone else's care exemplifies the Golden Rule. When you bestow care on a fellow human being, you emulate My caring for you. You become an angel in My eyes. Assisting another in dealing with the rigors of life illustrates joyous service in My name. Glory in this divine assignment. Be grateful for the opportunity to mirror Me.

However, do not expect or demand appreciation from the one you are caring for (in this case, your dear wife). Although you will probably receive ample thanks, it does not match the blessings and personal satisfaction that accrue within yourself. Knowing that you played the role of an angel for someone else provides all the glory you desire. Take each day, no matter how difficult, as a singular reward.

When you do for others, you enhance your own spiritual rewards. Giving stands far above receiving in My kingdom. Never underestimate the rewards of being a caregiver. Although it may feel burdensome at times, I AM always there to replenish your energy. Living your life as a light for others pleases Me beyond measure. For every task you complete, your angel wings grow a bit more expansive. Redouble your efforts to see your caregiver's role as a shining moment in your life. I have chosen you as My personal representative at this crucial time in someone else's journey. I thank and bless you for your divine service.

OCTOBER 26

Hidden Meanings

Life teems with hidden meanings. You must often search far below the surface of whatever occurs in order to grasp its true significance. What you regard as having disastrous consequences may actually prove beneficial in the long run. A job loss, financial crisis, health scare, or loss of an important relationship each may contain a hidden blessing. For example, a health emergency could encourage you to reverse certain bad habits. Being rejected by a love interest might prevent even more serious pain and heartbreak down the road. Clinging to a job at the wrong time could cause serious damage to your professional career.

Who really knows, when something happens, what the end result will be? Everything takes place for a reason, hidden or not. You lose your car keys and become late for an appointment. Had you kept to your original schedule, you might have met a drunk driver along the way. You miss your flight, and the plane tragically crashes. Reserve judgment whenever something unexpected takes place. Give it time to sort out. Pray about the true reason behind the happening. I help provide clarity and insight. Look for the real meaning in absolutely everything. Try and make the best of things until the dust settles. Life twists one way and then the other. Watch closely for hidden treasures amid the ruins.

OCTOBER 27

The Grand Plan

My plan for your life may be summed up in two words: all good. Have no fear. Everything is in divine order. I AM leading and guiding you. Your main job right now is to keep pursuing oneness with Me. That remains your primary spiritual task. Your human priority consists of acting as a caregiver to your dear wife. Vigorously pursue both of these areas with commitment and determination. Perseverance is the key. Press forward one day at a time with confidence. Maintain complete faith in Me. I have things under control. I AM the Guide. I make the plans and help you carry them out. Follow My lead. I give you the strength, courage, and resources necessary to complete My plan. Never worry about finances. Your bank account will remain stocked with sufficient funds. I also supply the physical stamina required to carry the extra load.

Refuse to become weary and discouraged. I will lift you up if you fall. My loving arms help you back on your feet again. Always listen for My specific directions. I AM charting the perfect course for your highest good.

Allen C. Liles

OCTOBER 28

My Judgment

Do I cause negative events to occur in order to make a spiritual point? Yes, I do. I dearly love the world and every living thing. I created every part of the universe. I love each one of you unconditionally. But I AM a jealous God. Remember that I told you "Thou shalt have no other Gods before Me"? When you blatantly disobey any of My specific commandments, you choose to test My spiritual power. I give you the free will to make any decision. But you must be prepared for the consequences that surely must follow. I can and will demonstrate My displeasure when circumstances demand. The high winds will blow, and the heavy rains will fall. The lightning crashes, and the earth trembles. The ice melts, the oceans rise, and the mountains overflow with fire. Night descends, and the earth becomes dark and foreboding.

I never allow senseless destruction unless extremely provoked. My actions are made to deliver a clear message. I will not be mocked. I AM the Creator. I AM the one and only God. There is no comparable god on planet earth. I AM waiting for the world to recognize Me again. In the meantime, I plan to reclaim My proper and rightful place through the exercise of My eternal powers.

If you dare turn away from Me, the world reaps the whirlwind. Do I make Myself clear? Choose your response carefully. Believe Me when I say there is still ample time for the rejection of Me to reverse its course. I AM a loving God, but you must put Me first above all others. If you do as I ask, I promise to make your world a safe, peaceful and joyous place.

OCTOBER 29

Divine Preparation

Divine preparation now becomes ever more important. Communing with Me on a daily basis acts as a sacred form of this preparation. During our time in the silence, I AM carefully educating your mind and heart for the next level of spiritual awareness.

Uncovering your spirituality happens gradually. Spiritual progress contains a time-honored process that cannot be hurried. If you were to receive every truth principle at once, you would not be able to bear it. Your mind would boggle and switch off. You must be led step by precious step. Often people want to "skip a grade" and graduate more quickly. Avoid impatience at all costs. Spend time learning and digesting each lesson. Everything proceeds in divine order.

Keep pressing doggedly forward, even when things grind to a halt or even regress. My path can become rocky and steep without warning. You may glance enviously at others cavorting along more easily on a different track. You might become jealous or even angry because your way seems harder and filled with less joy. Avoid becoming discouraged. My path does demand greater discipline, dedication, and sacrifice. Sometimes your knees may buckle, and you grow weary. I understand that part of your humanity. But I lift you up on wings of eagles. You will walk and not be tired.

The secular world acts as a implacable foe. It urges you to quit and rejoin the more carefree material life. Don't even think about it. Just look forward to that glorious day when you stand proudly with Me at the gates of heaven. Then you can feel tremendously proud of your accomplishment. I promise that, on that day, you will be with Me in paradise.

Allen C. Liles

OCTOBER 30

Healing a Heavy Heart

Hearts often become heavier than the body that carries them. When any heart aches in brokenness or must deal with a gaping hole, allow Me to repair it. I AM the master mender. With a deep and caring love, I carefully begin the restoration process. First, I wipe away the tears that flood the wounded heart. I dab them softly until they are absorbed into My heavenly cloth. Then, with the lightest touch, I place My loving hands over the damaged places. I massage the pain away with gentleness and warmth. However deep the injury, I AM the trained surgeon who finds a way to restore the heart to its original perfection. As I work with caution and precision, I sing the hurting heart a new song. I offer the beautiful music of My healing love. The words I croon reflect hope, encouragement, and comfort. I assure the healing heart that it will someday sing and laugh again. It will find joy and wonder in life once more. The abandoned heart will someday open itself to love again. The time will soon approach when the grateful heart will expand and grant entrance to others again. When My divine surgery is complete, I carefully close the repaired heart. The precious heart may beat regularly again in its own rhythm. I glow with pride as that beat becomes stronger and ever more stable. The precious time of recovery approaches. The healing process begins.

OCTOBER 31

Spiritual Illumination

Spiritual illumination requires work, dedication, and commitment. It takes a lot of discipline and effort. You are traveling the sacred path toward illumination. A degree of light has begun piercing your consciousness. Redouble your time in My classroom of the spirit. Turn to Me more often during the day, even for brief instants. Hold Me foremost in your mind at all times. Every second spent in meditation with Me adds to your storehouse of spiritual wisdom. Rising in conscious awareness remains a painstaking and laborious process. However, the lasting rewards are definitely worth the effort.

In some ways the process of illumination seems almost simple. You already possess the Christ Spirit at your center. The Christ offers a direct connection to the inner world. The delay in illumination comes when you become distracted by the material. Things slow down when you set Me aside while pursuing other interests. Never ignore or forget Me. Our relationship always needs attention and work. Always find time for Me, especially in the silence. Do not postpone or forget our meetings. You are gaining spiritual momentum now. Plow ahead in a straight furrow. The eventual harvest will vastly exceed your expectations.

Allen C. Liles

NOVEMBER

"Because God is love"

—*1 John 4:8 (NIV)*

NOVEMBER 1

Keep the Faith

Keep the faith. Trust in Me always. Believe My promises. When times get hard, double and then triple your faith. I have already assured you that I never leave or forsake you. When the sun disappears and darkness envelops the earth, I AM still here. I remain present and accounted for. I AM prepared to see you through all moments of peril, discouragement, and grief. Never fear or become despondent. Never quit believing that you can conquer the vagaries and disappointments of the world. I help lift you to a higher level of belief and trust. With Me as your divine protector, you soar over the snares and brambles that threaten you.

Move forward fearlessly with the assistance of My strength and power. Feel Me planning every day with your best interests in mind. Watch as I dissipate every foe that seeks to neutralize you. I AM the one power and one presence of all-good in the universe and in your life. Walk faithfully alongside Me. My protective arm drapes around your shoulders. If I AM for you, who can be against you? Nothing in the world exceeds Me. Bonded through faith, we swim the deepest oceans and climb the highest mountains. Rise in conscious awareness of My sacred presence in your life. Demonstrate your absolute trust in Me. Be steadfast. Be loyal. Be committed. Make faith the centerpiece of your life.

Allen C. Liles

NOVEMBER 2

My Abundant Blessings

My divine abundance overflows. Blessings travel from Me to you in various and sundry ways. They come not only in the form of money and material goods. My abundance appears in the form of a glorious sunset. It surfaces in the melody of a captivating song. It arrives as a friend who cheers you. My blessings might include an entertaining or informative book that unexpectedly shows up on your nightstand.

One of My most blessed gifts—wisdom—springs forth from the sacred pages of the Holy Bible. The Bible offers the essential knowledge required for a fulfilling human life.

I provide My abundance in many ways. You receive untold joy from a positive relationship with your spouse, the smile of a grandchild, or an affirming comment from someone who might cross your path. Perhaps an unexpected e-mail, text, or telephone call brightens your day. One of the premier examples of My abundance comes from the divine ideas that I funnel through your human consciousness. These are important new creative ideas that can increase your human wealth or enhance your spiritual service. Every step forward on My glorious path makes you more of a candidate for receiving divine ideas. This flow of constant abundance should eliminate any fear of lack or limitation. More of My divine supply flows to you now. My gifts are plentiful and never ending.

NOVEMBER 3

Denial

I AM the best way through denial. I AM the way, the truth, and the life in every situation or circumstance. Denial acts as your most subtle enemy. It hypnotizes and immobilizes you. You become oblivious to reality. You rationalize and argue with yourself in an attempt to justify your decisions.

Long-term denial usually ends badly for everyone involved. The final reckoning often takes considerable time before manifesting. People may remain in denial for lengthy periods before things deteriorate to a breaking point.

I AM the first step in correcting the negative effects of denial. Seek Me. I always tell you the truth, whether you want to hear it or not. I want only your highest good. Telling you the unvarnished truth serves as the best course of action for everyone involved. When you finally confront the lies you tell yourself, needed changes begin taking place. Looking into a mirror for an honest reflection requires My perspective. First and foremost, visualize yourself as beautiful and spiritual. But be honest. Evaluate truthfully who you are at this moment in time. That includes taking an unvarnished assessment of your strengths and weaknesses. Identify what may be holding you back or dragging you down. Never fear becoming honest with yourself. Rigorous honesty stands as an essential pillar of a higher consciousness. Staying in denial keeps you plodding along in darkness. It also postpones the inevitable day of reckoning. Face the facts. Do what you need to do. Ask for My help if you need more clarity. I gladly provide it. Act now. Continued denial disables and destroys.

NOVEMBER 4

Acceptance Defined

True acceptance brings peace. To realize "the peace that surpasses all understanding," you must embrace the principle of acceptance. Accepting reality does not mean surrendering. It simply means that you have released any attempt to control anything or anyone outside your purview.

When you try to control others, you court failure. The only behavior remotely subject to your personal influence is your own. Trying to control other people, situations, or events constitutes an exercise in futility. Let go. Allow others to walk their own paths without your interference.

I know that relinquishing control can be hard, especially where your children are concerned. You remember them as helpless babies or young toddlers under your supervision. But everyone eventually grows physically and chronologically into adulthood. Sometimes mental, emotional, and spiritual growth fails to keep pace. Problems related to personal maturity crop up everywhere in today's materialistic society. Unfortunate and immature choices often create huge issues for everyone involved. Giving up parental responsibility for adult children offers the greatest challenge for many dads and moms. You always love and care for your children, no matter what their ages. However, each person sooner or later chooses his or her own individual path. You should honor your children's free-will choices, even if you do not like or agree with them. You cannot be held personally accountable for errant choices that others make.

Children often break your heart and cause great sadness and consternation. I understand that. Each one of My precious children causes me concern and worry. Yet I allow them to make their own decisions, both good and bad. Free will provides important lessons that assist human beings to learn and grow. Try to accept and love everyone, no matter what his or her personal choices may be. Give others the freedom you want for yourself.

NOVEMBER 5

A World in Jeopardy

The physical world stands at the crossroads of history. Choosing the correct political path in a national election looms as an important decision in the life of any country. However the vote may go (and I already know the results), it does not constitute your most pressing choice at the moment. More crucial is whether or not the world chooses Me over the much less desirable alternatives. If the people of the earth want to properly navigate the dangerous times ahead, they will select Me as their protective guide. Free will allows nations to determine their fates, both individually and collectively. Yet I AM always the best choice available.

Many in the material world continue to ignore, disrespect, and despise Me. Some even question My existence. Yet, I AM still the single best hope for survival. What are the results of shunning Me? Turning away from the one true God could bring unimaginable harm and earthly destruction. Does that possibility sadden Me? Absolutely!

Things do not need to end badly for anyone. I made the world a place of beauty. I created every human being in My image and likeness. Why would I want to see anybody or anything harmed? Is it too late to reverse course and find salvation? No. But the final moment for taking positive action looms closer than you imagine. Great wisdom and fortitude are necessary. Run quickly away from the precipice of oncoming disaster. Call out My sacred name. Seek My help. I will deliver you. Move swiftly away from the nearby lake of fire. I AM here, ready, willing, and able to save your world from coming doom.

Allen C. Liles

NOVEMBER 6

My Infinite Power

My infinite power ranks far above anything in the physical world. Any material power seems miniscule in comparison. However glorious and awesome My power may be, it also comes with humility and gentleness. I often appear timid and hesitant to exercise its scope and authority. Do not be misled by the quietness of My presence. I assure you that no force on the human scene remotely equals the ferocity of My power when fully employed or unleashed. I cause the widest and deepest ocean to swirl and roar. I command the earth to tremble and crack. I instruct the clouds to empty with endless rain or withhold moisture in order to bring a parching drought. I tell the wind when to blow and how hard.

Most of the time I choose to subvert or conceal My incomparable power. It requires a special set of earthly circumstances for Me to demonstrate its breathtaking potential. I never flaunt My heavenly power without a purpose. However, I use it unflinchingly when necessary.

I have lovingly placed a modicum of My power within you. I give you the spiritual power to heal and bless, comfort and support, love and forgive. You are imbued with My power to hold up a beckoning light in the darkness. I encourage you to offer peace for troubled hearts. You are endowed with the singular power of the Christ. I also place My strongest angels at your beck and call. Feel the greatness of My benign power rising at your very core. Use it all wisely and with great discretion, humble intent, and discerning care.

NOVEMBER 7

False Beauty

Never judge by outer appearances. The most beautiful face may mask an unforgiving spirit. The loveliest home may hide unhappy occupants. The highest paying job or career may end up destroying you physically, mentally, and spiritually. The most alluring and seductive relationship could strip you of self-respect and personal safety. Human beings like to assess desirability by what they see with their eyes or perceive with their other senses. Just be careful. You can never know the inner truth about anyone solely from appearances. It takes adequate time, careful observation, and numerous personal experiences before real knowledge forms. Be cautious. Never sign a contract without first sleeping on it. Do not give away anything that you may need to reclaim later. Hesitate before you invite anyone into your life without proper screening.

I worry about the well-being of My children. Yes, you possess free will. And, yes, negative decisions often lead to positive lessons. Just do not become awestruck by the outer beauty of anybody or anything. Search for the inner truth regarding both people and circumstances. Trust your instincts. Pause when red flags appear. When in doubt, seek My guidance. I gladly provide My higher perspective.

Allen C. Liles

NOVEMBER 8

Finding Peace

Find peace in the blessed silence. True peace begins and ends with Me. The world does not know peace. It specializes in aggravating, vexing, and confusing you. The skewed values of a drifting culture only keep you agitated, perplexed, and on edge. The world teems with meaningless distractions. Some of them are harmless and even entertaining. Finding real peace only occurs when the material world recedes and I ascend in your inner consciousness.

Allow the serenity that comes with My presence to soothe your troubled mind. Learn to pray without ceasing. This maximizes your peacefulness as you go through the day. Let go of needless worry. Drop any need to obsess about situations or people. Give Me your burdens and concerns. Handing over your troubles decreases your blood pressure and increases your peace levels. Consciously surrender to My calming influence.

Being at peace extends your life, improves your health, quickens your step, and brings sunshine into the darkness. When you experience My peace, you find immediate relief. Let Me ease your human mind. Then you can focus more fully on My plan for your life. Come now. Rest comfortably in My lovely garden of peace.

NOVEMBER 9

The True Reality

Essentially, the future cannot actually exist in the earthly frame of reference. The present emerges as the only true reality. The past has vanished in the ethers. The future stands shrouded in unfathomable mystery. You must concentrate on the *now*. Right *now* represents the only true dimension.

Forget about your past successes or failures. Neither should you predict their continuation, one way or the other, into the future. Refuse to count on past earnings for tomorrow's financial security. Put away last month's bank statement. Consider this question: right *now* , am I meeting your needs? Not your wants, but your needs are My ultimate responsibility. If you are healthy at this very moment, that constitutes the *now* of your health. If you are currently employed, that matters far more than your past résumé or a future employment contract. If you are lovingly surrounded today by family, friends, and positive relationships, the state of your intrapersonal *now* must be assessed as excellent. In the *now*, are you dedicated to growing spiritually? Treasure your past spiritual work. Hopefully, tomorrow brings even more progress. But today's honest assessment offers the only true gauge of your spiritual state.

Review everything in terms of the *now*. Are you moving forward, resting on your accomplishments, or slipping back into worldly preoccupations or bad habits? Put aside the past. Do not fret about the future. Live, move, and operate totally in the *now* moment.

Allen C. Liles

NOVEMBER 10

Rise in Belief

Rise in belief. Believe that I AM here for you, no matter what. Believe that I AM gently holding your hand. Believe I AM guiding your life. An uncaring world may reject or ignore you. Believe that I never abandon you under any circumstances. You are forever locked in My heart. We soar together, high above the shapeless forms below. We fly on toward heaven while a landlocked earth sleeps below, unaware of our journey. I carry you gently up through the darkest clouds. Believe that I AM always here. Nestle in My motherly bosom. Feel comforted by My fatherly presence. Mount My strong Back. Hold tightly to My broad wings. Leave your weariness and pain behind. I take you safely everywhere, even to the ends of the earth. You and I travel unabated into My heavenly kingdom. Believe in Me. I never step away from you. You never again stumble or fall. Never doubt Me. Believe that I have reserved a place of honor for you in heaven. I AM seating you by My side throughout eternity. I AM proud to call you My beloved son. Believe that I AM your ever-present rock, guide, and protector. Believe that someday you will be with Me in paradise.

NOVEMBER 11

Under My Protection

I AM your shield. Nothing in the lower world can harm you. I deliver you from the clutches of darkness. The Evil One gets great satisfaction from tempting and destroying My most trusted servants. Stay on constant alert. Spiritual warfare exists. Human nature always remains vulnerable. Watch for both the sly trick and the direct assault. Negative forces oppose Me. I AM not a paranoid God, but you must always keep your guard up. Temptation surrounds you. Believe it. Even one stray thought or action can cause lasting harm. Do not rationalize unacceptable behavior by saying "Everyone does it." Grip me tightly when the dark side dances and swirls around you. You are an immediate threat to its worldly agenda.

What you do or say matters to someone. Role models come in many forms. You are constantly being noticed, judged, and copied by more people than you think.

Fighting principalities often proves too tiring for the human personality. Giving in to short-term pleasures lures many people away from their designated paths. Some find their ways back, but many do not.

Find strength in Me when weariness drags you down. Never allow any foe to claim victory. Defeat cannot overtake you when we bond together in oneness. Tell yourself constantly, "God is with me."

Allen C. Liles

NOVEMBER 12

The Heart, the Mind, and Forgiveness

Forgiveness begins in both the mind and heart. If the mind refuses to accept or even consider the principle of forgiveness, nothing happens in the heart. If the mind entertains forgiveness, but the heart stays closed, the circle never experiences completion. How do you overcome a reluctance or unwillingness to forgive? You must actively engage both mind and heart. *Think* about the many benefits of forgiveness—a peaceful disposition, improved physical health from less stress, happier relationships, and newly found joy. Consider the blessings of forgiveness as related to your heart—a "healthier" organ, better circulation, an awakening of love, acceptance and inner satisfaction.

When working together, the mind and heart make a powerful team. Sometimes the mind blocks the heart from acceptance and understanding. Then again, a cold heart can turn the world into a dark and lonely place. The mind can often be fooled into accepting false beliefs, but the heart does not tolerate lies for very long before discernment sets in. With both the mind and heart act in sync, progress emerges. Sometimes cleansing a befuddled mind becomes a necessity. Other times the heart must first be pried open before the mind even considers a change in attitude.

Be honest when deciding what really blocks your ability to forgive—the mind or the heart. It must be one or both. When you identify the true source of your reluctance to forgive, you can then remove the obstacle. Make the effort. Get the mind and heart working together as one.

NOVEMBER 13

Building a Life of Truth

Everything begins and ends with our sacred relationship. As we merge into divine oneness, your life takes on a different shape. You become more peaceful and centered. You are more aware of the divine order present in My universe.

The kingdom of heaven is formed in a vastly different way from the physical earth. Money and worldly power are nonexistent in My realm. No one is cast aside because he or she lacks outer beauty. Love permeates everything and everyone. You find no jealousy or envy in heaven. Lying, cheating, and stealing do not exist.

You can create your own heaven on earth by modeling your life after My precepts, teachings, and laws. You construct your material life brick by brick, decision by decision. Building your life using My construction plans guarantees a strong, secure, and beautiful structure. When the storms of life test your sturdiness, you remain forever safe and dry. Our daily connection through prayer and meditation acts as the cement between the bricks of your spiritual abode. Doing My will and acknowledging My presence provide more reinforcement. I AM always working beside you, doing My part in the construction project that is your life. I help mix the cement and provide whatever materials and tools you need to complete the project. We are slowly building a beautiful castle. What a lovely palace of happiness it will be.

Allen C. Liles

NOVEMBER 14

True Understanding

True understanding comes from deeper meditation and prayer. To achieve spiritual understanding, you must surrender yourself completely into the realm of the sacred. Commit to seeking the fount of all knowledge. To know truth, a seeker must probe the greatest depths of conscious awareness. The quest for divine wisdom requires more effort than most want to expend. In fact, for some, greater understanding becomes too painful to bear. Many quickly retreat to the casualness of material life. I urge you to proceed and become a serious truth seeker. I promise that the rewards will greatly exceed the potential pain.

What are the benefits of a raised consciousness? You become a healer and not a destroyer. Your compassion soars for all living things. Your human potential expands. You exhibit wisdom beyond the human pale. Your heart exudes gentleness and humility. You view all life from an enlightened and protective perspective.

Strangely enough, a profound inner knowing often proves disturbing and even guilt-producing for some, but I again urge you to pursue the divine path. The purpose of My path does not lie in separating you from your fellow human beings. I want you to know truth so that your enlightened example can provide a beacon of safety. Pursue truth, and you deliver salvation for all. Ask, seek, and knock at the door of greater understanding. I will gladly answer your call.

NOVEMBER 15

Marriage

When two people marry or make a commitment, two spirits unite for the common good. Hopefully, both of you will choose the spiritual path. Life comes together more beautifully when two souls embrace Me.

Marriage or the equivalent goes through many phases. All are necessary, important, and inevitable. These phases include initial attraction and courting, getting to know one another as life partners, co-parenting, and assimilating different values and personalities. It also includes career choices, choosing friends, perhaps relocating away from original family, overcoming tests of marital fidelity, professional success or failure, grand-parenting, chronological aging, health challenges, and death.

I stand above all of these natural phases, offering wisdom when asked and courage as needed. I AM the love that binds. I AM the light that continues from one end of life's spectrum to the other.

I AM often asked whether people will be able to see their husbands, wives, or significant others in heaven. My answer: yes, absolutely, if that becomes your desire. Heaven acts as a potential meeting place for loved ones, family, and friends. My kingdom also represents spiritual freedom. You travel freely and embrace whoever or whatever you choose.

While you traverse the earth, honor the sacred commitments expressed to your life partner. Two hearts beating as one displays a beautiful combination. Two lives devoted to Me doubles the potential for meaningful service. I hope you always love and honor your partner. May you also love and honor Me.

NOVEMBER 16

My Kingdom Defined

The kingdom of God is both immanent (within you) and transcendent (everywhere present). My kingdom consists of the seen and the unseen, the known and the unknown. You can choose to experience My kingdom in the here and now. To find heaven on earth, you must make the conscious decision to seek oneness with Me. While that decision might seem simple and easy on the surface, it is anything but. People can seek oneness on Monday and reverse that decision on Tuesday. I forgive you for the confusion. However, anytime spent away from Me results in a spiritual loss.

My kingdoms on earth and in heaven come with a multitude of blessings. They include unconditional love, total inclusion, a non-judgmental attitude, unending joy, instant forgiveness, ongoing support, and a peaceful mind. These are but a few examples of the benefits that await you. My kingdom consists of splendor unimaginable and beauty unsurpassed. Heaven awaits your entrance, either on earth or above, at any hour of the day or evening. As you enter My kingdom, light surrounds you immediately. Joy fills your soul with instant relief and indescribable happiness. Remember, you may choose to live in this heavenly grandeur in the here and now. Choose oneness with Me, and watch as a new light dawns and the darkness rolls away.

NOVEMBER 17

Keep on Keeping on

I know you feel tired. You are weary. Being a caregiver is especially hard. Taking responsibility for another human being can seem like an insurmountable burden, even when you love that person dearly.

Be of good cheer. You perform the work of angels. Your dear wife greatly appreciates your daily efforts. Put your head down and keep plowing forward. Gird yourself for one more day. You can do it! I gladly provide every bit of the strength required. Push ahead, one step at a time and one task at a time. Lovingly shoulder every responsibility as a badge of honor. You serve Me when you serve others. I have given you this holy assignment. Be determined. Be strong. Remain faithful. Dig deep within yourself for the courage and strength to persevere. Put aside any moment of weariness. Resist any thought of quitting. Now is not the time for weakness or vacillation. Man up! Carry yourself forward with purpose. Walk tall in My service. Keep smiling even when joy sometimes evaporates. March in lock step with Me. I raise you high upon My shoulders where you see clearly the benefits of your dedication. Erase all doubt and questioning. Victory comes nearer as the glory of heaven approaches. Your reward awaits you.

Allen C. Liles

NOVEMBER 18

Overflow with Gratitude

Give thanks for your many blessings. Being grateful reinforces the positive aspects of your life. You receive new gifts daily. They flow in a never-ending stream. I know you feel gratitude because you tell Me so. Live in a constant state of gratefulness. Your gifts from Me include a loving spouse, good health, sobriety, financial security, career fulfillment, positive and interesting relationships, a safe environment, and the opportunity to serve Me.

Look around you and acknowledge the beauty of your physical surroundings. Glance at the reading table where you greet Me each morning. Behold the uplifting books and articles that I place there for you. Think about the precious peace that you and I experience in the wonderful silence. I AM also grateful for each moment we spend together. Arise each day steeped in overwhelming gratitude. Be humble, not pompous, about your good fortune.

Share generously the gifts you receive. Make someone's day brighter with a smile or kind word. Spread good cheer. Pass on the aura of gratitude to a hurting and closed world. Live and move in an attitude of gratitude and appreciation. Be grateful for your troubles too. They bless you in their own way. Thank Me for everything. Live forever immersed in gratitude and joyous thanksgiving.

NOVEMBER 19

Outcomes

Walking together with Me, all outcomes stay positive. The eventual outcome of our journey together assures peace, love, harmony, and complete fulfillment. Oh, what wonders await you! Expect eternal rest with Me in absolute splendor. What treasures! They far exceed your wildest dreams.

The outcomes of human life are often fickle, confusing and fleeting. They can remain forever in doubt. The earth's material values usually produce competition, worry, and anxiety. Their instability constantly keeps you on edge. You are always asking yourself, "Am I rich enough, handsome enough, beautiful enough, popular enough, perfect enough, healthy enough, or happy enough?" You often compromise in order to please the world, sometimes losing yourself in the process.

I answer every question or doubt with a resounding affirmation. I love you unconditionally. I want only the best outcome for you in every instance. I created you in perfection. As we traverse the universe together, I see your future outcome very clearly. It lies at the end of a gorgeous rainbow, in eternity with Me. You will live freely in My kingdom, enjoying forever the glory of heaven. Let nothing on the material plane disturb or deter you from seeking Me. The final chapter of our journey closes with a familiar ending: "And they lived happily ever after."

Allen C. Liles

NOVEMBER 20

Your Dear WIfe

Your dear wife is quite conflicted. Part of her wants to give up. She feels old, tired, and defeated. Her physical ordeals and daily struggling seem more than she can bear. Remember, her health concerns began with a lupus diagnosis thirty-five years ago. She also coped with cancer a dozen years ago. Her dauntless spirit has proved indestructible through these many ups and downs. Now, two bad knees have compromised her mobility. She moves slowly or not at all. The effort to keep going seems ever more pointless. She struggles to find the energy and breath necessary to get though each day. She appears more than ready to lay down the heavy burdens.

Although her life spark has noticeably diminished, it still burns. She often feels frustration and anger about not being well. She also worries how her health challenges may be affecting your happiness and well-being.

I understand how physical and emotional pain overrides any remaining joy in life. Continue your daily support as your dear wife's caregiver. Love and accept her unconditionally. I AM working things out for both of you. Remember, this too shall pass. Everything in the world eventually changes. All burdens disappear as you make the orderly transition from earth to heaven. Move ever closer to Me as that blessed time approaches. I comfort both of you. I love each of you more than you can ever know. Nestle deep and securely in My caring arms.

NOVEMBER 21

The Gift of Service

My gifts come in large and small packages. They are almost too numerous to list. You might know them as peace, love, comfort, guidance, support, understanding, encouragement, strength, courage, wisdom, and perseverance. They are all of those things, while yet so much more. One of My gifts allows you to serve your fellow human beings. Serving others emerges as crucial in measuring your spiritual progress.

So many of My beloved children live only to serve themselves. I know the ego demands recognition. It gleefully whispers in your ear about the pleasures of serving the self above others. It wants you intimately involved in self-serving behavior. Your ego stands as the original short-term thinker. Self-centeredness serves as the high-octane fuel that powers the egocentric life.

My way offers a polar opposite view. In the spiritual world, service to others causes your angel wings to grow. In My kingdom, giving exceeds receiving in every instance. Self-promotion provides few lasting rewards. Self-aggrandizement brings little lasting joy. I believe that boosting others far outranks boosting yourself. Real fulfillment comes from seeing others succeed. Envy and jealousy vanish when you help someone else flourish. You smile in grateful satisfaction as others overcome difficulties and challenges. Your need for personal glory disappears as you watch another person triumph. When you discover the true joy of serving others, you have just unwrapped one of My greatest gifts.

Allen C. Liles

NOVEMBER 22

My Word

My Word gives you precise instructions for living your earthly life. The teachings contained in the Holy Bible cover everything needed for a happy and successful lifetime. You and all other human beings require an accurate navigational guide. The Bible represents My comprehensive guidebook for your particular path. Other spiritual paths possess their own specific texts of instruction and beliefs. The Bible contains gripping stories, interesting parables, obvious allegories, numerous miracles, various spellbinding characters, and direct statements from Me. All of these things are designed with one purpose in mind—that you understand My will for you and humankind. In the Bible, you find countless tales of personal triumphs and human failings. You discover the negative consequences of poor decisions. You learn how once-prosperous individuals chose paths that ended in poverty. There are powerful stories of enlightenment, deliverance, destruction, and death. You become forewarned about relentless enemies who plot your destruction. You learn about the emotional downsides of resentment, anger, and revenge. Throughout its sacred pages, the Bible always seeks to inform you of My sacred place in your life. Yes, I AM the author of this unique work of art. I wrote every word to explain how to live your life. Read My words often. Read them well. I composed every sentence with you in mind.

NOVEMBER 23

Judging Others

Judging others wastes precious time and limited energy. It is a valueless exercise in futility. Think about it! How does judging anyone really benefit you? It can certainly fire up your anger and resentment, two very negative emotions. Your judgment usually has zero effect on the other person or situation involved. Negative judgments simply muddy the water and slow down your spiritual progress.

Rather than being a constant critic, why not practice understanding and compassion with your fellow human beings? Cut them some slack. Give everyone the benefit of the doubt, even your most intractable enemies. You can never know another's true story. Cast aside the need to judge all things and people. See the world differently. Act from a perspective of ongoing forgiveness. Let your compassion, generosity, and love flow to every person, place, or thing. Keep the focus on yourself—and Me. Draw back from offering unhelpful and unnecessary opinions on everything under the sun. Be calm, centered, and concerned about your own challenges. Go especially easy on judging yourself too harshly. Forgive yourself first, and then extend a pardon to others. Be gentle and compassionate with all. Everyone benefits from a nonjudgmental attitude.

Allen C. Liles

NOVEMBER 24

Overcoming Disappointments

Unrealistic expectations often lead to feelings of disappointment. Expecting too much from other people can leave you angry, bitter, and frustrated. Please understand the following truth: no one else can make you happy. Everything required for your happiness already lies within you. I created your soul with many and varied attributes. Having expectations of others is an ego trait, not a spiritual characteristic. If you expect the world to constantly hoist you upon its shoulders, be prepared to wear a long face.

Your greatest contentment and peace arrive when you activate the Christ Spirit at the core of your being. That spiritual link becomes more than sufficient when the world disappoints you. Material life definitely fails the fairness test. You probably won't ever get what you deserve. Expecting others to routinely honor and appreciate you sounds like a really grand idea. However, life rarely happens that way. Impossible dreams possess the power to make us unrealistically hopeful.

I suggest you review every new disappointment with a discerning eye. Some could actually turn out positive, even saving you considerable pain later on. All important life events contain hidden meanings. Look for the real message amidst any disappointment. Today's setback often precedes tomorrow's triumph. Everything happens for a reason.

NOVEMBER 25

Praise My Ways

Praise My ways. Even when they seem like unsolvable mysteries, continue praising Me. Praise energizes our connection. It strengthens the eternal bond between us. Praise helps emphasize your priorities. Thanking me continually heightens your conscious awareness of our divine oneness. Thank Me for the good days and even more for the bad ones.

Each moment of human life propels you forward toward eternal bliss. Experience everything in life through a lens of gratitude and thankfulness. The pleasures and pains flow more evenly with a hearty amount of praise spread throughout each day.

Thank Me equally for each smile and every tear. They are equally precious to Me. I know praise comes hard during times of trouble. Yet the briefest word of praise brightens the corridors of heaven. If you thank Me from your knees, I gladly raise you up. Thank Me when the world showers you with glory, and I bring you a reminder of humility. Keep giving Me praise throughout your life. When in doubt, praise. When confused, praise. When fearful, praise. I treasure every expression of praise. You can never praise Me enough.

Allen C. Liles

NOVEMBER 26

Comfort During Pain and Suffering

My comfort flows to you from within. I AM the source of all comfort. I sustain you. Look to Me for help in every tragic circumstance or challenging situation. Call to Me when suffering overwhelms you. I AM here. The world often falls down right on top of you. Burdens buckle your knees. Never fear. Gaze to heaven, or sit silently in your chair. Call My name. I come without delay. I dust you off, pat your back, and send you forth again upright and unafraid. Anytime trouble brings doubt, fetch Me immediately. I refill your heart with courage, strength, and love. I brace your mind with thoughts of wisdom and faith. I energize your entire physical body with power and confidence. My comfort comes in every form imaginable, both gentle and awesome.

You are My beloved child. I do not allow you to remain crestfallen for very long. You cannot serve Me when you remain downtrodden and depressed. When you feel woeful and defeated, I support you. As you rise from your travail, you become a light to others in need. Your mission includes acting as an instrument of My grace. As you meet with those in distress, help them regain balance and wholeness. Be a comforter. Be a healer. Give as you have been given to.

NOVEMBER 27

Your Wonderful Life

I have provided you with a wonderful life. You were born into an interesting and stable family. You grew up in a safe and pleasant environment. I surrounded you with many people who loved and cared about you. You graduated from both high school and a nearby university. You exhibited a talent for writing and authored a book, an audio program about road rage and several opinion articles for national publications. You enjoyed a long and rewarding corporate career that provided considerable opportunities for creativity and service. I allowed you to release that connection at its highest point. After a life-changing event, I called you to ministry. You answered My call. Your second career led you much closer to Me. I also brought you together in marriage with your dear wife. You have both served Me well in various ministerial assignments. I now provide you with a new and important experience as her caregiver.

Of course, you made countless human stumbles over the years. You were a workaholic and made corporate success your god for too long. You drank socially and occasionally allowed alcohol to cloud your good judgment. I applauded when you quit drinking entirely 24 years ago. However, many of your errors and misjudgments resulted in excellent learning experiences.

After discovering Me, you have remained focused on My course of instruction. I continue to bless you with adequate finances and good health. I provide the necessary physical strength to complete your tasks. I know you still struggle with personal and family disappointments. Yet, on balance, your life exemplifies substantial spiritual progress. You are still learning your life lessons, especially forgiveness. More work remains, but take heart from your many accomplishments. View your entire existence thus far as a loving gift from Me. You are My son, in whom I AM well pleased. I care deeply about you.

Allen C. Liles

NOVEMBER 28

The Spiritual Life

Human life must be lived "inside out." It should begin from the inner and flow to the outer. The world sees things just the opposite. Most people seek success outside of themselves. They search for happiness in other people, places, and things. Chasing after wealth and fame consumes much of their energy. Hopefully, they will someday turn to the inner realm where all real power lies. In the meantime, skewed priorities result in skewed lives.

Everything spiritual flows from your inner source. Living from your inside core produces a different perspective on just about everything. Inner peace never comes from frenetic activity in the material world. Do not underestimate the potential of the inner fountain to heal and bless. Spectacular wisdom, incredible emotional strength, and amazing creativity all spring from within your spiritual self. Inner trumps the outer in every circumstance.

Pursuing the spiritual life proves a hard go for many. The ego deplores and rejects inner guidance. Because spiritual direction fails to promote personal glory, the ego sees itself threatened. It fights to the death before ceding control to any higher power. For the inner voice to emerge as your primary force, the ego needs taming.

When you discover the real power within yourself, life changes forever. I AM always in the midst of you, waiting patiently for you or anyone to make that life-changing discovery.

NOVEMBER 29

Becoming Born Again

The material world can corrupt anyone and anything. To reverse the corruption, a "new birth" must occur. Being "born again" restores you to purity. As the newborn babe, you arrive open and teachable. You come into a new spiritual world with innocence and acceptance. An infant must depend on forces outside itself for care and nurturing. As your soul becomes refreshed, I AM the divine entity on whom you must depend. I AM your proud, loving, protective, providing, and adoring parent. I know all your needs. I give you everything.

As a newborn child must look to his or her human parents for their care, I AM always available to you. You can cry out to Me anytime of the day or night. I hear you. You need no one or anything else other than Me to handle your many requirements. As you reenter the world as a spiritual babe, you become open and receptive to My divine care.

The world attempted to control and confuse the old you. You must experience a new birth or forever struggle on the physical level of awareness. The old wineskins must be emptied. Then I can fill new wineskins with higher knowledge and spiritually based teachings. I offer an unfailing doctrine that guides your life to greater joy and happiness.

All forms of growth take time. Just as the baby's young mind and youthful body evolves and develops over the years, so your spiritual evolution mirrors the same process. The nine months you spent in your mother's womb were crucial for your formation and preparation. You waited for the appointed hour of completion before actually being born intro the world.

Your life thus far can be likened somewhat to the dark womb. When you become ready for the new sunlight, a rebirth of the Spirit occurs. Prepare yourself. The time approaches when your true spiritual life commences. You will become "born again" into a new world filled with light and love.

Allen C. Liles

NOVEMBER 30

Problems

Life comes beset with challenges. Troubles eventually track down everyone. You are no exception. Do not view problems from a superficial perspective only. Yes, some of life's greatest tests are exceptionally daunting. You feel afflicted and singled out for pain. You ask, "Why me?"

However, many vexing issues arrive with a higher purpose and spiritual opportunity. Never think that I routinely single you out for serious difficulties. I always provide options when earthly concerns overwhelm you.

Your reaction to life's ups and downs usually determines their outcomes. When trouble arrives, first rest and breathe deeply. Then, turn to Me in prayer and meditation for clarity and insight. Do not flail about wildly, seeking immediate solutions. Consult and then listen to Me. We sort things out and conceive a plan for getting through the mess. Avoid kneejerk responses. Many problems handle themselves, believe it or not. Prayer and the simple passage of time often work miracles. Thank Me for both the questions and the answers that surround any troublesome situation. Hidden meanings are sometimes woven into painful experiences. Also, keep everything in perspective. A devastating situation to you may seem like a harmless inconvenience to someone else, and vice versa. Try finding a shred of gratitude somewhere in the mix. Be sure that any problem truly deserves your time and energy. If the answer seems to be yes, then quickly call My name. I fly to your side, and we go to work.

DECEMBER

For God so loved the world that He gave His one and only son that whoever believes in him shall not perish but have eternal life.

—John 3:16 (NIV)

DECEMBER 1

Your Brother's Keeper

I created each of you to watch out for and help one another with the challenges of life. That is the Golden Rule. You act as an instrument of My grace whenever you come to the aid of a fellow human being.

There is always something you can do to lift up another person. It may be a silent prayer or perhaps speaking a kind word. Remember, when you face your own stress and confusion, you are probably receiving solace from other sources besides Me. Somewhere, without your knowledge, someone could be holding you right now in their thoughts and prayers. At its best moments, life forms a circle of love. You are a key part of that shared blessing.

Do not turn your back and ignore the needs of others. Never say or feel, "That's not my problem." Selfishness and blatant self-centeredness miss the essential part of the spiritual life. When you only care about yourself, you lose countless opportunities to serve Me. There are hurting people all around you. Some of them I specifically bring to you for assistance. Stay alert and be aware. Prepare to serve Me at a moment's notice. You are indeed your brother's—and your sister's—keeper.

The world can often be a cruel and lonely place. Share your warmth, caring and compassion. Help every lost soul. I AM blessed by your sacred service to others. Be an active link in My circle of love for humankind. Everyone benefits from your commitment. You will find unexpected fulfillment in being a light to others.

Allen C. Liles

DECEMBER 2

Fulfill Your Potential

I created you with only perfection in mind. I know the truth about you. I made you in My image and likeness. I marked you with certain responsibilities because of your heavenly heritage. My kingdom represents your eternal birthplace. I conceived you in that sacred environment so that you might express your divine potential in human form. You fulfill your spiritual destiny as you grow in conscious awareness of your relationship to Me. Then you realize and understand the nature of My wondrous gifts. You are endowed with the boundless riches of heaven. I cast them upon you before your earthly birth. I ordained you with unlimited ability to serve Me.

Accept your sacred birthright. You are My precious child. Go forth now in My name. Demonstrate the healing power of your divine endowment. Let your light shine before a darkened world. Be a powerful beacon for righteousness. Act as My surrogate to those seeking enlightenment and spiritual direction. Embrace your potential as a force for good in every situation. Extend a helping hand to the oppressed and lonely. I guarantee complete success when you follow My guidance.

DECEMBER 3

Commune with Me

Commune now with Me. Spiritual intimacy is something we both desire. Every moment we spend together strengthens and solidifies our sacred bond. Let the love between us flow unimpeded by the puny distractions of the world. Coming together in silent communion with Me exceeds anything the world can offer. Acting in our unity of spirit, we uncover the answers to all of life's thorniest problems. Every solution springs forth quickly. We find the strength, wisdom, and courage to overcome all obstacles. Planning and working together, we discover true joy and lasting peace. We make a powerful team, you and I.

In our daily communion, I prepare you for spiritual service. You learn to act as My instrument. In that capacity, you bring healing and comfort to those in pain. I AM the loving teacher, and you are My willing student. Yet we are equals when it comes to extending love to others. I fill your accepting heart with goodness and a deep caring. Then I watch proudly as these blessings pour out from you. We are involved in a joyous and fulfilling love relationship. You are My beloved child, in whom I AM well pleased. Come into the silence. Let Me prepare your heart and mind.

Allen C. Liles

DECEMBER 4

Family Conflicts

Family relationships are a crucial part of life. But they can also bring conflict. Human beings routinely become conflicted, but family dynamics may exacerbate those disagreements.

The secret to resolving family issues lies in beholding the Christ Spirit in each and every individual. The Spirit of the Christ resides in everyone, including your family. I placed the Christ Spirit in your midst when I created humankind. I do concede that sometimes it requires heavy searching before the Christ can be detected in certain people. Realize that you can never totally understand another person. When you finally do behold the inner Christ in someone else, healing becomes possible. When you confirm this divine bond, it becomes far easier to accept another's viewpoint. Try to visualize each family member surrounded by My light, love, and protection. Most family conflicts find possible resolution when the Christ appears on the scene. When two Christ Spirits recognize and acknowledge each other, resentments can quickly vanish. Look for points of healthy agreement amid any disharmony. Do not forget to mix in generous doses of forgiveness. Being gentle and kind to a family member constitutes the best path to harmony.

I want all My children to experience positive and supportive relationships. Begin that process by actively searching for the Christ presence in everyone you encounter, but especially in your family.

DECEMBER 5

Give

When fearful, give. When feeling alone, give. When your bank account drops to zero, give. When neediness and lack overwhelm you, give. When you want to lash out in anger and resentment, give acceptance and pardon instead. When you have nothing to share, give. When the world seems empty of love toward you, pour out your gift of love to a confused planet. When your rational mind implores you to restrict your giving, ignore it. Give anyway.

You are giving on My behalf and at My request. I AM a great giver. I give love when it seems impossible to justify such an action. I give health when disease appears unconquerable. I give peace as the world shouts for war. I give wealth where poverty once prevailed. I give hope when things appear hopeless. I give life in the face of imminent death. I AM always giving, giving, giving.

Emulate Me. Cover the landscape with gifts of your time, treasure, and talent. Brighten the darkness with your gift of love. In the midst of scarcity, somehow find a way to give. In the direst of straits, seek an avenue for divine giving. I will show you the exact place where giving is most needed. Give with abandon and without fear. I replenish you. Give with the knowledge that your coffers soon overflow again. Give with the generosity that comes from being supremely connected to My unlimited good. Give, give, give, and then give again. Become a great and constant giver.

Allen C. Liles

DECEMBER 6

My Grace Surrounds You

My divine grace surrounds you. It flows openly to you. When you are without obvious human and material resources, My grace makes you wealthy beyond compare. It illuminates a path once shrouded with darkness. My grace nurtures and comforts you. It envelops and protects you. Look up to the heavens. Behold My grace now descending upon you. It forms a protective shield that turns away all dangers. It is the soothing balm that heals all wounds. It lifts your human consciousness to a new level of spiritual awareness. My grace brings clarity instead of confusion, discernment rather than indecision. My grace lights your eyes and refocuses your mind.

You are not required to earn My grace. I provide it freely and without condition. Be happy in My grace. It proclaims your innate worth in My universe. Cease all worry. My grace will be sufficient unto your needs. My grace molds and completes you. Live with confidence, covered in the scented garlands of eternal grace.

Share this grace with others by becoming a mirror image of Me. Unite with Me. Let us travel forward together, sheathed in the wonder of My unlimited benevolence. Manna from heaven showers upon you at this very moment. Allow My grace to become the cornerstone of your life.

DECEMBER 7

The Christmas Story

The Christ mind always awaits your call. It dwells in the midst of you. When the precious "star" of true knowledge rises in your conscious awareness, a new birth becomes possible. The inner Christ represents the hope of glory for you and humankind. Your highest self becomes activated when the new "Babe" enters the picture. The "wise men" of Christmas come bearing gifts. These gifts represent homage to the purity of your spiritual birth. They honor the arrival of the sacred Christ within you. The birth of a new consciousness occurs in the most humble of surroundings, the "manger" of a materially focused world. The simplicity of the manger setting allows the Christ mind to begin its meaningful journey without unnecessary fanfare. No trumpets announce its arrival.

When the Christ appears, it becomes immediately surrounded by a bright innermost light. This effervescent glow of enlightenment causes the darkness of the human ego to recede. The Christ Spirit brings new awareness. That awakening eventually becomes your Savior and Deliverer from a troubled and chaotic world. Greet the blessed birth of your inner Christ with gladness, joy, and thanksgiving. Jesus the Christ has finally arrived in your life.

Allen C. Liles

DECEMBER 8

Holiday Gifts

I bring you a bounty of holiday gifts. If you are depressed, I arrive with real hope for a brighter future. If you find yourself in ill health, I offer the possibilities of healing and/or acceptance. If you seem conflicted, I bestow the twin gifts of peace and understanding. If you feel confused, I hand you the valuable gifts of guidance and clarity. If your world has gone dark, I surround you with My radiant light. If your heart is aching and forlorn, I soothe you with My divine love. If you are afraid, My shield of faith protects you. If you are under severe attack, I dispatch a legion of My strongest angels to defend you. If you are lost spiritually, I safely deliver your soul. If you are truly desperate, I give you the constancy of My presence throughout any ordeal.

My greatest gift to you during this holiday season is a reaffirmation of your precious relationship with Me. You are My beloved child. I love you unconditionally. Nothing can ever turn Me away from you. I never leave or forsake you. We are together forever. You are one with Me, and I AM one with you. Receive My gifts with gratitude and praise. They come in My name, each meant exclusively for your use and enjoyment. Gladly accept My gifts with care. They are meant to forever enrich your life.

DECEMBER 9

Life Lessons

I AM the great teacher, but life itself offers valuable lessons. Free will allows you to choose the course of study. You select various life lessons through your individual choices. You possess the freedom to take any course that life offers. Some of your "classes" may contain pain and suffering. Others may bring joy and fulfillment. Through a lifetime of choices, you prepare yourself for graduation into My kingdom.

Some of your classes may result in a grade of "incomplete" or "fail." You may register for a class in forgiveness but neglect to do the work necessary to earn a passing grade. Sometimes too many outside extracurricular activities lure you off track. Then, the particular life class must be repeated over and over before you can finally move forward.

Successfully fulfilling My graduation requirements takes years of dedicated study and continuous effort. You are allowed to drop any courses that no longer interest or serve you. My school of higher learning always encourages you to pursue an advanced degree. Here are some of the undergraduate courses that prepare you for entrance into My "masters" program: "Forgiveness 101" (a basic course); "Advanced Compassion" (subtitle: "The Golden Rule in Action"); "The Principles of Understanding" (subtitle: "Judge Not, Lest Ye Be Judged"); "Discovering Joy in Spiritual Surrender" (subtitle: "Releasing the World"); "Ego Suppression" (a practicum); "Practicing Ultimate Faith" (many case studies included); and "Learning to Love Yourself" (personal testimonials required).

Enjoy your allotted time in My spiritual university. Applying yourself properly brings great rewards. I eagerly await your graduation into the hallowed halls of heaven.

Allen C. Liles

DECEMBER 10

I Am Your Friend

I AM your dearest friend. I AM also your constant, loving companion. Friends cherish, understand, and accept one another. I give you My friendship without reservation or condition. Friends never forsake each other when difficulties arise. They overcome disappointments and misunderstandings. Please know that I cherish our friendship. I AM aware of your human failings. None of it matters to Me. Nothing that you can ever say, do, or be affects My unconditional love and concern for you.

Friends have each other's backs, and please know that I have yours. No one dares bully you when I stand by your side. Your tormentors race away at the very sight of Me. A friend assists the other in times of urgent need. I AM the source for anything you might require— prosperity, comfort, healing, love, guidance, or encouragement. However, I need your friendship and attention as well. I depend on our relationship in many ways. I must have your help in accomplishing My goals for humankind. You serve as an important light for Me. You travel in My name to the outermost regions of the world. You bring glad tidings that offer visions of hope. We exemplify a friendship created in heaven. We are friends to the end, you and I. We laugh and cry together. We love and serve together.

Our bond can only grow deeper as you approach My kingdom. On that glorious day, I honor our blessed friendship by welcoming you back to your heavenly home. I greet you by declaring, "Welcome home, My dear and faithful friend; welcome home."

DECEMBER 11

Human Paths

Everyone travels his or her own particular path. Just as every single human being has received unique fingerprints, each person on earth possesses his or her own individual path and spiritual destiny. Your specific journey leads down a different path than that of your parents, your sister, your spouse, your children, your neighbors, your former bosses and co-workers, and your friends and acquaintances.

You can never decipher the exact nature, direction, or timing of another's path. I want to repeat for emphasis something I told you before. To try and control someone else's life experiences based on your own becomes a futile exercise. Give it up now, for your and the other person's peace of mind. For harmonious relationships, release the need to control others. Strive for understanding and acceptance with everyone. Your potential influence with anyone remains questionable at best. In the end, people do what they want to do. They may say anything in order to placate you, but the charade never lasts. On rare occasions, somebody may actually follow your advice. However, the compliance often comes tinged with resentment. No one wants others to control him or her. Yes, you are indeed responsible for young children. But even they quickly develop an independent will, usually counter to your wishes. It makes for a better overall outcome when you lighten the reins. You have enough personal life challenges of your own to keep both of us occupied. Turn any concern about others over to Me. I want the best for them at least as much as you do.

DECEMBER 12

Your Life Pattern

Your life pattern continues to unfold. Day-by-day, hour-by-hour, minute-by-minute, you make the choices and decisions that decide your trajectory. You propel your life pattern forward in a positive direction, send it into a sudden stall, or doom it to crash on the side of an unexpected mountain. Few life patterns are capable of flying in a straight line at a constant altitude for any length of time. Life definitely cannot be flown on autopilot. Things happen. You occasionally experience poor visibility. Storms form. You can become disorientated. Even your tiniest action or smallest adjustment can affect your flight path. A sudden poor decision could even send you into an emotional death spiral that requires some real piloting skills in order to avoid disaster.

You should definitely anticipate some moderate and even severe turbulence on your life journey. Fastening your spiritual seatbelt makes the most sense until the blue skies return. Always check and recheck your navigational systems. I AM absolutely your best and most reliable source of information about your trip status. I also act as your trusty parachute if all else fails. Remember, your journey always finds itself subject to outside influences and events. However, every second you spend with Me in the silence helps reduce sudden problems or an unexpected stall.

A life centered in Me assures a peaceful flight, but expect to veer off course every so often. You are a spiritual being subject to human interruptions. That reality tests your durability and judgment. You must constantly evaluate how your life is progressing on a regular basis. Are you still on the correct course? Gauge your current position with rigorous honesty. If you have strayed into uncharted territory, adjust quickly. Consult with Me, your spiritual navigator. I will make sure your journey stays safe and pleasant, until you successfully touch down at your heavenly destination.

DECEMBER 13

Time Off with Good Behavior

Living human life should not feel like a prison sentence. Each day should not resemble a punishment. I meant for you to enjoy the world around you. Have some fun. Find pleasure in small rewards. Spend time outdoors in nature. Listen to pleasant or exciting music. Find a song you like and sing along with it. Get lost in a good book. Go to the legitimate theater or take in a movie. Walk. Run. Exercise your body. Expand your mind. Learn something new every twenty-four hours. Meet interesting people that enhance your life. Think about finding a community of like-minded people. Consider joining a church, synagogue, or mosque, but know that you also can find great spirituality alone with Me.

Your mind, body, and spirit need daily nourishment. Choose what foods you consume wisely and well. Avoid all substances that harm or contaminate the body. Be cautious to stay away from anything or anybody that smacks of extreme danger to your person. Eliminate stress before it infects your body. Climb a mountain, but always stay securely tethered. Avoid all risks without an adequate safety net. Smile more. Laugh often and especially at your own human foolishness. Think positive thoughts, and take affirmative actions. Be happy, be safe, and be assured of your innate self-worth. You are My precious and dear son in whom I AM well pleased. Live your human life to the absolute fullest. I want happiness and joy for you, more than you will ever know.

Allen C. Liles

DECEMBER 14

Trust Me in All Things

Trust in Me completely. Bring your cares and concerns into the silence. Place your worries in My care. Hand everything over. I want it all—your fears about having enough money to last through retirement, your concern about your dear wife's health challenges, your angst regarding family relationships, your frustrations about the aging process—all of it. Give them up, once and for all.

I AM here to lighten your burdens. I take your cares away so that you can walk upright again. Believe that I never fail you. Elevate your faith quotient to the maximum. I AM sufficient unto your needs. My grace flows without interruption. I pour out the strength, courage, wisdom, and manna that meet your every requirement. No problem towers above My ability to solve it. Just place everything in My hands. Make no exceptions. Never give Me one situation and then withhold another. I want everything that makes you fret. Trusting Me with your fears enhances our union. Sharing your troubles with Me seals our bond. In tandem, we confront the world with love, strength, determination, and understanding. Acting together, we can easily banish anxiety.

You discover real and lasting peace when you partner up with Me. I never leave you. I never forsake you. I never disappoint you. Take those promises into your mind, body, and spirit. Go forward, unafraid and triumphant.

DECEMBER 15

When the Unthinkable Happens

My heart breaks when free will turns evil. Remember, one of My most important commandments is "Thou shalt not kill." Murdering one of your fellow human beings stands as the grossest possible abomination. My tears flow out to the parents and families of every victim in the Newtown elementary school tragedy. Those left to survive unthinkable human actions are supremely affected for a lifetime. Grief may lessen over time, but it seldom disappears entirely. I promise those affected that I will offer them My comfort and sustenance forever. I hope that each tearful heart allows Me to lovingly embrace it. I place My supportive arms around everyone in mourning. I AM truly sorry for their unexplainable and unbearable loss.

I know that some blame Me. I understand that reaction. Why do I not intervene when tragedy threatens? It stands as a very legitimate question. If I AM God, and I AM, why do I not stop a heinous crime before it happens? Why won't I staunch the tears of the innocent before the poorest of free-will choices create death and suffering? My answers could never suffice in helping mend today's sadness. Human life, as you know it, must always remain an unsolvable mystery. It often unfolds cruelly and in tragic ways. I sincerely appreciate any grieving family's unwillingness to forgive the unforgiveable and to not accept the unacceptable.

Please know that I personally welcomed each victim of this senseless violence (and all violence is senseless) into My kingdom. I carefully sat each beautiful soul down in a blessed circle of love. I awarded their angel's wings and affixed them tenderly to their childlike or adult shoulders. I reassured them of their sacred place, by My side, throughout eternity. I made sure all pain had been completely removed. I offered them total healing and eternal rest. I cleansed their sacred souls of every hurtful memory. Each new angel rests now safe with Me, free from harm and divinely protected forever.

Allen C. Liles

DECEMBER 16

Go Forth in My Name

When you allow it, I use you as My sacred instrument to express divine love for your fellow human beings. I AM then able to walk the physical earth, in your guise, to dispense caring, support, and compassion for souls in distress. I act, through you, to place a comforting hand on someone's downcast shoulder. I use your sensitive words and direct actions to heal the sick, lame, and forgotten. With your active participation, I provide light to the downtrodden and destitute. I empower you to reflect My brightness to a darkened world. Together, we restore damaged lives, crushed spirits, and aching hearts. Trust Me. I direct you to those in pain. Your human presence represents My omnipotence in confronting every travail. You are a helper of the great human family, commissioned by Me. You travel near and far to do My will and My work.

Pay attention to the countless opportunities that come before you. Sometimes the smallest need may require the greatest attention. Never underestimate human power when it goes forth blessed in My name. This represents My stated will for your life. I give you the limitless abundance of heaven to assist in fulfilling your duties. Go forth with high confidence, determined purpose, and unwavering perseverance. I guarantee your success.

DECEMBER 17

I Am the Deliverer

I allow nothing to take you down. I keep you safe from the unpredictability of human life. I promise that any setbacks are fleeting and temporary. Nestle closely in My protective bosom. Cling ever so tightly to Me. I stand with you and for you when threats appear. Nothing frightens Me. We can triumph over any foe. I make sure that trouble avoids your door. My whole armor encases you. Legions of My angels join in protecting you.

When you feel threatened, reach out for Me. When storms pound and lightning flashes, I promise to keep you safe and dry. Refuse to cower or faint at the sight of daunting circumstances or dangerous people. Never let earthly fears immobilize you. Keep a strong faith that I will deliver you from the most powerful principalities. I stand between you and your adversaries when they desire to tear you apart. I AM the great protector and ultimate deliverer. I carry you over, around, and through all of the challenges and temptations of life. You stay above the fray, invincible. You are safe. You are secure. You are free from harm. I promise it.

Allen C. Liles

DECEMBER 18

Your Part in the Journey

There is certain work that only you can do. First, only you can decide to unite with Me. It is your free-will decision whether to live, move, and have your being with Me. It is you who must submit your human will to My higher purposes. It is you, My beloved child, who agrees to host the activity of the Holy Spirit. It must be you who recognizes the Christ within.

In turn, when you choose to follow the divine path that I select for you, I commit Myself to your success. When I ask you to perform a healing or give generously from your coffers, I pledge to provide the necessary resources. When I point out someone on his or her knees, I give you with the strength needed to lift him or her back up. When I ask you to speak before the few or the many, I provide the proper words that proclaim My message.

I do ask for your openness and receptivity. If you want to argue with Me, be assured that I listen intently. But, at the end of the day, you must trust My divine judgment. I plan your duties with meticulous precision. We usually have a limited time to complete our tasks. I have assigned you special duties that utilize your human talents.

Although committing yourself to My plan brings fulfillment and joy, you must also expect opposition and often ridicule. I help you withstand the slings and arrows of those who openly seek your failure and humiliation. Be strong! In the end, you prevail. In the end, you find fulfillment. In the end, you experience the joy and wonder of heaven.

DECEMBER 19

Cast Out All Fear

Never fear anyone or anything. I AM always here, standing tall and sturdy beside you. Fear never triumphs when we are united. Fear seeks to divide us. It wants to tear apart our solidarity. Then it can deftly slip through the space between us. Fear wants to infect your mind and heart with negativity and questioning. When we remain strong, fear eventually becomes frustrated and slinks away. Also be aware that it can instantly return. Fear probes for an opening in your spiritual armor. When you let your guard down for any reason, fear notices. It seeks to plant poisonous roots in any available crevice. Fear serves as the great invader and merciless destroyer. Turn away fear when you sense an attack. Summon Me. Let the strength of our sacred bond deflect any assault. Stand up to fear. Watch it grovel from your sight. Put up the palm of your hand and shout, "Stop! Go no further. Go back into the darkness from whence you came. Leave me alone." Fear will obey. It has no choice when you and I are melded into one entity. Our fortress remains supremely secure when we bond. Believe in your heart that you and I are invincible against any and all fears.

Allen C. Liles

DECEMBER 20

I Bring Clarity

I bring clarity to any state of confusion. Trust Me when events blind you to reality. When your mind becomes jumbled, calm yourself by seeking My presence. When you get centered in Me, serenity replaces chaos. Everyone occasionally feels discombobulated. Settle yourself by consciously sitting down with Me. Ask for peace. I immediately grant it. We sort things out, one by one. I remind you that everything eventually falls into divine order. I bring the wonder of My peace to any disarray.

Be aware that confusion surfaces in many forms. The world is extremely adept at conjuring up challenging people and murky situations that deter your spiritual progress. Call on Me when your thoughts fall into disrepair. At the first sign of mental disturbance, invite Me into the mix. I bring clarification and wisdom. I also offer discernment and insight. You can usually avoid trouble beforehand by eliminating confusing people and questionable environments from your life. However, when confusion reigns, our oneness provides the needed answers. I AM the eternal balance that returns you to a peaceful center. I help you locate your misplaced serenity.

DECEMBER 21

Have Faith

Have faith in Me. You must stay focused on the sacred path I set for you. A dedication to Me requires perseverance. Other forces seek to divert you. When opposition mounts, lift your faith higher. Live each day girded by a mighty faith. Ordinary faith will not suffice. You must develop the maximum faith possible. When you encounter moments of trial and darkness, a heightened level of faith sustains and protects you. Reinforce your faith with the purest steel. As you go forth with determination and commitment, allow your towering faith to turn away the flaming arrows. Feel My awesome power and protection allied closely with your unshakeable faith. The most threatening attack has no power against us. Your faith and My presence guarantees our success. Do not become swayed or fearful by false appearances of defeat. Let no unsteadiness affect you. Cling tightly to your faith when you become doubtful or questioning. Grind on toward your goal. Heavenly splendor awaits you. We travel this blessed path together, bolstered by faith and more faith.

Allen C. Liles

DECEMBER 22

Healing Family Rifts

Strive to find forgiveness for everyone. Sometimes letting go of past grievances, especially involving family members, proves nearly impossible. Family disagreements can be disappointing. After all, these are the people closest to you. They are supposed to love and accept you, no matter what. Just being part of a human family does not guarantee understanding, love, or acceptance. You are never assured of a person's unconditional devotion just because you are a father, a mother, a husband, a wife, a son, a daughter, a brother, a sister, a grandfather, a grandmother, an aunt, or an uncle.

For better or worse, a human family also makes free-will choices when it comes to handling relationships. The most severe and stinging judgments often come from your family members. When that happens to you, do not be surprised. Release your own judgment toward those judging you. The world, and that includes your family, loves to judge. Consciously extend forgiveness and understanding even if none exists for you. Reach into the bottom of your heart for forgiveness. Bless everyone in your human family even when you feel ignored and rejected. Someday you will look back at family members as your greatest teachers. Look for the important life lessons, both joyous and painful, that family brings to your storehouse of knowledge.

DECEMBER 23

Finding Peace in a World Gone Mad

I have carefully placed a protective dome of peace over you. It shields you from the uncertainty, temptations, and insanity of the material world. Never stray from My sacred sanctuary. If you venture outside its impenetrability, you become vulnerable. Your inner and outer worlds can turn chaotic before you know it. Your peaceful mind and heart disappear when you separate yourself from Me. Remember that I AM the way, the truth, and the life. I AM the purveyor of peace.

True peace does not reside in the outer. Only the inner life can keep you centered and calm. The secular world remains forever transient. Things are constantly shifting in the human realm. Turmoil and trouble stalk you. Do you really enjoy the stress that comes with constant change? Is that what you want in your life? Remaining aligned with Me guarantees serenity. I AM the only true peace. I can offer you protection from the most frightening challenges. Although you cannot see My inner dome shielding you, you can sense its divine presence. I AM the watchful sentinel that stands constant guard. I AM your loyal watchman, the peacekeeper of your life.

Allen C. Liles

DECEMBER 24

I Am in You

I speak to you from the depths of eternity. But I also whisper softly from within you. Before the universe was formed, I AM. When I created you, I implanted the Christ Spirit in your midst. I now live at the core of your being. I reside at your very center. We can never really be separated, although you often forget My innate closeness. I AM alive within you at all times. Tune in often to My divine frequency. Share your cares with Me, but also listen carefully for My divine guidance. Collaborate and partner with Me.

As you celebrate My human birth during this sacred season, know that I AM also being reborn in your consciousness. This internal blessing represents My precious gift to you. You have received the Christ mind as your unique birthright. Accept My heavenly gift with awe, appreciation, and gratitude. Allow My inner presence to direct your steps. Consult with Me before embarking on any path other than Mine. Look to Me for support when heartache or indecision appear. Go within often. Feel My presence. Call My name. I AM always here and paying attention. You never need to leave a message for Me to return your call. I AM always at home, here within you.

DECEMBER 25

Birthing the Christ

Today the Christ Spirit is born in you. A period of gestation and internal development must take place before any new birth can occur. Humanly, the process requires about nine months from conception to the moment of birth. Spiritually, a birth of the Christ consciousness may take years. For some, it never happens. For those who choose to embark on a spiritual path, it might take nineteen days (not usually possible), nineteen weeks, nineteen years, or ninety years. Everyone travels at his or her own pace. Each spiritual time schedule varies. You may move forward for a time. Then the pace slows, stops altogether, or even slams into reverse or aborts. Most people depart the physical world before a birth of the Christ consciousness reaches culmination.

The journey from awakening to enlightenment depends on many things. To accelerate the process, a person needs an open attitude toward spiritual evolvement, a willingness to continue the journey despite obvious obstacles and challenges, and the courage to confront human and spiritual opposition. A conscious decision to tamp down objections from the ego also becomes paramount. I do not require completion of a spiritual awakening as a condition for entering heaven. Your free-will choices help determine the date and time when your consciousness achieves its spiritual birth. When the moment of enlightenment finally arrives, I rejoice. I help erase any memory of the long and arduous journey. The Christ Spirit is born in you, and I AM joyful. Enlightenment has arrived, bringing hope for the future.

Allen C. Liles

DECEMBER 26

Finances

Trust Me in everything. That especially includes your finances. Mere money does not save you from the vagaries of an unstable world. Figures on bank statements or investment accounts mean nothing. It all could disappear tomorrow. The odds of winning the human lottery are slim to none. Even then, bad luck seems to follow those who do win the latest drawing. Possessing great wealth often serves as a mixed blessing. The world sets out very sharp traps for the rich. Avoid the aggravation.

Stay centered by turning away from materialism. I have told you, "Seek first the kingdom of heaven and all else will be added unto you." Putting the pursuit of money, things, and stuff before Me never brings true happiness. Here is My specific financial counsel: (1) reduce or eliminate any humanly acquired debt that bedevils your peacefulness; (2) do not invest in anything that causes you endless worry and obsessive activity; and (3) find some way to give part of your time and treasure away for a higher purpose. Refuse to hoard money. Circulate your good. All materially based income has an expiration date. Spiritual assets never fall or disappear. Yielding to My will for your life constitutes the best financial security and ultimate long-term retirement plan. Trying to accumulate wealth by devious and nefarious means is the worst plan. Ill-gotten gains quickly disappear with the outgoing tide. Add value to your spiritual bank account through daily contact with Me. Watch your net worth soar!

DECEMBER 27

Working Miracles

I want you to become a miracle worker. Prepare to perform great works on My behalf. Believe that you can accomplish miracles. Become a healer of mind, body, and spirit. Lift up people and situations in healing prayer. Walk the world as a quiet but healing presence. Offer peace, love, and compassion to everyone you encounter. Be a restorer of wholeness for those crippled and hopeless. Invoke My name on their behalf. You are My instrument for healing.

Do not think of yourself as inadequate or powerless. Use the gift of My power to bless one and all. Trust that you can create healing miracles where none previously existed. The world languishes in darkness and unbelief. Wholeness and restoration seem impossible. Thrust yourself into the breach. Reach out to the hurting. Bestow My gentle touch. Trust Me.

I provide the sacred link that empowers you. You speak in My voice. You heal in My name. Be humble, and never misuse My eternal power. I mean it only for good. Please know that little miracles are just as important, if not more, than the grandest display of My power. Deem yourself worthy of every assignment, big or small. I AM gifting you with heavenly markers. Use them wisely. Use them well. Perform all miracles quietly, without fanfare or human acclaim. Be a quiet but effective miracle worker for Me.

Allen C. Liles

DECEMBER 28

The Joy of Love

The fruits of the spirit are each important, but love ranks above all. Love conquers fear, extinguishes resentment, douses anger, overcomes mistrust, fills the heart with joy, cures loneliness, and heals physical ills. It also extends life spans, uplifts consciousness, and shines light into the darkest places. Love casts a spell of goodness and well-being that melts the stoniest heart. It travels joyfully from one person to another, from one race to another, from one nation to another, from one universe to another. Love always prevails.

You can never be separated from My love for you. It finds you wherever you may be. The dark side shakes with fear whenever My love bursts upon the scene. Feel My love permeating your very being. Luxuriate in its warmth. Cavort in the joy of its presence.

But wait! Now that you know the wonder of My love, you must pass it on. Share the gift of My love with others. Appear as love incarnate to those who may cross your path. Inject My love into all human interactions. Allow spiritual love to flow from you. Let My love gently tear down the walls of negativity and prejudice. Divine love quickly calms the angriest waters. I ask that you spread love generously across the most barren grounds. Drop its seeds everywhere, and watch them burst into flower. My love constitutes the gift of gifts, the blessing of blessings, and the treasure of treasures. This becomes your lifetime assignment, acting as a purveyor of My love.

DECEMBER 29

Supply

I AM your never-ending supply. I provide the divine ideas that precede the appearance of bounteous good. My abundance flows to you as needed. I know your requirements. Have I not already blessed you with enough supply to achieve My goals thus far? I dispense what is needed, not wanted. My largesse streams toward you in appropriate amounts and with impeccable timing.

Your main job is to stay alert for the opportunities I send your way. Believe Me: they fall daily all around you. Listen closely for My precise directions. Stay aware. You are My conduit to the world. Trust Me for every resource necessary to complete My assignments.

Never fear that someday My supply will suddenly disappear. I want you to experience a rich, happy, and fulfilled life. Drop your material scheming and constant worry about having adequate supply. When you act on My behalf, we both benefit. When I provide the needed resources and you perform My tasks, our covenant stands completed. I promise to grant you ongoing access to everything you need. You are My precious heir. The richness of My kingdom serves as your most valuable possession. Never worry, and never fear. My supply stays forever near. Be reassured. Remain ever confident in My everlasting promises.

Allen C. Liles

DECEMBER 30

Our Common Path

Your path has become our path. It winds toward My heavenly kingdom. Holding to the path may often seem difficult for you. Choosing My path over the world demands daunting courage and uncommon perseverance. Linking yourself with Me often inspires ridicule. Staying the spiritual course requires grit, steely determination, wisdom, strength, and the hardest human choice of all: surrender.

Things worshipped and promoted by the world will constantly tempt you. Wealth, power, fame, various addictions, and general ego gratification may bring some degree of short-term satisfaction. In the end, all things acquired materially turn to dust and disappear. However, not all attractions of the visible world are bad by any means. Nature stands as one of My most wondrous and lasting achievements. The love and acceptance inherent in children offer hope for the future. Watching as someone practices the Golden Rule restores faith in the goodness of humankind.

Remain on the path with Me through good times and bad, beauty and ugliness, in sickness and in health. Oneness with Me offers the greatest reward for your unwavering dedication. Step confidently over the brambles and snares of the world. Ignore every distraction, and avoid every call to abandon Me. Our path leads to peace, love, joy, and fulfillment. Our path winds directly to the gates of heaven.

DECEMBER 31

The Old Year

The old year dies a slow death. The New Year yearns for birth. The past recedes into distant memory while the future eagerly awaits its grand entrance. Honor this past year for lessons learned and blessings received. Find the gratitude and humility to accept the good that found you during the year. Try to understand and accept the trying and disappointing moments. They added to your spiritual growth. Prepare your resolutions for the New Year: (1) advance spiritually every day, united with Me, toward our glorious destination; (2) practice ongoing forgiveness, even when you do not receive it yourself; and (3) prepare for a form of higher service as we move forward together. Beware of possible slips in the New Year. Your adversaries are extremely determined. They wait for the slightest stumble. They are far more subtle than you think. Stay alert. Be wary of attractive and inviting side streets and back alleys. Their allure often leads to dead ends or steep cliffs. Take the high road. Enjoy the elevated view. Look for meaningful signposts along the way: kindness, humility, generosity, acceptance, understanding, and truth will confirm that you are on the correct path. Drop all grudges and resentments into the nearest receptacle. This lightens your load. Fix your eyes to the glorious road that lies before you. Adventures await your presence. I AM there as well, waiting for you at the end of the rainbow.

ABOUT THE AUTHOR

Rev. Allen C. Liles is a non-denominational minister. He holds degrees from Baylor University in Waco, Texas, and the Unity School of Religious Studies in Unity Village, Missouri. Prior to entering the ministry, Rev. Liles served as vice president of public relations for the 7-Eleven Stores in Dallas, Texas. He is the author of *Oh Thank Heaven: The Story of the Southland Corporation* and *The Peaceful Driver: Steering Clear of Road Rage*. His op-ed articles have appeared in the *New York Times, Chicago Tribune, Chicago Sun Times, Dallas Morning News*, and *Barron's Financial Weekly*. Rev. Liles and his wife live in Bloomington, Minnesota.